Sheffield Hallam University
Learning and IT Services
Adsetts Centre City Campus
Sheffield   S1 1WB

101 804 293 8

D0419795

Business Tenancy Renewals

/FEK LOAN

Renewals

A Surveyor's Handbook

Adam Rooney

and

Julian Cridge

SHEFFIELD HALLAM UNIVERSITY
LEARNING CENTRE
WITHDRAWN FROM STOCK

RICS
BOOKS

Acknowledgements

Crown Copyright material is reproduced with the permission of the Controller of HMSO and the Queen's Printer for Scotland.

Published by RICS Business Services Limited
a wholly owned subsidiary of
The Royal Institution of Chartered Surveyors
under the RICS Books imprint
Surveyor Court
Westwood Business Park
Coventry CV4 8JE
UK
www.ricsbooks.com

SHEFFIELD HALLAM UNIVERSITY
WL
346 .043462
RO
ADSETTS LEARNING CENTRE

No responsibility for loss occasioned to any person acting from or refraining from action as a result of the material included in this publication can be accepted by the authors or publisher.
ISBN 1 84219 241 8

© RICS Business Services Limited (RBS) February 2006. Copyright in all or part of this publication rests with RBS, and save by prior consent of RBS, no part or parts shall be reproduced by any means electronic, mechanical, photocopying or otherwise, now known or to be devised.

Typeset by Columns Design Ltd, Reading
Printed and bound in Europe by the Alden Group, Oxford

Contents

Legislation

The following Acts and Statutory Instruments are referred to in the publication. Where an Act or Statutory Instrument is mentioned frequently, it is referred to by the abbreviation in brackets that follows.

Access to Justice Act 1999
Arbitration Act 1996
Civil Evidence Act 1995
Companies Act 1985
Costs of Leases Act 1958
Courts and Legal Services Act 1990
Human Rights Act 1998
Interpretation Act 1978
Landlord and Tenant Act 1927
Landlord and Tenant Act 1954 (LTA 1954)
Landlord and Tenant (Covenants) Act 1995
Law of Property Act 1925
Law of Property (Miscellaneous Provisions) Act 1989
Leasehold Property (Temporary Provisions) Act 1951
Recorded Delivery Services Act 1962
Rent Act 1977
Supreme Court Act 1981
Trusts of Land and Appointment of Trustees Act 1996

Civil Procedure Rules 1998, SI 1998/3132 (CPR)
Landlord and Tenant Act 1954 Part 2 (Notices) Regulations 2004, SI 2004/1005
Regulatory Reform (Business Tenancies) Order 2003, SI 2003/3096

Code of Practice for Commercial Leases in England and Wales (2nd edition)
Protocol for the Instruction of Experts to give Evidence in Civil Claims, June 2005
RICS practice statement, *Surveyors Acting as Expert Witnesses*

UK legislation passed after 1988 is published by the Office of Public Sector Information on www.opsi.gov.uk and UK legislation prior to 1988 may be purchased through The Stationery Office Limited on www.tso.co.uk.

Preface

This handbook on lease renewals for business tenancies has been designed to be user friendly and practical. I therefore hope the reader will find the language clear, unambiguous and straightforward so that the information can be easily absorbed and used effectively. The contents and approach have been specifically targeted at the surveyor although there is no reason why others will not find this handbook equally useful and informative.

The landlord and tenant relationship is one that often evokes considerable emotion, particularly when the end of a lease is in sight and the opportunities for a new lease are being considered. This should be a time when the relationship brings forward a desirable outcome that suits both parties and not one which sets the landlord and tenant apart. When problems do arise, it is often through misunderstanding, ignorance or lack of preparation. This handbook can hopefully redress these problems by considering all aspects of the business of lease renewal from many angles.

The two authors, Julian Cridge and Adam Rooney, have gone as far as possible in covering the subject matter comprehensively and then further still by providing examples of situations which often arise and how they should be tackled. The user of this handbook will therefore benefit from not only the handbook's technical depth but also the practical solutions to common areas of conflict.

I have thoroughly enjoyed being a member of the writing team. Both Julian and Adam have made my job relatively easy by covering the subject matter so fully and nearly always providing the script in accordance with quite a short and strict timetable. Importantly, they have also been willing to incorporate market practices and word their text so that it meets the needs of practitioners.

Often it is only when barristers, solicitors and surveyors come together on a subject that a truly comprehensive picture is provided. I believe that in this respect the reader will find this handbook punches well above its weight and will become a companion that will always be kept close at hand.

Graham Chase
Consultant Editor

Introduction

In the years immediately after the Second World War, the commercial sector in England and Wales was struggling back to life. The numerous air raids, rationing and general shortages affecting industry and the population as a whole had all taken a heavy toll on businesses of all sizes and property in both cities and towns was scarce. This, combined with little security of tenure, allowed landlords to demand rent at levels that threatened newly-emerged and long-established enterprises alike.

Recognising these difficulties, the government of the day brought in temporary legislation in the form of the *Leasehold Property (Temporary Provisions) Act* 1951. This provided the necessary breathing-space in which to formulate and then enact more permanent provisions.

And so the *Landlord and Tenant Act* 1954 hit the statute book on 30 July 1954 and remained there essentially unchanged until 1 June 2004.

In the early 1990s, partly because of the property market changes since 1954 and partly because of Lord Woolf's Civil Justice Reforms, both landlords and tenants were keen on change. The 1954 Act, for example, contained the absolute requirement for the tenant to have to litigate to seek a renewal lease even when the landlord did not oppose renewal, which was clearly outmoded. Equally, a tenant's ability to at least delay its landlord's development proposals by playing the litigation system was also seen as contrary to the 1954 Act's aims.

In 1992, as part of its periodic review of the 1954 Act, the Law Commission reported a number of proposals that recommended changes to the legislation. It was not until 2001 that the government started to consult on these ideas.

This consultation resulted, on 1 December 2003, in the publication of the *Regulatory Reform (Business Tenancies) Order* 2003. Sweeping changes were made to the *Landlord and Tenant Act* 1954. Gone was the need to apply to court for a contracting-out order, as was the obligation for the tenant to apply to court for a new tenancy if both parties were continuing to negotiate. The reforms brought about a number of other important changes, all of which are dealt with in this book.

This book has been written principally with surveyors in mind. We have, throughout the various stages of writing the book, worked closely with our consulting editor, Graham Chase, a surveyor of many years and president of the Royal Institution of Chartered Surveyors from July 2006. Graham's welcome guidance has ensured that the text remains grounded in the practical, rather than flying off into the theoretical.

Where possible, we have included detailed legal guidance for surveyors. However, this book is not a replacement for expert legal advice. In the same way that a solicitor should not give valuation advice, a surveyor should not seek to litigate matters on behalf of their client and nor should a surveyor attempt to advise a client about complex legal issues. If in doubt, expert legal advice from a solicitor or barrister should always be sought.

Finally, a grateful and deserved 'thank you' to our family, friends and colleagues for their encouragement and consideration whilst we were writing this book. We wish to record our particular appreciation to Julia Killick and Graham Chase for their constant guidance and support, and to Claire Mulville for her help in compiling the appendices.

Adam Rooney and Julian Cridge

1

Deciding whether LTA 1954 applies

The *Landlord and Tenant Act* 1954 (LTA 1954) regulates the majority of business tenancies, providing in a single statute the law governing their continuation, renewal and termination. In overview:

- A business tenancy will **continue** indefinitely (beyond any contractual expiry date) unless and until it is determined in accordance with LTA 1954.
- The court can **renew** a business tenancy, on such terms as it thinks fit, on an application made by the landlord or the tenant.
- A landlord can only **terminate** a business tenancy against the tenant's wishes if it successfully challenges the tenant's claim for an order for the grant of a new tenancy, or establishes the right to a termination order. In either case the onus is on the landlord to establish one or more of seven grounds of opposition to the grant of a new tenancy. If the landlord succeeds in establishing certain grounds, then the tenant is entitled to compensation.

However, not all business tenancies are covered by LTA 1954 and since those that are benefit from important protection, it is vital to identify the tenancies to which LTA 1954 does apply.

Section 23(1) of LTA 1954 provides that the Act:

'... applies to any tenancy where the property comprised in the tenancy is or includes premises which are occupied by the tenant and are so occupied for the purposes of a business carried on by him or for those and other purposes ...'

Section 23(1) therefore contains a number of elements, each of which are examined in further detail throughout this chapter.

These elements are that:

- LTA 1954 only applies to a tenancy (section 1.1);
- the property comprised in the tenancy must include premises (section 1.2);
- the premises must be occupied (section 1.3) by the tenant (section 1.4); and
- the tenant must occupy the premises for business purposes (section 1.5).

These elements are supplemented by other parts of LTA 1954, as well as by case law, and must all be satisfied for LTA 1954 to apply.

From time to time, one or more elements may not be satisfied, so that a tenancy can move in and out of the protection of LTA 1954 over a period of time. The tenant may cease to occupy the premises, for example, or continue to occupy but cease to do so for business purposes – in such cases, LTA 1954 does not apply. The impact of a tenancy moving in and out of the protection of LTA 1954 is dealt with in section 1.6.

Even if each of the elements is satisfied at any given time, LTA 1954 does not apply at all:

- to tenancies of farmland, mines, for specified public uses or granted to employees as part of their employment package;
- if the parties have already agreed in writing to a further tenancy of the property once the current tenancy comes to an end. The tenant does not need to claim security of tenure under LTA 1954, because it has already secured a further tenancy of the business premises;
- where a public body owns the land and that body certifies that LTA 1954 should not apply as a matter of national security or other public interest;
- if the tenant has applied for and been granted a new tenancy by the court, but then tells the court of a change of mind and the court revokes its earlier order. Effectively, this prevents the tenant from changing the decision again and seeking to claim the protection of LTA 1954 a second time;
- if the parties have 'contracted out' of the provisions of LTA 1954 (this is dealt with in more detail in chapter 2); or
- to fixed term tenancies of less than six months' duration (unless the tenant has already been in occupation for longer than that or is the successor to someone who operated the same business in the premises for a longer period).

1.1 LTA 1954 applies to any tenancy

The LTA 1954 sets out (in section 69(1)) exactly what types of tenancy are included for these purposes, but it is also necessary to refer back to general landlord and tenant law to understand the extent of the definition in section 69(1).

Basic landlord and tenant law: what is a tenancy?

A tenancy comprises several necessary elements[1]:

- A contractually binding agreement. There can be no contract if no consideration (e.g. rent) is provided or the parties to the agreement do not intend to create a legal relationship between them. The agreement should also not be referable to any other relationship between the parties.
- One person (the landlord) must grant to another (the tenant) exclusive occupation (sometimes referred to as exclusive possession) of the land. The grant of the right to exclusive occupation is usually given in return for the promise to pay a rent, but a rent is itself not a necessary element of a tenancy.
- The right to exclusive occupation must be conferred for a fixed or renewable period or periods.

Whether or not any particular agreement constitutes a tenancy is a question of law. It is not necessary to show that the parties intended to grant a tenancy as opposed to any other interest in the property: they might call their agreement a tenancy, but if it does not comprise one or more of the above elements, it is not a tenancy and their labelling is irrelevant. It has sometimes been suggested that what the parties call their agreement should be ignored, but their 'label' does need to be considered with the agreement as a whole, as it can sometimes be a good indication of what the parties actually intended.[2] This is particularly the case where both parties are substantially of equal power and have had full legal advice.[3]

Exclusive occupation

Exclusive occupation means the right to exclude everyone from the property, including the landlord (except where he or she exercises limited rights of entry, for example to carry out repairs). Whether or not a particular agreement grants a right of exclusive occupation is a question of fact.

The court will usually decide that question by investigating the degree of control and use that the person granting the right retains over the premises under the agreement. If that person retains a significant degree of control or use, the court will probably find that the agreement does *not* confer exclusive occupation.

This is what distinguishes a tenancy from a licence. LTA 1954 does not apply to licences. The distinction is not always easy to draw in practice, however, underlined by the fact that a number of cases in this area have been determined in the House of Lords. The practical difficulties are outlined in the following example.

> *For the last five years, T has occupied a grocer's stall in a shopping centre owned by L plc. There are ten permanent fixed stalls in the concourse, each of which has always occupied the same space. T always uses the same stall and when it is not in use roller blinds are pulled down and T locks the stall so no one has access to it. T occupies the stall pursuant to an agreement, which provides that:*
>
> - *T has to pay a weekly fee, in advance, for the use of the stall.*
> - T will be permitted to trade from one of the stalls in the centre each day but no guarantee is made on stall allocation.
> - *T must obtain permission from L plc about what is sold from the stall and the stall needs to be set up in a certain way. If T does not obtain permission, L plc can remove any goods from the stall that are not authorised to be sold.*
> - T can only get access to the stall during 'trading hours' for the shopping centre.
>
> In this example, T appears to have exclusive occupation of the grocer's stall, but the question is rather what rights have been conferred on him by the agreement entered into with L plc. It may be difficult for T to argue that the agreement conferred a right of exclusive occupation, because a number of factors militate against that conclusion, including:
>
> - the agreement reserves the right to L plc to move T to other premises, i.e. another stall;
> - there is a degree of control over what T can use the stall for. If T had real exclusive occupation of the stall, L plc would not be able to dictate what was sold and the manner in which it was sold. More importantly, L plc would not be able to enter the stall and remove unauthorised goods.; and
> - there is a limitation on hours of use. This is not necessarily determinative, but is a relevant factor.

Where there is any doubt about whether or not an arrangement constitutes a tenancy, it is advisable to proceed on the basis that it is. Any steps necessary as a result of LTA 1954 should be taken 'without prejudice' to the contention that LTA 1954 does *not* apply. Legal advice should always be sought in such circumstances at the earliest opportunity.

The statutory definition of 'tenancy'

Section 69(1) of LTA 1954 requires that a tenancy be created by a 'tenancy agreement' and extends the definition to cover underleases and agreements for lease or underlease made in writing.

Mortgage terms confer a right to possession in favour of the mortgagor (the lender) for the life of the term, which could be viewed as the grant of a tenancy. Similarly, during the mortgage term, the borrower can formally recognise the lender as his landlord, which process is known as attorning tenant to the mortgagee. LTA 1954 expressly excludes both situations from its definition of 'tenancy'.

Usually, a tenancy will be made in writing and will contain all its terms within one document. If all the terms are not found in that document, they must be incorporated into it by reference to the document in which they are found. These requirements do not apply if the tenancy is for a period (or initial period if there is a right to renew) of less than three years. A short tenancy can therefore be created orally (see the *Law of Property Act* 1925, section 54(2) and the *Law of Property (Miscellaneous Provisions) Act* 1989, section 2).

The question arises whether such tenancies fall within LTA 1954.

Section 69(2) of LTA 1954 provides that:

'References in this Act to an agreement between the landlord and the tenant ... shall be construed as references to an agreement in writing between them.'

Since section 69(1) refers to a 'tenancy agreement', this might appear to exclude from the operation of LTA 1954 short tenancies and others (such as those created by estoppel) which are not reduced to writing.

There is no decided authority on this point. However, the authors consider that LTA 1954 does apply to these short and other types of tenancy, for the following reasons:

- the LTA 1954 states that it does not apply to fixed-term tenancies of six months or less, so if Parliament intended to exclude tenancies of three years or less, it could have said so; and
- certain sections of LTA 1954 expressly refer to agreements between landlord and tenant (section 32, for example, refers to an agreement between them as to the property which constitutes the tenant's holding). Section 69(2) operates only in relation to these particular sections. Section 69(1), in contrast, refers only to a tenancy agreement, not a tenancy agreement 'between the landlord and the tenant'.

The special case of tenancies at will

In practice, tenancies at will arise in three situations:

- Where a prospective tenant is allowed into exclusive occupation of premises under an agreement for lease or pending further negotiation or execution of a lease of those premises,[4] provided the negotiations or execution are not allowed to drift[5].

- Where a person is allowed into exclusive occupation of premises under a tenancy agreement and has paid rent, but for some reason (because the tenancy agreement has been signed by someone who did not have actual or ostensible authority to do so for example) the lease is void.
- Where a tenant (who is not protected by LTA 1954) holds over after the contractual expiry of the previous tenancy, with the landlord's agreement, on terms that the landlord may recover possession on demand or the tenant may give up possession without giving notice.

In the first and second cases, a 'tenancy at will' may arise by operation of law. Where a tenancy is created in this way, there is no underlying 'tenancy agreement' (as required by section 69(1))and accordingly LTA 1954 does not apply.

In the third case, the tenancy at will is invariably created by express agreement, usually before the previous tenancy expires. The essential element of such a tenancy, however, is that the landlord is entitled to possession on mere demand. This is obviously inconsistent with the provisions of LTA 1954, which provide that a landlord may only end a business tenancy in accordance with LTA 1954. The courts have held that the existence of this inconsistency must mean that Parliament did not intend LTA 1954 to apply to tenancies at will.

Subtenancies

It is possible for LTA 1954 to apply to a subtenancy, even if it does not apply to the head tenancy out of which the subtenancy is created and even if the subtenancy is unlawful. The same is not true, however, if the purported grant of a subtenancy is effectively an assignment of the head tenancy[6]. This occurs if the subtenancy is granted for a period that is equal to or exceeds the remaining term of the head tenancy[7].

On 1 July 2004 L granted a one-year tenancy of a clothes shop to T. The tenancy was contracted out of LTA 1954. A couple of weeks later (but before T moved stock into the shop and started to trade) a friend, S, expressed an interest in taking the property. T orally agreed that S could move into the property, provided rent was paid periodically to T, and that S would not be required to leave 'for at least a year'. S subsequently moved into the premises, began to trade from them, and paid rent to T each month.

T's promise not to require S to leave 'for at least a year' means that the term offered to S was longer than T's interest in the premises. As a matter of law, S took an assignment of the remainder of T's term, which was contracted out of LTA 1954.

If T had not said that S could remain in the premises 'for at least a year', T would have granted a valid periodic subtenancy of the premises to which LTA 1954 would apply. It would not matter, for these purposes, whether or not the head tenancy prohibited the grant of a subtenancy, although on the grant L may have then had the right to forfeit the head tenancy (which would have the effect also of determining the subtenancy). Unless L forfeited or served a notice on S to determine the subtenancy under section 25 of LTA 1954, the subtenancy would continue even after T's head tenancy expired at midnight on 30 June 2005.

It may seem unjust for LTA 1954 to protect unlawful subtenancies. Effectively a landlord could be left with a subtenant with rights under LTA 1954, whereas the landlord expected that someone with no such rights would occupy the premises. However, there may be a remedy, because if the head tenancy prohibits the grant of a subtenancy (with or without consent), the landlord may forfeit the head tenancy or (if for any reason the landlord waives or loses the right to forfeit and the underlessee knew that the grant of the underlease was in breach of the head lease[8]) seek an injunction requiring the subtenancy to be surrendered.

1.2 The property comprised in the tenancy must be or include premises

Use of the word 'premises' suggests that LTA 1954 only applies when the land comprised in the tenancy has actually been built upon, but case law has given the word a wider meaning to extend also to bare land. In fact, LTA 1954 has been held to apply to tenancies of racehorse gallops, brick pits and car parks.

Some care needs to be taken where the rights involved are rights of way rather than rights of occupation, which can also be leased. Unless the right of way is *additional* to some right of occupation, LTA 1954 does not apply to the right of way at all.

1.3 The premises must be occupied

Although LTA 1954 does not define what is meant by 'occupied', the courts consider that premises are 'occupied' if the tenant carries on some business activity on the property[9]. Since this is a question of fact, there is no exhaustive list of the factors that will be taken into account. Nevertheless, a review of the case law suggests that the following elements will be important:

- *Whether the occupier is physically present or not.* Physical presence may not always be necessary. A person can occupy a warehouse, for example, by storing goods there on a permanent basis, although rarely visiting the premises.
- *What control the occupier exercises over the premises.* Where a local authority, for example, was the tenant of a park that was used by the general public, it was still deemed to occupy the space because it was responsible for maintaining the gardens and policing access to the park, which was only permitted during daylight hours[10].
- *What use the occupier makes of the premises: whether the tenant actually need be present on the premises to use them.* An internet service provider, for example, may use premises to site computer hardware that is crucial to the business, whereas the business could be maintained from offices or home elsewhere. This contrasts with a restaurateur operating from premises, who will need to be on site in order to run the restaurant business.
- *What time is devoted to the activity carried on at the premises?* Premises need not be occupied for 24 hours, 7 days a week, but there does need to be a 'thread of continuity' of occupation. This means that LTA 1954 can apply to premises, which are used for seasonal business. It is not sufficient, however, for these purposes, to intend to restart the business again at some future time if, in the interim, the business cannot be carried on (see the following example for further details).

Companies will be considered as being physically present in premises if their directors or employees are there in the capacity of office-holder or in the course of their employment. Similarly, it is possible for a person to occupy premises through a manager or agent. This is considered further in section 1.4.

Where an occupier is absent from the premises but continues to assert rights over them (including an intention to return once practicable), the reasons for absence become important. If the tenant cannot physically be present at the premises (if, for example, they have been destroyed by fire), then absence is excusable and LTA 1954 will still apply. If, however, the tenant has voluntarily absented for whatever reason, the court is unlikely to find that the tenant occupies the premises and LTA 1954 will not apply – it is the tenant's intentions in this case which are paramount rather than whether there is a reasonable prospect that the tenant will return to the premises.

T is unable to carry on business from his shop because the neighbouring premises have been destroyed by fire and his own premises have become unsafe. T writes to his landlord stating that 'he wants to get back in to trade as soon as possible', retains the keys, and leaves some of his stock there. T is absent for six months and LTA 1954 still applies to the tenancy. The Act would also apply if T had merely closed the shop for two weeks so that his staff could take their annual holidays.

T runs a casino business, which he wants to run from different, better premises, but it is only possible to obtain a gaming licence for one set of premises, so T ceases to occupy the old premises in order to apply for a licence for the new one. If T is not granted a licence for the new premises, the intention is to continue business from the old premises. LTA 1954 ceases to apply to the tenancy of the old premises once T moves out as the absence is voluntary, albeit taken (in T's view) in the best interests of the business.

My client leases a garage from which he runs a car repair business. The tenancy includes a right of way over land at the back of the garage, along which he can gain access. At the end of his lease, my client will be entitled to a new tenancy of the garage under LTA 1954. What happens to the right of way?

Although it is not possible to 'occupy' a right of way, your client's right is also protected (as the court has held in a number of cases). If your client's right of way had been separate and nothing to do with the tenancy, however, the position would be different. This may seem strange because without access, your client cannot get to the garage and enjoy the rights that are protected by LTA 1954. Changes were made to LTA 1954 on 1 June 2004 and it had been hoped that those changes would extend the provisions of LTA 1954 to leases of rights such as rights of way (called incorporeal hereditaments), but they have not.

Ceasing to occupy at the end of the contractual term

Despite a period of non-activity, a tenant may still be treated as occupying the premises if absence or non-activity can be seen as part and parcel of the normal business activity of winding down the business in order to quit the premises[11].

The court will determine this question of fact by having regard to the following[12]:

- What was the purpose of leaving the premises unattended?
- What was the intention behind the decision to leave the premises unattended?
- Was the period of inactivity reasonably incidental to the winding down for the purpose of handing the premises back on the day the tenant was required to quit?
- Was the period of absence part of the overall thread of occupation of the premises, looked at as a whole?

1.4 The tenant must occupy the premises

The premises are, in most cases, occupied by the tenant and in these circumstances, there is no doubt that the requirement is satisfied. It is worth noting, however, that it is the *tenant*, not the occupier, who is entitled to protection of LTA 1954. That does not mean that the tenant needs to *physically* occupy the premises in order to claim that protection. Different scenarios are considered below.

Companies

Occupation by a company that is not the tenant will be treated as occupation by the tenant where the actual tenant has a 'controlling interest' in that company (sections 23(1A) and 42 LTA 1954).

A person is considered to have a controlling interest in a company if, were they a company, the company in actual occupation would have been their subsidiary. 'Subsidiary' here has the meaning given by section 736 of the *Companies Act* 1985, which states that company X is deemed to be a subsidiary of company Y if:

- company Y either:
  - holds a majority of the voting rights in company X;
  - is a member of company X and has the right to appoint or remove a majority of its board of directors; or
  - is a member of company X and controls alone, pursuant to an agreement with other shareholders or members, a majority of the voting rights in it; or

- company X is a subsidiary of any company that is itself a subsidiary of company Y.

T is the tenant of a grocer's shop. If the grocer's business is actually run from the premises by Fruit and Veg Limited, of which T is the only shareholder, then LTA 1954 applies to the tenancy. However if the grocer's business is actually run from the premises by Fruit and Veg Limited, of which T holds only 25 per cent of the shares, then LTA 1954 does not apply.

If the tenant is a company, LTA 1954 will apply to its tenancy if the person in occupation is another company in the same corporate group or (if its controlling shareholder is an individual) by that individual or by another company under the control of that individual.

Fruit and Veg Limited is the tenant of a grocer's shop. If the grocer's business is actually run from the premises by Mr A, who is the company's only shareholder then LTA 1954 applies to the tenancy. LTA 1954 will also apply in the situation where the grocer's business is actually run from the premises by Green Grocers Limited and Mr A is the only shareholder in both Fruit and Veg Limited and Green Grocers Limited.

Occupation by one person where more than one are entitled to occupy

Difficulties may also arise if the tenant is actually two or more individuals, such as where a husband and wife take a tenancy of premises jointly. Unless the premises are occupied by *all* of the joint tenants, save in the next two exceptions, LTA 1954 does not apply[13].

Occupation by beneficiaries under a trust

Where the tenant is a trust, occupation by one or more of the beneficiaries under the trust will be treated as occupation by the tenant, and LTA 1954 will apply (section 41(1)), provided the beneficiaries are entitled to occupy the premises under the trust. Where the trust is written, the trust document may provide that the beneficiaries are entitled to occupy trust property and, in all other cases, the trustees may permit them to do so.

A tenancy is granted to Mr and Mrs T as joint tenants, who run a bar business from the premises. They hold the premises on implied trust. Mr and Mrs T split up, and Mrs T now runs the bar alone, but Mr T has not consented to this, as he wants to run the bar himself with his new partner. LTA 1954 does not apply to the tenancy, because although there is a trust under which both Mr and Mrs T are beneficiaries, Mrs T is not entitled to occupy the premises as she has not secured agreement to do so from the other trustee (Mr T).

Occupation by one or more partners

If at some point a property has been occupied for business purposes by a partnership, LTA 1954 may continue to apply even though – at the relevant time – not all of those partners continue to occupy it for the purpose of the partnership business or some other business purpose (section 41A).

In order to apply in these circumstances, LTA 1954 requires that:

- the premises be let to joint tenants;
- at some point during the course of the tenancy, all joint tenants must have occupied the property for the purpose of carrying on business there in partnership;
- the tenancy was a partnership asset at that time;
- a business is now carried on by at least one of those joint tenants (even if they are no longer in partnership or are carrying on a different business); and
- none of the other joint tenants occupies the property under the tenancy for business purposes.

A and B are solicitors and take a joint tenancy of an office. After a couple of months, they enter into partnership and agree to treat the tenancy of their office as a partnership asset. A year later C joins the partnership and, in due course, B retires from the partnership. If A and C continue to occupy the office for the purpose of running their law firm then LTA 1954 applies, even though one of the joint tenants (B) does not occupy the premises, and C (who is not a joint tenant) is now carrying on business there.

It would not matter for these purposes if, after B's retirement, A and C had dissolved their previous partnership and now carried on some other business. What is needed is continuity of at least one business tenant (in this case A), and it is this tenant who enjoys the protection of LTA 1954.

Unincorporated associations (clubs)

Tenancies cannot be granted to unincorporated associations, but can be granted to its officers as trustees for the club membership as a whole. In such case, occupation of the premises by one or more club members permitted by the trustees and carrying on a business will mean that the LTA 1954 applies.

Where the landlord tries to grant a tenancy to a club (without naming any individuals), the tenancy will in fact be granted to the person who signs it on behalf of the club. In this case, it would be for that person to show that they in fact held the tenancy on trust for other club members and that those members occupied the premises in order to benefit from the protection of LTA 1954.

Managers

Where a tenant claims to occupy premises by virtue of their being managed on his or her behalf by some other person, the terms of the management agreement require careful scrutiny to ensure that, in reality, the manager is not in fact operating their own business. The courts are more likely to find that the manager is operating their own business if the agreement looks like a subtenancy.

The sort of thing which might suggest that the manager were operating their own business rather than that of the tenant include where, under the agreement or in fact, the manager:

- takes the profits;
- is at complete liberty to conduct the business in whatever manner they see fit;
- pays for all the goods supplied for the purposes of the business and is liable for all the outgoings such as any ground rent, business or water rates;
- makes capital contributions to the business or otherwise assumes or shares in the business risk.

Tenant shares occupation of the premises with another

It does not matter if the tenant shares occupation with someone else, provided the other requirements for the application of LTA 1954 are satisfied. Difficulties will arise where the tenant sublets the whole of the premises, because subtenants will occupy for themselves rather than for the tenant (even if the tenant's business is to sublet the premises concerned). The prospect of establishing that LTA 1954 does apply may depend on the nature of the subtenancy, i.e. whether it is for business or residential purposes. For example:

- In the case of **business sublets**, if the tenant sublets the whole of the premises, then LTA 1954 does not apply to the tenancy. If part only of the premises is sublet, then LTA 1954 does apply but the tenant is only entitled to a new tenancy of that part of the premises that the tenant continues to occupy not to the part that is sublet. The distinction between lease and licence again becomes relevant, because if the tenant shares occupation with a person who is a licensee rather than subtenant, then LTA 1954 can apply to the whole[14].
- In the case of **residential sublets**, the tenant and subtenant can occupy the same space, the former for the purposes of LTA 1954, the latter for the purposes of any applicable residential statute (such as the *Rent Act* 1977), provided the business tenant retains sufficient access and control over the suboccupied area. This is a question of fact and degree. If there is insufficient access or control, then the position is the same as for business sublets[15].

1.5 The premises must be occupied for the purposes of a business

The use of the word 'business' suggests that some commercial activity must be carried on by the tenant at the premises with a view to making profit, even if that aim is not actually realised.

Section 23(2) of LTA 1954 provides that 'business' includes:

'... a trade, profession or employment and includes any activity carried on by a body of persons, whether corporate or unincorporated ... '

Businesses carried on by individuals

Tenants who are individuals must carry on a trade, profession or employment and occupies the premises for that purpose. It is not sufficient to show that the individual carries out some other form of business activity. Difficulties can arise where individuals sell goods or provide services from their homes. Whether or not what they are doing constitutes a trade, profession or employment is a question of fact and degree.

A is an accountant, but in his spare time he enjoys painting pictures, which he does in a small studio at the back of his house. He often gives away paintings to those who express an interest in them and, from time to time, he will sell them for a small sum. LTA 1954 would not apply to the tenancy of his house. Nor would it apply to E, an elderly woman who takes in lodgers to her house for a small sum that only just covers her household expenses. She takes in lodgers for company – without them, she would not be able to afford her outgoings and would have to move to a smaller property.

LTA 1954 would, however, apply to T, who rents a large 7-bedroom house in the countryside and regularly provides bed and breakfast for visitors to the area. This nets T a large profit and is the only source of income.

Businesses carried on by bodies of persons

'Activity' means some general use by the persons occupying, which is similar to the notion of 'trade, profession or employment', and not some particular, casual operation[16]. It is the activity that is important.

LTA 1954 still applies[17] even if:

- the tenant company does not list the objective of making profit in its articles of association; or
- the tenant cannot or does not distribute any profits.

LTA 1954 does not apply if the activity carried on is merely for pleasure and social enjoyment.

It is worth noting that a social members' club which 'trades' with its members (by providing them with a bar or catering service, or letting them use its facilities for a fee for example) does carry on the required business activity.

T carries on business as a pharmacist. Whilst doing building work to the premises from which T runs that business, he takes a tenancy of adjacent premises for storage of building materials. LTA 1954 does not apply to the tenancy of the second premises as dumping building materials on these premises is not a business activity, nor was this part of T's business (which is, after all, to run a pharmacy).

T is the trustee of a tennis club and (on behalf of the club) rents a clubhouse and courts. The club sells food and refreshments to its members at cost, but does not make a profit. The members of the club are carrying on the activity of a lawn tennis club, so LTA 1954 does apply to T's tenancy, even though that activity is not carried on commercially[18]. However if the only service provided by the club to members is use of the courts and no fee is paid for that use or for membership then LTA 1954 would not apply.

Whose business?

The business carried on must be that of the tenant, but it is not necessary that the business belong to the tenant alone. If a tenancy is a partnership asset, and one or more of the partners occupies the premises for the purpose of the partnership's business, this will be deemed to be occupation for the purpose of the tenant's business.

A, B and C are architects who work in partnership with one another. A works in a separate office from B and C, which he leases in his own name but has agreed with B and C should be treated as an asset of the partnership. LTA 1954 applies to A's tenancy, even though the business which he carries on there is not only his own business, but also that of the partnership of which he is part with B and C.

Tenant comprises more than one person

Difficulties arise where the tenant comprises more than one individual, and each carries on a different business from the premises. Whilst some suggest otherwise[19], the authors consider that there is no reason why LTA 1954 should not apply in such case.

It is correct that LTA 1954 refers to 'a business' (rather than just 'business' or 'and businesses'), but section 6 of the *Interpretation Act* 1978 provides that in any statute, unless the contrary intention appears, words in the singular include the plural. Taking this into account, it would be curious if two businesses were not protected by LTA 1954 just because they happened to operate out of the same premises, even though both joint tenants had a right to be there and to use those premises as they wished. Had Parliament intended to exclude this situation from the operation of LTA 1954, it could have chosen different words.

A lease is granted to Mr and Mrs T as joint tenants. Mr T runs a mail-order business selling wine from the office at the back, whereas Mrs T runs a bar from front of house. They hold the premises on implied trust and because Mr and Mrs T are agreed that each of them can run their separate businesses from the same premises, so LTA 1954 applies to their tenancy.

Groups of companies

LTA 1954 will apply where one company carries on its own business in the premises, even if the actual tenant of those premises is another company which runs its business elsewhere, provided the two companies are in the same group (under section 42(2)).

As discussed earlier in this chapter, the two companies will be in the same group if:

- one is the subsidiary of the other;
- they are both the subsidiaries of another company; or
- the same person has a controlling interest in both of them.

It may be that this 'group sharing' of the premises follows an assignment of the tenancy from the tenant to the company now in occupation. For the purposes of LTA 1954, this assignment is ignored, so that the 'tenant' will still be treated as the original tenant, not the assignee (under section 42(2)).

This may seem odd, but follows from clear wording of LTA 1954. It is unlikely that this is what Parliament intended[20], but similarly unlikely that a court could be persuaded to look at the intention behind the provision, because there is no ambiguity in it.

What are relevant 'purposes'?

If LTA 1954 is to apply, the tenant must occupy the premises concerned (or someone must do so whose occupation is treated as being equivalent to occupation by the tenant), but the tenant need not carry on business there. It is not necessary to show that occupation is necessary for the business concerned, rather that occupation furthers the tenant's business activities[21].

T owns and runs a hotel and rents a nearby cottage where some of the staff live. Whilst it is convenient for T that the staff live nearby, the fact that they live in the cottage rather than elsewhere does not assist the business, so LTA 1954 does not apply to the tenancy of the cottage. However, a medical school, that is the tenant of a nearby flat where some of its students live, provides the students with accommodation because this assists in their education. As the school provides this education in the course of its business LTA 1954 applies to the tenancy of the flat between the medical school and its landlord.

Mixed residential and business use

According to the *Mixed Use Development: Practice and Potential* report from the Office of the Deputy Prime Minister, the number of properties with mixed use is set to increase. In theory, LTA 1954 can apply to the tenancy of a property that has mixed use, and LTA 1954 will apply if the business activity is a significant purpose of the occupation, and not merely incidental to it[22]. This is a question of fact and degree.

T takes a tenancy of a house, with the intention of carrying on a chiropractic practice from the study during the working week. LTA 1954 applies to her tenancy. It would not, however, apply if T merely brought work home from her chiropractic practice and worked in the study of the house, even if emergency patients have, in the past, been treated at the house.

Difficulties can arise where the user of premises changes over time, particularly when premises that are originally let for residential use are then used, in whole or in part, for business purposes.

Business use must be permitted under the lease

If any business use of the whole property is prohibited under the lease, then LTA 1954 does not apply (section 23(4)). A lease will either state this expressly ('not to use for business purposes') or by implication ('not to use for anything other than residential purposes').

If the absolute prohibition on any business use relates to part only of the property, LTA 1954 can still apply.

Where business use is not excluded, it may be limited ('not to use for any purpose other than B1 and B2 user'). In this case, application of LTA 1954 depends on the wording of the restriction:

- if there is a limitation against use in any one or more of the classes of business in section 23(2) of LTA 1954 (trade, profession or employment for individuals; business activity for others) and the actual use is in breach of the prohibition, LTA 1954 does not apply; but
- in all other cases where business use is limited, even if the actual use is in breach of a prohibition, LTA 1954 does apply.

What happens if the landlord has permitted a use that is otherwise in breach of covenant?

LTA 1954 may apply if:

- the *immediate landlord or predecessor in title consents* to the actual use prohibited by the tenancy agreement. Consent may be express or inferred from positive conduct on the landlord's part[23]. Any subsequent variation of the lease which permits the actual use has the same effect;
- the *immediate landlord acquiesces* in the actual use prohibited by the lease. An immediate landlord will be taken to acquiesce in a breach if he has knowledge of it, but subsequently takes a step that affirms the relationship between himself and the tenant (such as the waiver of a right to forfeiture which might have arisen or service of a notice under LTA 1954).

If a landlord acquiesces in a prohibited user, but then sells the interest in the property to a third party, the consent on acquiescence of the predecessor in title is not binding, and if the then immediate Landlord chooses not to consent or acquiesce in breach of the user covenant, LTA 1954 will not apply.

T is the tenant of a grocer's shop, but the premises are actually used to run a restaurant business. The lease contains a clause that: 'the premises shall be used at all times as a grocers shop and for no other purpose'. LTA 1954 applies, even though the operation of the restaurant business is in breach of covenant. If the lease had instead contained a clause that 'the premises shall not be used for any trade, profession or employment save for that of grocers shop', then LTA 1954 would not have applied.

1.6 Relevant time for deciding whether LTA 1954 applies

During the course of a tenancy, and depending on the circumstances, the tenancy can move in and out of LTA 1954 protection. The application of LTA 1954 is therefore transitory. This generally has little effect, but it continues to be of importance:

- if the landlord and tenant wish to surrender the tenancy. LTA 1954 contains special provisions about agreements to surrender;
- if the landlord or tenant wish to serve a notice (under LTA 1954 or otherwise); and
- when the contractual tenancy expires, and a statutory continuation tenancy arises under section 24 of LTA 1954.

Agreement to surrender the tenancy

Whether or not LTA 1954 applies at the time of any agreement to surrender affects the validity of the agreement. This is dealt with in greater detail in chapter 2.

Need LTA 1954 apply when a notice is served?

A notice served under LTA 1954 will not be valid if LTA 1954 does not apply at the time the notice is served[24], but will take effect if LTA 1954 does – at some later stage – apply again[25].

T ceases to occupy a business premises on 1 January 2005. On 2 January 2005, the landlord serves a notice under section 25 of LTA 1954. The notice has no effect because LTA 1954 does not apply on the date of service. But then if T went back into business occupation on 1 March 2005, the notice served on 2 January 2005 would then (retrospectively) take effect.

Notices to quit and break notices

A tenant can serve a notice to quit (to determine a periodic tenancy) or a break notice (to determine a fixed-term tenancy) at any time (provided, under section 24(2)(a) of the LTA 1954, the tenant has been in occupation of the premises for at least a month). These can be served regardless of whether or not LTA 1954 applies, as the Act has no impact on the validity of either notice, and the tenancy will end on expiry of the notice.

A landlord can serve a notice to quit or break notice, but it will not bring the tenancy to an end if LTA 1954 applies (section 24(1)). The only circumstances when a landlord's notice to quit or break notice will bring the tenancy to an end are where:

- the notice is served at a time when LTA 1954 does not apply. The fact that LTA 1954 applies again after the notice is served does not prevent the notice from taking effect (section 24(3)(b)); or
- if LTA 1954 does not apply at the time when the notice expires.

When does the current tenancy end?

If LTA 1954 ceases to apply before expiry of the contractual date of termination, then the current tenancy will end on the contractual date of termination (if it is for a fixed-term) or on expiry of a notice to quit (if it is periodic), even if a notice has been served under LTA 1954 and/or an application made under LTA 1954 to the court (section 27(1A)).

L lets premises to T for a fixed term expiring on 1 June 2006. On 1 December 2005, T serves a section 26 request on L, giving 30 November 2006 as the date of commencement of the new tenancy. On 10 March 2006, before the contractual term had expired, T ceases to occupy the premises, so the tenancy ends on 1 June 2006, notwithstanding that T had served a section 26 request.

If the tenant has already made an application to the court, steps need to be taken to bring the fact that the tenant no longer occupies the premises to the attention of the landlord. If no steps are taken, such that the landlord reasonably believes that the tenant continues in occupation, the tenant may not be able to adduce evidence denying actual occupation as at the contractual date of termination. The effect of this is unclear, but it is likely that the tenant will be allowed to adduce evidence of cesser of occupation only from the date on which the landlord is first notified, and the consequences of this may be that the tenancy will not end until the statutory period expires (see below).

Where a tenancy is for a fixed-term, a landlord will usually serve a section 25 notice specifying in that notice a date for termination which is the same as the date on which the fixed-term actually ends. In such case, there is no 'gap' between the expiry of the contractual date of termination and expiry of the statutory period, which is the period ending on the date of termination specified in the landlord's section 25 notice or date immediately before the date of commencement specified in the tenant's section 26 request (See chapter 6 for more information). If LTA 1954 ceases to apply where there is no gap between expiry of the fixed term and of the statutory period, the tenancy ends on expiry of the fixed term, as stated above.

In the situation where LTA 1954 ceases to apply after expiry of the contractual date of termination but before expiry of the statutory period and before any application is made to the court, then if the tenant remains in occupation for business purposes on expiry of the contractual termination date, a continuation tenancy arises by reason of section 24 of LTA 1954. If LTA 1954 subsequently ceases to apply (and for as long as it ceases to apply):

- no application can be made to the court; but
- the tenancy continues (section 24(3)(a) of LTA 1954).

The question therefore arises as to when the continuation tenancy ends. This is usually when the statutory period expires but could be earlier depending on action taken by the landlord or the tenant.

L lets premises to T for a fixed term expiring on 1 June 2006. On 1 December 2005, T serves a section 26 request on L, giving 30 November 2006 as the date of commencement of the new tenancy. On 10 June 2006, after the contractual term had expired, T ceases to occupy the premises. The tenancy ends on 29 November 2006.

If the tenant wishes to end the tenancy before the statutory period expires then they can serve a notice to quit (to end a periodic tenancy) or break notice (to end a fixed-term tenancy), and the tenancy will end on expiry of such notice if it is before expiry of the statutory period.

If the tenancy is for a fixed term and has no break provisions, the tenant can bring the continuation tenancy to an end before the statutory period by giving not less than three months' written notice to the immediate landlord (section 27(2) of LTA 1954).

L lets premises to T for a fixed term expiring on 1 June 2006. On 1 December 2005, T serves a section 26 request on L, giving 30 November 2006 as the date of commencement of the new tenancy. On 10 June 2006, after the contractual term had expired, T ceases to occupy the premises. On 12 June 2006, T serves notice on L under section 27(2) of LTA 1954 expiring on 12 September 2006. The tenancy ends on that date, notwithstanding that the statutory period has still not expired.

If the landlord wishes to end the tenancy before the statutory period expires then, as stated above, a landlord cannot normally end a tenancy by serving a notice to quit or break notice, but if LTA 1954 ceases to apply this becomes possible. In those circumstances the tenancy will end on expiry of the landlord's notice if it is before expiry of the statutory period.

If the fixed-term tenancy has no break provisions, the landlord can bring it to an end before the statutory period by giving between three and six months' written notice to the tenant (section 24(3)(a) LTA 1954). The fact that LTA 1954 may, once again, apply after service of the notice does not affect the operation of any notice (section 24(3)(b)).

L lets premises to T for a fixed term expiring on 1 June 2006. On 1 December 2005, T serves a section 26 request on L, giving 30 November 2006 as the date of commencement of the new tenancy. On 10 June 2006, after the contractual term had expired,

T ceases to occupy the premises. On 12 June 2006, L serves notice on T under section 24(3)(a) of LTA 1954 expiring on 12 September 2006. The tenancy ends on that date, notwithstanding that the statutory period has still not expired.

Whereas a tenant may have no reason to serve a notice if the statutory period expires before any such notice would, a landlord does. If no notice is served to the landlord and LTA 1954 again applies to the tenancy because, for example, the tenant resumes occupation for business purposes, the possibility of determining the tenancy by service of a notice to quit or break notice will be lost[26].

If a notice is served by the landlord, and LTA 1954 subsequently reapplies, the tenant could in theory make an application for a new tenancy (which would have the effect of continuing the tenancy beyond the date of expiry of the statutory period). Rather than ending on the date three months from the final disposal of those proceedings, however, the continuation tenancy would instead determine on expiry of the landlord's notice.

L lets premises to T for a fixed term expiring on 1 June 2006. On 1 December 2005, T serves a section 26 request on L, giving 30 November 2006 as the date of commencement of the new tenancy. On 10 September 2006, after the contractual term had expired, T ceases to occupy the premises. On 12 September 2006, L serves notice on T under section 24(3)(a) of LTA 1954 expiring on 12 December 2006. T does not resume occupation. The tenancy ends on expiry of the statutory period, 29 November 2006, notwithstanding that the landlord's notice has still not expired.

In the above example, if T resumed occupation on 1 November 2006 and made a claim for a new tenancy on 2 November 2006, the tenancy would end on expiry of the landlord's notice, 12 December 2006.

If an application has been made to the court, and LTA 1954 then ceases to apply, the tenancy will nevertheless continue for a period and ends on the later of the date:

- three months after final disposal of the proceedings; or
- on which the statutory period expires.

The claim will be disposed of when the court makes an order:

- striking-out the claim;
- discontinuing the claim;

- giving (summary) judgment on the claim or allowing an appeal; or
- dismissing the claim or an appeal.

Usually, the 'final disposal' date is 14 days after the date of such an order (see chapter 6), which is the time within which it can be appealed.

If LTA 1954 ceases to apply, but a claim has already been made to the court, what happens to the proceedings?

Tenant has claimed an order for the grant of a new tenancy

Usually, a tenant will discontinue a claim if they no longer occupy for business purposes. If the tenant does not, the court should strike out the claim as an abuse of process (whether of its own volition or, more typically, on an application made by the landlord). It is a continuing condition of the tenant's right to a new tenancy that at all times during the course of the proceedings the tenant holds a tenancy to which LTA 1954 applies (and continues to apply)[27]. The court has no jurisdiction to make an order for the grant a new tenancy if – at any time during the course of proceedings – LTA 1954 does or has not applied, even if the landlord wants the court to grant a new tenancy.

Landlord has claimed an order for the grant of a new tenancy

The landlord cannot discontinue a claim without the tenant's agreement (section 24(2C) of LTA 1954). This will normally be given, but if the tenant refuses to agree or has disappeared, the landlord should apply for an order dismissing the claim, with an order for costs against the tenant.

If the landlord does not take steps to discontinue a claim where the tenant has agreed to this, the tenant should inform the court that it does not wish to take a new tenancy and in such event the court must dismiss the landlord's claim under section 29(5) of LTA 1954.

Landlord has claimed a termination order

A termination order is one that has the effect of terminating the current tenancy without the grant of any new tenancy, introduced with effect from 1 June 2004 (this is dealt with in greater detail in chapter 9)

The Landlord cannot discontinue a claim without the tenant's agreement (section 26(9) of LTA 1954). This will normally be given, but if the tenant refuses to agree or has disappeared, the landlord should apply for an order dismissing the claim, with an order for costs against the tenant.

Continued

LTA 1954 is not clear as to whether, after a landlord's claim for a termination order has been dismissed, LTA 1954 can then re-apply and/or whether the tenant would be able to make a claim for a new tenancy if the statutory period had not yet expired. The authors consider that even if LTA 1954 could re-apply, the tenant could not then make a claim for a new tenancy, because section 24(2B) of LTA 1954 provides that such a claim may not be made if a claim for a termination order has been made and that claim has been served.

If the landlord refuses to apply for a claim to be dismissed, the tenant must wait for that claim to be tried. If the tenant is prepared to consent to an order, this should be offered by the tenant at the earliest opportunity in order to protect against future costs (see the section on offers to settle in chapter 7).

2

Excluding LTA 1954 protection

Contracting out is the statutory process set out in section 38A of the *Landlord and Tenant Act* 1954 (LTA 1954) where a landlord and tenant agree that LTA 1954 protection will not apply to a particular tenancy. In other words, they agree that the tenancy can be surrendered early or that the tenant will not have the right to compensation or to renew the tenancy once it ends. Once a contracted-out tenancy comes to an end, the tenant no longer has a right to occupy the premises and the landlord is entitled to possession.

It is important to note that *both* parties must agree to the tenancy being contracted out. Whilst it is true that a landlord cannot force a prospective tenant to accept a contracted-out tenancy, often the prospective tenant does not really have any choice. Either the tenant accepts the contracted-out tenancy or it will have to risk not being granted one.

Of course, this position can change depending on the relative negotiating strengths of the parties. Also, a tenant who already holds a business tenancy protected by LTA 1954 can (subject to the landlord's ability to oppose renewal on any of the statutory grounds) insist on being granted a new protected tenancy.

Specifically, contracting out excludes the provisions of sections 24 to 28 of LTA 1954 from the tenancy. These are the provisions which, broadly speaking ensure that a business tenancy continues after the contractual tenancy expires, and allow the parties to apply to court for a renewal tenancy.

Where the parties agreed to grant or surrender business tenancies before 1 June 2004, contracting out was achieved by applying to court for an order authorising the agreement to contract out. From and including 1 June 2004, the contracting-out procedure was changed to a system of warning notices and declarations from the landlord and tenant respectively. (These issues are looked at in more detail later in this chapter.)

The general rule is that any agreement to contract out of LTA 1954 is void (section 38(1)). However, this rule is relaxed in certain defined circumstances, which then permit contracting out.

This chapter explains:

- what agreements can be contracted out (section 2.1);
- why landlords or tenants should exclude protection (section 2.2);
- the old contracting-out procedure (section 2.3); and
- the new contracting-out procedure (sections 2.4 and 2.5).

In reality, surveyors will not normally be advising their clients on the intricacies of the contracting-out process. As will be seen, the new post 1 June 2004 procedure is fraught with potential difficulties. The provisions are seemingly straightforward but actually do not cater for a number of common commercial property transactions, such as option agreements and guarantors who are required to take a new tenancy on the tenant's insolvency.

At the time of the consultation on the new procedures a large number of representations were made to the government about the procedure's failings. The government has promised to review the new procedure.

What follows is an overview of the contracting-out process. Its main purpose is to allow surveyors to identify whether a tenancy has been properly contracted out of LTA 1954. Because of the potential pitfalls, expert legal advice should be obtained when dealing with the new contracting-out procedures.

2.1 Agreements landlords and tenants can contract out

Contracting out applies in two situations:

- to the grant of a new tenancy of premises (whether or not they are already occupied by the tenant); and
- to an agreement for the surrender of an existing tenancy that is protected by LTA 1954.

The first situation is straightforward, as a new lease cannot be excluded from LTA 1954 protection unless the contracting-out requirements are met. However, the second situation is less straightforward and requires some explanation.

Agreements to surrender

An agreement to surrender is an agreement (whether oral or written) for the tenant to surrender the tenancy to the landlord 'at some future point in time' – where future does not have to mean weeks, months or years and can include hours, minutes or even seconds.

Under LTA 1954, if the agreement to surrender has *not* been properly contracted out, then it is void and unenforceable. There is, though, nothing to stop the parties achieving a surrender either by deed or by operation of law.

It is 1 January 2006. L is the landlord of T who has three years left of a five-year tenancy. T no longer wants the tenancy and L agrees to accept a surrender of it. If L and T agree on 1 January 2006 that T will leave on 1 February 2006, but then on 1 February 2006 T decides to continue with the tenancy, L cannot enforce the terms of the agreement as it is an unauthorised agreement for surrender and is void.

However if on 1 January 2006 L and T signed a deed of surrender which is stated to take effect immediately and then T decided not to move out, L is within rights to enforce the deed of surrender and evict T. This is because the deed of surrender was not an agreement to surrender the tenancy at a future point in time, but a document evidencing the actual surrender of the tenancy there and then.

Another instance where L would be allowed to evict T would be if after agreeing on 1 January 2006 that T will leave on 1 February 2006, T moved out and handed the keys back to L who then changed the locks. Even if T were to decide later in the day to return to the premises, L is able to refuse, despite the fact that the surrender arose as a result of the unauthorised agreement on 1 January 2006. This is because the actual surrender occurred by operation of law when T moved out and L changed the locks.

It is important to note that this rule only applies to tenancies that are protected by LTA 1954. If the tenancy has *already* been contracted out, it is not necessary to also contract out the agreement to surrender.

2.2 Why exclude protection of LTA 1954

The position of landlords and tenants has changed since LTA 1954 was introduced. The rental market is more evenly balanced, with supply currently outstripping demand in a number of areas, and business tenants are often in stronger negotiating positions than landlords. The value to tenants of the statutory right to a renewal tenancy usually results in a higher rent and given the market, some tenants prefer to pay a cheaper rent. They do not see the right to a new tenancy as a part of their future business plans and so are not willing to pay for it.

Equally, landlords are increasingly wanting to maintain flexibility in their portfolios. Gone are the days when a 14- or 21-year tenancy was the norm. Shorter, contracted-out tenancies allow landlords to more easily move with market demands. A contracted-out tenancy means that a landlord is certain of regaining possession. The landlord is then better able to plan for the refurbishment or even entire demolition and redevelopment of properties.

Landlords usually do not want to be left with subtenants (especially subtenants of part) when the head tenancy comes to an end and contracting out is therefore often a precondition to subletting the whole or part of the business tenant's holding. As is discussed in chapter one, a subtenant that remains in business occupation after the head tenancy ends is entitled under LTA 1954 to remain in occupation, even if the subtenancy was created unlawfully.

2.3 Contracting out before 1 June 2004

Surveyors are often asked to advise on existing tenancy arrangements when managing or acquiring premises. As part of this process it is important that a surveyor can recognise whether a business tenancy is protected by the LTA 1954 or not. So, whilst it is no longer possible to use the old contracting-out procedure (subject to the transitional provisions detailed in section 2.6), a surveyor still needs to be aware of that procedure's requirements.

The pre-1 June 2004 procedure applied to the granting of new tenancies and agreements to surrender existing tenancies protected by LTA 1954.

Granting of new tenancies

Where the parties agreed that the new tenancy should be contracted out, they would jointly apply to court. They would seek the court's authorisation to their agreement to exclude the provisions of sections 24–28 LTA 1954.

The application had to be made *before* the new tenancy was entered into and the proposed new tenancy had to be one for a fixed period of time, such as five years, 25 years or even nine months. It could not be a periodic tenancy that ran, for example, from quarter to quarter.

The parties would jointly confirm to the court that they had agreed the new tenancy was to be contracted out and then the court would then make an order authorising that agreement.

Reference to the agreement to contract out and to the court order was then included within the terms of the tenancy agreement itself or was endorsed on the tenancy agreement.

Agreement to surrender existing tenancies

The procedure was virtually identical to that for granting new leases. The parties applied jointly for the court to authorise their agreement to surrender the tenancy, but unlike the grant of a new lease, the agreement to surrender did not need to contain an endorsement or clause confirming the agreement to contract out. So long as the agreement to surrender mirrored the one ordered by the court, then the agreement was lawful.

I am reviewing a small commercial property portfolio with a number of leases that were completed in the 1980s. How can I tell whether they have been contracted out of LTA 1954?

Check the tenancy agreement itself. Is there a clause that refers to the tenancy having been contracted out? The wording of these clauses differ but they usually look something like this:

'Having been authorised to do so by an order of the [XXXX] County Court made on [date] under the provisions of section 38(4) of the *Landlord and Tenant Act* 1954 as amended the parties hereto hereby agree that the provisions of sections 24 to 28 of that Act as amended shall be excluded in relation to this lease.'

If the tenancy agreement does not contain a clause similar to this or does not have similar wording endorsed somewhere on it, then the lease is probably protected by LTA 1954. However, to be certain you will need to see a copy of the court order authorising the contracting-out agreement.

2.4 Contracting out on or after 1 June 2004

As before 1 June 2004, the ability to contract out applies both to granting a new tenancy and agreeing to surrender an existing, protected tenancy. The new provisions are contained partly in section 38A LTA 1954 and partly in schedule 2 to the *Regulatory Reform (Business Tenancies) Order* 2003.

In simple terms, the new procedure, contained in section 38A LTA 1954, requires the landlord to serve the tenant with a notice that warns the tenant that it is going to lose LTA 1954 rights. The tenant replies with a declaration confirming that it has received the landlord's notice and the declaration also states that the tenant accepts the consequences of the tenancy being contracted out/surrendered.

For the grant of a new tenancy

There are two different procedural requirements depending on how much notice is given before the new tenancy is granted.

If the landlord gives at least 14 days notice, the landlord is required to serve the tenant with a notice in the prescribed form (see appendix 9A) not less than 14 days before the date on which the tenant enters into the tenancy, or, if it is an earlier date, before the tenant becomes contractually bound to enter into the tenancy.

There is debate amongst commentators as to what 'contractually bound' means. Some argue that a tenant is contractually bound to take a tenancy when it enters into a conditional agreement for lease. Therefore, they say, that the contracting-out landlord's notice/tenant's declaration procedure must be followed before entering into an agreement for lease. Others say that this is not the effect of the legislation so that the contracting-out procedure only needs to be followed just before the agreement for lease goes unconditional. The authors' view is that the former, more cautious approach should be adopted.

If the new tenancy contains obligations on a guarantor to take a grant of a new tenancy on the tenant's insolvency, then some commentators believe that the guarantor must also be served with the landlord's notice and then required to give the tenant's declaration. Others believe that this is only necessary if and when the guarantor is later called on to take a new tenancy. The authors believe that the former approach is the more sensible. However, expert legal advice should be obtained when dealing with the new contracting-out procedures.

The notice will give the landlord's name and address, and will also tell the tenant that the tenancy will have no security of tenure.

The tenant (or their authorised agent) must then make a declaration in the prescribed form (see appendix 9C), which states the tenant's name, the address of the proposed demised premises and the duration of the proposed tenancy. The declaration confirms that the tenant has received and read the landlord's notice, and that the tenant understands the consequences of entering into a contracted-out tenancy.

A reference to the landlord's notice and the tenant's declaration must be contained in or endorsed upon the tenancy agreement (and not the agreement for lease) – this is according to paragraph 5 to schedule 2 of the *Regulatory Reform (Business Tenancies) Order* 2003. The tenancy agreement must also, according to paragraph 6 to schedule 2 of the 2003 Order, contain a clause referring to the agreement to exclude the provisions of section 24–28 LTA 1954.

Recommended wording required by the *Regulatory Reform (Business Tenancies) Order* 2003

For the declaration and clause required to be included in a tenancy agreement, there is no prescribed wording that must be used. The following wording (or wording like it) would meet the requirements:

Exclusion of statutory provisions

1. The Tenant confirms that before [the date of this Lease]/[it became contractually bound to enter into the tenancy created by this Lease]:

(a) The Landlord served on the Tenant a notice (Notice) dated [XX] in relation to the tenancy created by this lease in a form complying with the requirements of schedule 1 to the *Regulatory Reform (Business Tenancies) (England and Wales) Order* 2003 (Order).

(b) The Tenant, or a person duly authorised by the Tenant, in relation to the Notice made a declaration (Declaration) dated [XX] in a form complying with the requirements of schedule 2 of the Order.

2. The Landlord and Tenant agree to exclude the provisions of Sections 24 to 28 (inclusive) of the *Landlord and Tenant Act 1954* in relation to the tenancy created by this Lease.

As can be seen, the suggested wording is quite lengthy. However, because the LTA 1954 imposes the requirements listed above, it is vital to ensure that the tenancy agreement shows that these have been met. In explanation:

- points 1 (a) and (b) above provide the reference to the notice and declaration required by paragraph 5 to schedule 2 of the *Regulatory Reform (Business Tenancies) Order* 2003. The first sentence also confirms that the notice/declaration were made/given before the tenancy/agreement for lease were completed; and
- point 2 is the parties' agreement to exclude the provisions of section 24–28 LTA 1954, required by paragraph 6 to schedule 2 of the 2003 Order.

If the landlord were to give less than 14 days notice the procedure is the same as above *except* that the tenant's declaration is different – the tenant must make a statutory declaration (one which is given before a commissioner for oaths, solicitor or similar person, but not before the tenant's own solicitors' firm) in the prescribed form (see appendix 9B).

Agreement to surrender

The procedure for an agreement to surrender is almost identical to that used for the grant of a new tenancy. (This process is discussed in chapter 3.)

The longer procedure involves the tenant being served with a notice in the prescribed form (see appendix 9D) not less than 14 days before the date on which he or she enters into the agreement to surrender or (if earlier) becomes contractually bound to do so.

The notice gives the landlord's name and address and warns the tenant that occupation of the premises will not be permitted after the date for surrender given in the agreement. The tenant is also told that there is no entitlement to compensation, unless agreed otherwise.

The tenant (or their authorised agent) must then make a declaration in the prescribed form (see appendix 9E). In the declaration the tenant confirms receipt of the landlord's notice, as well as confirming understanding of the consequences of entering into the agreement to surrender. The declaration also states the tenant's name, the address of the demised premises and the tenancy's commencement date.

It is important to note that (unlike the new tenancy contracting-out procedure) there is no need to refer to the landlord's notice/tenant's declaration in the agreement to surrender.

If the landlord gives less than 14 days notice the procedure is the same as above *except* that the tenant's declaration is different – the tenant must make a statutory declaration (one given before a commissioner for oaths, solicitor or similar person, but not before the tenant's own solicitors' firm) in the prescribed form (see appendix 9F).

Which procedure?

You may be wondering why there is one procedure where a landlord gives 14 days or more notice and another for where the landlord gives less notice. In its journey through parliament, a great deal of concern was raised about taking away the court's ability to refuse a contracting-out order (even though this was rarely, if ever, exercised).

In the explanatory notes to the *Regulatory Reform (Business Tenancies) Order* 2003, the government indicated that it expected the '14 days or longer notice' procedure to be adopted in most cases and that the 'less than 14 days notice' procedure would only be used on the 'rare' occasions when the parties did not have 14 days between agreement of the lease terms and execution of the lease itself.

In reality, the 'less than 14 days notice' procedure will be normally used. It is unlikely that parties will want to hang around for 14 days before executing the tenancy agreement once its terms have been finalised.

General issues

The regulations in the *Regulatory Reform (Business Tenancies) Order* 2003 do not make it clear whether the terms of the proposed tenancy/agreement to surrender must have been agreed before the landlord's notice is served. There has been a great deal of discussion as to whether a notice can be served at heads of term stage or only once the agreement's terms are finalised.

The authors believe that it is safer to serve the landlord's notice once the terms of the new tenancy/agreement to surrender have been finalised – as the legislation states that the landlord's notice must be served before the 'tenant enters into the tenancy to which it applies'. The prescribed form of notice warns the tenant not to 'commit to the lease' without reading the notice carefully. This seems to suggest that Parliament intended the tenancy terms to have been finalised. Further, it is sensible to attach the draft tenancy/agreement to the landlord's notice and the tenant's declaration. In this way there can be no doubt as to which precise agreement the contracting-out procedure relates to.

Where there are joint landlords, then the landlord's notice must name both landlords. There is, though, no need for each landlord to separately serve a notice on the tenant. However, where there is more than one proposed tenant then each tenant should be served with a landlord's notice and each should complete their own declaration – the notice should be addressed to *all* of the proposed tenants

I am acting for a landlord and have just received the tenant's declaration in reply to the landlord's notice. The tenant's declaration is signed by the tenant's agent and not the tenant itself. Does this invalidate the declaration?

Continued

No. So long as the declaration states that the person signing it has the tenant's authority to do so, then you are entitled to rely on the declaration. In fact, the prescribed form actually has a sentence that deals with this. However, you should not rely on the declaration if you have reason to believe that the person who signed the declaration did not have the tenant's authority. You should then ask the tenant to make and sign his or her own declaration.

2.5 Variations to the contracted-out agreement

What effect any variations to the agreement will have on the validity of the contracting-out process will depend on when the variation took place. These rules apply equally to new tenancy agreements and agreements to surrender. It also applies whether the pre- or post-1 June 2004 contracting-out procedure was adopted. This is because the principles are essentially the same, although there have not yet been any reported cases concerning the post 1 June 2004 contracting-out procedure.

Variation after contracting-out procedure complete but before agreement is entered into

If there is a variation after the contracting-out procedure has been completed, but before the agreement has been entered into then it is possible for the parties to only make very limited variations to the draft agreement once the contracting-out procedure had been completed[28]. The words 'that tenancy' in the old legislation (compared with 'the tenancy to which it applies' in the amended legislation) meant that the agreement's terms had to be substantially similar to the draft agreement referred to in the contracting-out process.

The decision in *Metropolitan Police District v Palacegate Properties Limited*[29] means that minor/insignificant variations would not affect the validity of the contracting-out process, whereas major/significant ones would. This is of fundamental importance, as if a new tenancy agreement has not been effectively contracted out, the tenant will enjoy the protection of LTA 1954.

The Court of Appeal indicated that a 'minor' variation would be one which had no bearing on the tenant's need for security of tenure or on understanding of the consequences of contracting out – one example would be if a draft tenancy agreement was varied to change the rent payment date from, say, the 1st to the 10th of each month.

Conversely, the Court of Appeal indicated that a 'significant' variation was once which did impact on the tenant's need for security of tenure. This would include a variation that reduced the tenancy's length or significantly increased the rent.

In the past, parties tended to be less keen to go through the lengthy court process of obtaining another court order following a variation in the draft lease as this served only to increase the cost and time of getting the new lease in place.

Since 1 June 2004, the contracting-out procedure is now comparatively cheap and speedy – particularly if the 'less than 14 days notice' procedure is adopted. With this in mind, if there is ever any doubt as to whether a variation is 'minor' or 'significant', the best advice is to repeat the contracting-out process with the varied draft lease.

Some practitioners suggest that this is not necessary and that an additional 'deed of variation' can be completed before the new lease is executed. The authors disagree and believe this is a highly risky practice to adopt, as, firstly, there is no point drafting an additional document when the parties can just as easily amend the draft lease and serve new contracting-out notices for it, and, secondly, the contracting-out process does not apply to deeds of variation. The newly varied and then executed lease might then fall within LTA 1954 protection.

Variation after contracted-out agreement is entered into

Once the contracted-out agreement has been entered into, the parties are free to vary it whenever they agree to do so. The variation will not affect the validity of the contracting-out process *unless* the variation amounts to an implied surrender and regrant (by, for example, *increasing* the length of the tenancy or the size of the demised premises). If there is an implied surrender and regrant then the newly granted tenancy will gain the protection of the LTA 1954. This can be avoided by simply using the contracting-out procedure to grant a new lease incorporating the varied term length or demise.

2.6 Compensation

If a tenancy has been contracted out of LTA 1954 the tenant has no right to statutory compensation on quitting the premises at the end of the term. If a tenancy has not been contracted out it is still possible to modify or exclude the tenant's right to statutory compensation. (This is dealt with in detail in chapter 10.)

2.7 Transitional provisions

There are a number of transitional provisions contained within the new legislation, including:

- any agreement to contract out of the LTA 1954 which was authorised by a court order made before 1 June 2004 remains effective;

- many tenancy agreements contain a covenant requiring the tenant to ensure that any subletting is contracted out, but if the covenant requires the tenant to obtain a court order authorising the contracting-out (whether or not the tenancy agreement was entered into before 1 June 2004), then reference to a court order is to be construed as a reference to using the new contracting-out procedures; and
- The new legislation retains the old contracting-out procedure for agreements for lease entered into before 1 June 2004, which were often conditional on a contracting-out order being obtained for the new tenancy. Parties to agreements for leases entered into before 1 June 2004 must therefore still apply to court for an order authorising a contracting-out agreement.

3

How to end a tenancy

Nothing in the *Landlord and Tenant Act* 1954 (LTA 1954) prevents the termination of a protected tenancy by forfeiture (of the immediate tenancy or of a superior tenancy), surrender, or service by the tenant of a notice to quit or a break notice. In all other cases, however, the tenancy may not be terminated other than in accordance with LTA 1954, which means serving a notice under sections 25 or 27, or serving a request under section 26.

This chapter looks at the effect of LTA 1954 on ending business tenancies. It compares the different termination methods applicable to those tenancies that are the subject of LTA 1954 (so called 'protected tenancies') and those which are not (so called 'unprotected tenancies'), and examines the common law methods of termination by:

- forfeiture (section 3.1);
- surrender (section 3.2);
- notice to quit where the tenancy is periodic (section 3.3);
- break option where the tenancy is a fixed-term (section 3.4); and
- effluxion/expiry where the tenancy is a fixed-term (section 3.5).

The chapter also considers section 25 notices, section 26 requests and section 27 notices (sections 3.6 and 3.7).

It should be remembered that an unprotected tenancy is not just one that has been deliberately excluded from protection by the parties (as discussed in chapter 2). The phrase also includes tenancies that were originally protected but become unprotected, where the tenant does not fulfil all of the requirements for LTA 1954, such as if the tenant no longer occupies the premises for business purposes (as discussed in chapter 1).

3.1 Forfeiture

Forfeiture is the landlord's power to bring a tenancy to an end due to the tenant's breach of covenant (assuming the tenancy agreement contains a forfeiture clause). It can be exercised by peaceable re-entry or by the issue and service of court forfeiture proceedings. Its effect is to end all future rights and obligations under the tenancy, including the right to receive/obligation to pay future rent as well as the tenant's right to occupy.

The right to forfeit is unaffected by LTA 1954 so that it does not matter whether the tenancy is protected or unprotected. If the tenancy is forfeited the tenant can, in the usual way, apply to court for relief from forfeiture and the court will then exercise its discretion in deciding whether to grant relief and on what, if any, conditions.

What happens if a landlord seeks to forfeit where proceedings for or opposing the grant of a renewal tenancy are underway under LTA 1954?

The Court of Appeal has decided that so long as an application for relief from forfeiture is made without undue delay, then for the purposes of LTA 1954 the tenancy still exists. A landlord's application to strike out the claim for a renewal tenancy will not succeed unless it is obvious that relief will not be granted[30].

Until the tenant's application for relief from forfeiture has been dealt with, the court should be asked to adjourn the claim for the renewal tenancy. There is no point the parties wasting costs and court time dealing with the renewal claim if there is a risk that the tenant's application for relief might fail.

Effect of forfeiture on subtenancies

The forfeiture of a head tenancy destroys all interests granted under that head tenancy[31] – so if a head tenancy is reinstated following an application for relief from forfeiture, then all of the subtenancies are also reinstated.

Subtenants can also seek relief from forfeiture, but, if relief is given, it is by the grant of an entirely new tenancy to the former subtenant. The terms of that new tenancy are decided by the court and can differ from the original head tenancy.

Sometimes a subtenant applies for relief from forfeiture at a time when the subtenancy is being continued by LTA 1954 (i.e. where the subtenancy has expired). In deciding the terms for the new tenancy that will be granted as a result of the relief application the court will exercise its discretion. According to the Court of Appeal in *Cadogan v Dimovic*[32] it must do so within the constraints of LTA 1954 – as an example the new tenancy's length should not be more than 15 years (section 33).

Unlawful subtenancies

As discussed in chapter 1, LTA 1954 protection applies equally to lawful and unlawful subtenancies[33]. As a result, unless the landlord forfeits the head-tenancy, and assuming LTA 1954 does apply to the subtenancy, it will probably have no method of immediately terminating that subtenancy even though it is unlawful (subject always to the possibility that the court will grant an order requiring the unlawful sub tenancy to be surrendered)[34].

You may wonder what will happen if the superior landlord does not forfeit the head-tenancy or only discovers the unlawful subtenancy once the head-tenancy has expired. Once the landlord becomes the competent landlord (discussed further in chapter 4), it is possible to rely on the statutory grounds in section 30(1) of LTA 1954 to obtain possession from the unlawful subtenant. The ground most likely to be relied on is section 30(1)(c):

> '... that the tenant ought not be granted a new tenancy ... for any other reason connected with the tenant's use and management of the holding ...'

This is covered in more detail in chapter 7.

3.2 Surrender

A surrender is the consensual act of the tenant offering, and the landlord accepting, the return of the tenancy to the landlord thereby bringing it to an end. It can happen by the parties executing a deed of surrender. It can also happen by implication because of surrounding circumstances, where the tenant vacates the premises and the landlord accepts the keys back for example. An implied surrender is known as a 'surrender by operation of law'.

The parties can also enter into an 'agreement to surrender', to effect a surrender at some time in the future. However, as discussed in chapter 2, if the tenancy is protected by LTA 1954 the agreement to surrender will be void unless it is first contracted out.

Unprotected v protected tenancies

The effect of a surrender on unprotected and protected tenancies is the same – once a surrender takes place it ends all future rights and obligations under the tenancy, subject to any agreement to the contrary.

A surrender by deed or operation of law will also determine both protected and unprotected tenancies. However, there is an important difference between unprotected and protected tenancies when dealing with agreements to surrender:

- Landlords and tenants of unprotected tenancies are free to enter into an agreement to surrender at any time; but
- Landlords and tenants of protected tenancies *cannot* enter into an agreement to surrender unless they have first complied with section 38A(4) of LTA 1954. If they do not then the agreement to surrender will be void.

For protected tenancies and agreements to surrender, section 38A(2) of LTA 1954 provides that:

> 'The persons who are the landlord and the tenant in relation to a tenancy to which this Part of this Act applies may agree that the tenancy shall be surrendered on such date or in such circumstances as may be specified in the agreement and on such terms (if any) as may be so specified.'

In principle, therefore, nothing prevents the landlord and tenant from agreeing to surrender the tenancy, but section 38A(4) continues:

> 'An agreement under subsection (2) above shall be void unless:
>
> (a) the landlord has served on the tenant a notice in the form, or substantially in the form, set out in Schedule 3 to the 2003 Order; and
> (b) the requirements specified in Schedule 4 to that Order are met.'

The 2003 Order referred to is the *Regulatory Reform (Business Tenancies) (England and Wales) Order* 2003. (The form referred to is at appendix 9D.)

As discussed in greater detail in chapter 2, the requirements specified in Schedule 4 to that Order are that:

- before the tenant enters into the agreement for surrender, or becomes contractually obliged to do so:
- (a) the landlord must serve the notice under section 38A(4)(a) of LTA 1954; and

(b) if the notice is served 14 days or more before the tenant is to enter into the agreement, or will become contractually bound to do so, the tenant (or a person authorised by him) must make a declaration in the form, or substantially the form, of the declaration in paragraph 6 of Schedule 4 to the 2003 Order; or

(c) if the notice is served less than 14 days before the tenant is to enter into the agreement, or will become contractually bound to do so, the tenant (or a person authorised by him) must make a statutory declaration in the form, or substantially the form, of the statutory declaration in paragraph 7 of Schedule 4 to the 2003 Order; and

- reference to the landlord's notice and tenant's declaration or statutory declaration must be contained in or endorsed on the agreement to surrender.

3.3 Notices to quit (periodic tenancies)

A notice to quit is used to bring an unprotected periodic tenancy (one without any fixed length, which, for example, runs weekly, monthly or quarterly) to an end. Either landlord or tenant can serve it and so long as it is of the correct length and expires on the last or first day of the period, it will bring the periodic tenancy to an end.

A tenant of a protected tenancy can serve a notice to quit to bring it to an end (much like the break option discussed in the next section). If the landlord has already served a section 25 notice the tenant can still serve a notice to quit to end the tenancy earlier than the date given in the section 25 notice.

Except in exceptional circumstances (see section 1.6), a notice to quit served by a landlord will not bring a protected tenancy to an end, as section 24(1) of LTA 1954 ensures that the tenancy continues unless and until determined in accordance with LTA 1954. The landlord must rely on one of the other common law methods (if applicable) or serve a section 25 notice relying on one or more of the statutory grounds in section 30(1) of LTA 1954 to end a protected periodic tenancy.

3.4 Break options

A break option is the right for the party with the benefit of the option to bring a fixed term tenancy to an earlier end. The option is usually contained within the tenancy agreement itself (as 'the break clause') and can only be operated by very strictly complying with the procedure set out. The normal procedure requires a break notice to be served, expiring on the break date, but there are often preconditions that must also be complied with before the break notice expires.

If a tenancy is unprotected and a valid break notice is served, it will bring the tenancy to an end on the break date specified by the tenancy agreement. All future rights and obligations under the tenancy come to an end on the break date, but, depending on the terms of the tenancy, past breaches can usually still be claimed for.

The effect of a break notice on a protected fixed term tenancy depends on whether the tenant or the landlord exercises the right to break.

If the tenant exercises the break option, the effect on the tenancy is the same as if it were an unprotected one. This is because section 24(2) of LTA 1954 specifically allows the tenant to end a protected tenancy using a break option contained in the tenancy agreement. The one exception to this rule is that the tenant cannot serve a break notice to bring the tenancy to an end during the first month of the tenancy (section 24(2)(a) of LTA 1954)[35].

If the landlord exercises a break option the only effect is to bring the fixed term of the contractual tenancy to an end. Section 24(1) of LTA 1954 makes it clear that the tenancy will continue and it becomes known as a continuation tenancy. Practically, the only way for the landlord to force the tenancy to end is to forfeit it (if there is a breach and the tenancy gives the landlord a right to forfeit) or to serve a section 25 notice, opposing renewal on one of the statutory grounds in section 30(1) of LTA 1954 (for more information see chapter 7).

Unlike the tenant, and depending on the wording of the break clause, a landlord can use a section 25 notice both to effect the break and start the tenancy renewal/opposition process (this is detailed in chapter 4).

3.5 Expiry of the fixed term

When the fixed term of an unprotected tenancy comes to an end then the tenant's right to remain in the premises also ends. If a tenant does not vacate, they becomes a trespasser and are liable to pay the landlord mesne profits (or 'use and occupation charges'), which the court will usually determine to be equal to the current market rent for the premises.

If a landlord wants to regain possession once the tenancy expires, they can (subject to certain considerations) peaceably re-enter the premises and change the locks. If the tenant refuses to vacate and the landlord cannot peaceably re-enter (because, for example, the tenant leaves a person on the premises who would oppose entry by the landlord), then the landlord must issue possession proceedings.

The periodic tenancy trap

Landlords need to be careful not to demand rent from a person whose unprotected tenancy has expired or been brought to an end. To do so could imply the creation of a new, protected, periodic tenancy with all the rights to renewal and compensation that go with it.

Where the landlord is negotiating with a former tenant for the grant of a new tenancy the law will usually imply a tenancy at will between the parties whilst negotiations continue. However, landlords are best advised to write to their former tenants confirming the grant of a tenancy at will pending the agreement and grant of the new tenancy.

If the tenant just needs a few extra days or weeks to vacate the premises then this can also be provided for – a tenancy at will can be granted, rent can be charged and the landlord is entitled to possession on mere demand.

The advantage/disadvantage of the tenancy at will is that either side can give immediate notice to end it. It should, though, always be remembered that the courts will look behind the face of any agreement to find its true purpose. If a document or agreement described as a tenancy at will is in fact an ongoing periodic tenancy then the court will construe it as such[36].

As mentioned in chapter 1, section 24(1) of LTA 1954 continues a protected tenancy after its fixed term has expired. This is so long as the tenant is in occupation of the premises for the purpose of its business on the last day of the term. If the tenant is not (or it has served a section 27(1) notice expiring on that day), then section 27(1A) states that section 24 will not apply and so the tenancy will end on the last day of the fixed term.

Where the tenancy continues, the landlord and tenant can either leave matters as they are, negotiate a new tenancy, or serve a section 25 notice/26 request to bring the current tenancy to an end.

Where a tenancy is continued by LTA 1954, the landlord can still regain possession by forfeiture or surrender. The tenant can also bring the continuation tenancy to an end by serving notice under section 27(2), as detailed later in this chapter.

I represent a landlord who, ideally, would like to obtain vacant possession from a business tenant but he does not think he can rely on any of the statutory grounds of opposition. What should he do?

The landlord can either leave the current tenancy in place or serve a non-hostile section 25 notice to determine it. If the tenant does not make a claim for a new tenancy on or before that date, then he or she loses the right to do so and will have to leave.

If the landlord chooses to serve a notice, he may want to consider putting a rent stop on the account with effect from the date of termination specified in the notice. If he demands rent after the date specified without making it clear that he did not intend for the tenant holding over to regain protection under LTA 1954, there could be arguments about the creation of a new periodic tenancy subject to the Act. If those arguments succeed, the landlord would then have to go through the whole LTA 1954 process again, and the opportunity afforded by the tenant's failure to apply for a new tenancy will have been lost.

3.6 Section 25 notices and section 26 requests

Section 25 notices and section 26 requests have the effect of terminating the current protected tenancy on the termination/renewal date in the notice/request. Both have prescribed forms and only apply to protected tenancies. Chapter 4 considers them in more detail.

Section 25 notices

Section 25 notices can be served both before and after the fixed period of a tenancy ends and they can also be served when dealing with a purely periodic tenancy. The notice must be a minimum of six months and a maximum of 12 months long (section 25(2) of LTA 1954).

A section 25 notice can be hostile (served by a landlord who opposes the grant of a new tenancy on one or more of the grounds set out in section 30(1) of LTA 1954) or non-hostile (served by a landlord who does not oppose the grant of a new tenancy).

Assuming that no application is made to the court after service of a section 25 notice, the current tenancy will end on the termination date stated in the notice.

Terminating periodic tenancies or tenancies with break clauses

There are additional requirements relating to break notices and periodic tenancies, as the termination date is calculated slightly differently (section 25(3) of LTA 1954).

Periodic tenancies normally terminate on expiry of a notice to quit and it is not necessary to serve a notice to quit and a section 25 notice to end a periodic tenancy that is subject to LTA 1954. A section 25 notice alone will be sufficient provided that the termination date specified in that notice is not earlier than:

- six months nor later than 12 months after the section 25 notice is given; and
- the date on which the periodic tenancy could have been determined by a common law notice to quit.

T has a yearly periodic tenancy running from and including 1 January each year. The common law rule is that not less than six months' notice to quit must be given to expire either on the first or last day of the annual period. On 1 May 2005. Landlord, L, wanted to serve a section 25 notice on T giving the earliest termination date possible. L calculates that, excluding the day of service, a section 25 notice six months long would have a termination date of 1 November 2005.

However, because T's annual periodic tenancy cannot be brought to an end by common law notice to quit before 31 December 2005, a termination date of 1 November 2005 would invalidate the section 25 notice. L therefore correctly inserted a termination date of 31 December 2005 and serves the section 25 notice. This termination date is valid because it is more than six months after the section 25 notice is given and it is not earlier than the annual periodic tenancy could have been determined by common law notice to quit.

T's notice would also be valid if any termination date between 31 December 2005 and 1 May 2006 was used. The termination date does not have to be the same as the expiry date of the common law notice to quit, it just must not be earlier than that date.

Tenancies with break clauses can be terminated using a section 25 notice so long as the termination date is not earlier than:

- six months nor later than 12 months after the section 25 notice is given (or, if longer, the period of notice required by the break clause plus six months); and

- the date on which the tenancy could have been determined in accordance with the break clause.

A tenancy agreement contains a break clause requiring the landlord (L) to give the tenant (T) not less than nine months notice to exercise the break. L wants to serve a section 25 notice giving the earliest termination date possible. As of 1 January 2005 L calculates that, excluding the day of service, a section 25 notice six months long and served today would have a termination date of 1 July 2005.

However, because the break clause requires not less than nine months' prior notice, a termination date of 1 July 2005 would invalidate the section 25 notice. L therefore correctly inserts a termination date of 1 October 2005 and serves the section 25 notice. This termination date is valid because it is more than six months after the section 25 notice is given and it is not earlier than the date on which the tenancy could be brought to an end under the break clause.

Problems could arise if a break clause required a period of notice greater than 12 months, but section 25(3)(b) of LTA 1954 provides that instead of the termination date being not later than 12 months after the section 25 notice is given, it is not later than the period required by the break clause plus six months. So, if a break clause requires 18 months notice, the termination date in the section 25 notice can be between 18 and 24 months after the section 25 notice is given.

So long as it strictly complies with requirements of a break clause, a section 25 notice can also act as a break notice[37]. It will then bring the tenancy agreement to an end under the break clause and for the purposes of section 25 LTA 1954. It is, though, good practice to serve the section 25 notice with a covering letter stating that the landlord intends the section 25 notice to also act as a break notice.

It is also possible for a landlord to serve a formal break notice under the tenancy agreement first and then later serve a section 25 notice. If a landlord wants a section 25 notice to double as a break notice, the section 25 notice must strictly comply with the requirements of the break clause. For example, if the break can only be exercised if the landlord wants to increase the demise, a section 25 notice could not exercise the break as the landlord cannot make its wish to increase clear in the notice – in this type of scenario, the landlord should serve two notices: one notice complying with the requirements of the break clause; and the other complying with section 25 of LTA 1954.

Section 26 requests

Section 26 requests can only be served by tenants whose original tenancy was granted for a fixed term of more than one year (section 26(1)). Consequently, they cannot be served by periodic tenants or tenants who were granted a tenancy of a year or less. Like section 25 notices, the request must be of a minimum six months and a maximum 12 months in length. A landlord must serve a counter-notice to a request within two months if there is opposition to the grant of a new tenancy.

The request must specify the date of commencement of the new tenancy and assuming that no application is made to the court, the current tenancy will end on the date immediately before the commencement date stated in the request.

3.7 Section 27 notices

Section 27 notices are served by tenants of protected tenancies to confirm that they do not wish their tenancy to continue. The notices only apply for protected fixed-term tenancies and there are two types of section 27 notice: section 27(1) and section 27(2).

The section 27(1) notice will help a tenant that wishes to prevent a fixed term tenancy from continuing after the contractual expiry date (24(1) of LTA 1954). Section 27(2) notices are used by a tenant wishing to end the tenancy when the fixed term has already expired and the tenancy is being continued under section 24(1) of LTA 1954.

Neither notice can be served if the tenant has already been served a section 26 request (section 26(4) LTA 1954) and they also cannot be served until the tenant has been in occupation under the tenancy for at least one month. (Section 27 notices are discussed in more detail in the next chapter.)

3.8 Final disposal of court proceedings

Once court proceedings are issued for an order for the grant of a new tenancy or for a termination order, section 64 LTA 1954 usually has the effect of continuing the current tenancy beyond the termination date given in the section 25 notice or date immediately before the commencement date given in the section 26 request (in both cases, referred to as the termination date).

The current tenancy will terminate three months after the final disposal of the claim unless, as at that date, the termination date in the section 25 notice or section 26 request is more than three months away, in which case the current tenancy ends on that later date.

LTA 1954 defines the date of 'final disposal' of proceedings as being the earliest date on which the proceedings have ended and the time for appealing or further appealing has expired. Proceedings can end by the application being granted, dismissed, struck out, discontinued or a decision being made on any appeal. The usual time for appealing is fourteen days, so that the current tenancy usually ends three months and fourteen days after any final court order.

If the party making a claim or an appeal withdraws the claim or appeal, by serving a notice of discontinuance for example, then no (further) appeal period is allowed for and the three months then runs from and including the date of the withdrawal.

If the court makes an order for the grant of a new tenancy, the new tenancy normally starts on the day after the date on which the old one ends by reason of this final disposal rule. The parties are, however, free to agree a different start date for the new tenancy if they wish.

4

Dealing with notices

There are a number of notices that can be served under the *Landlord and Tenant Act* 1954 (LTA 1954), as mentioned in the previous chapter. There are prescribed forms for some of these notices and requests (found in the *Landlord and Tenant Act 1954 Part 2 (Notices) Regulations* 2004).

In each case, the parties must use the relevant prescribed form or a form 'substantially to the same effect'. If they do not, their notice will be invalid. Other defects in a notice could also render it invalid, which means care must be taken in preparing it.

This chapter explains:

- who needs to serve or be served with a notice:
  - the 'competent landlord' (section 4.1); and
  - the correct tenant (section 4.2);
- how to complete and respond to the different types of notice:
  - landlord's section 25 notice (section 4.3);
  - superior landlord's notice withdrawing a section 25 notice (section 4.4);
  - tenant's section 26 request for a new lease (section 4.5);
  - tenant's section 27 notice to terminate the tenancy (section 4.6); and
  - section 40 request for information, by landlord or tenant (section 4.7);
- the methods of serving notices (section 4.8); and
- problems with notices (section 4.9).

4.1 The competent landlord

The competent landlord is the only person entitled to serve a section 25 notice and the counter-notice in response to a tenant's section 26 request. Equally, the competent landlord is the only person upon whom a tenant can serve a section 26 request.

It is important to remember that the person who is the 'competent landlord' can change, and, at the very least, the identity should always be checked before serving any notices and before issuing any proceedings.

See the flowchart below for how to identify the 'competent landlord', under section 44 LTA 1954.

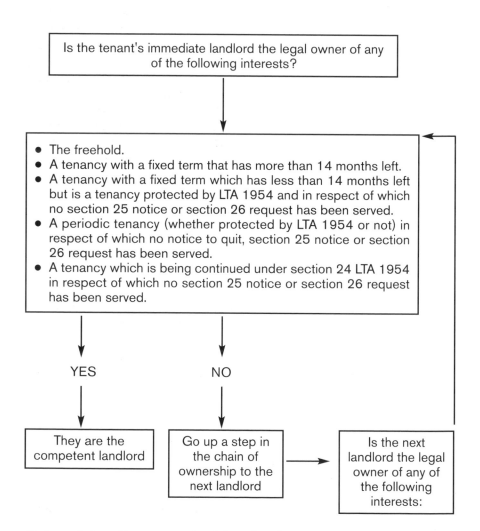

Determining the competent landlord

Issues that affect whether someone is a 'competent landlord'

Registered land: as can be seen from the flow-chart, only the legal owner of an interest can be a competent landlord. For all land registered at HM Land Registry (if the landlord's interest has been registered), only the person named on the Proprietorship Register is the owner of the legal interest. This rule applies even if the owner's name registered at HM Land Registry is incorrect or out of date (for example where the owner company has changed its name over time). The incorrect or old name should be used in any notice until such time as the Proprietorship Register has been amended or updated.

When land is transferred there are often delays before the new owner of the land is registered at HM Land Registry. However, even though they may have done everything necessary to complete the transfer, until the new owner becomes the registered proprietor it is the old owner (whose name still appears on the Proprietorship Register) that remains the competent landlord under LTA 1954. Therefore all notices and court proceedings must be served/issued in the old owner's name. Once the new owner has become the registered owner, then they must be substituted in place of the old owner in any existing court proceedings.

Equitable interests: the competent landlord must be the legal owner of the interest. A person cannot be the competent landlord if they only have an equitable interest[38]. The one exception is if the landlord is a tenant and holds its tenancy under an unconditional agreement for lease[39].

Trustees: as with equitable interests, the beneficiaries under a trust cannot be the competent landlord, only the trustees can.

Receivers and mortgagees: section 67 LTA 1954 confirms that mortgagees in possession or receivers appointed under a mortgage can be the competent landlord.

Severed reversions: where different persons own the same type of interest in different parts of the property demised by the tenancy, the 'competent landlord' means all of those persons collectively (section 44(1A) of LTA 1954).

Joint landlords: as with joint tenants, all joint landlords must act together in serving a notice.

> *Personal representatives:* if the competent landlord dies, then personal representatives become the competent landlord until the interest is passed on.
>
> *Chain of landlord interests:* a notice served by the competent landlord binds the interest of any interim landlord even if they have not consented to it (paragraph 3(1), schedule 6 of LTA 1954). However, the interim landlord is also entitled to compensation for any loss arising out of the giving of the notice (according to paragraph 4(1), schedule 6 of LTA 1954).

4.2 The correct tenant

Normally the tenant for the purposes of LTA 1954 will simply be the person(s) named in the tenancy agreement or to whom the tenancy was granted. However, there are a few special cases:

- *Joint tenants (other than partners).* If the tenancy has been granted to a number of joint tenants, then all notices served by them must name all of them[40]. Equally, if a notice is to be served on joint tenants it must name all of them[41].
- *Trustees.* Unlike joint tenants, it is not necessary to name all of the trustees so long as the notice makes clear that they are acting together. Calling the tenant 'The Trustees of [A's Trust]' will be enough. Also, one trustee can sign on behalf of the others, although it is advisable to make clear (either in the notice or in a covering letter) that the trustee has the authority of the others to do so.
- *Personal representatives.* Where a tenant dies, personal representatives become the tenant for LTA 1954 purposes.
- *Partnerships.* Sometimes the tenancy will have been granted to two or more people who operate their business under a partnership. If the partnership make-up changes, the 'tenant' must still be those named in the original tenancy agreement. Under section 41A of LTA 1954, however, if:
  - the tenancy was granted to at least two joint tenants and it demised property which was occupied for business purposes;
  - at some point during the tenancy, a business was carried on in partnership by the joint tenants and the tenancy was a partnership asset;
  - the business now being carried out (i.e. at the date of the notice) is being carried out (not necessarily in partnership) by one or more of the original joint tenants ('the business tenant'); and/or

- none of the other original joint tenants occupy the premises carrying on their own, other business

then the business tenant is the tenant for the purposes of serving/being served with notices and making court applications application under LTA 1954. If a tenant relies on section 41A then they become solely liable for the rent and other obligations under the tenancy from the termination date in the section 25 notice or from and including the renewal date in the section 26 request.

On 1 January 2005 A, B, C and D are granted a five-year tenancy of some High Street offices in which they establish their solicitors' practice. They run the business together as a partnership until 2006. A falls out with B and leaves the partnership but the others carry on. In 2010 C and D retire from the partnership and start up their own, new business selling golfing equipment elsewhere. B remains in the premises but retrains as a surveyor and runs a new surveying business from the premises.

At no stage has the tenancy been assigned and so all four of them remain the legal joint tenants. However, because of section 41A, B is treated as the business tenant for the purposes of the lease renewal process and can therefore serve notices and issue court proceedings in his own name, without naming or seeking consent from the other tenants. Equally B's landlord can issue notices and proceedings to B alone, although the landlord can also still name the original four tenants in notices and proceedings if he chooses to.

4.3 The section 25 notice

From and including 1 June 2004 the LTA 1954 prescribes two forms of section 25 notice (see appendices 3 and 4), whereas before there was only one. There is now:

- a prescribed form of section 25 notice for the landlord to end the current business tenancy and offer a new one ('a non-hostile notice'); and
- a prescribed form of section 25 notice for the landlord to end the current business tenancy and oppose the grant of a new one ('a hostile notice').

A section 25 notice cannot be validly served if a valid section 26 request has already been served (section 26(4) of LTA 1954).

Non-hostile section 25 notice

Along with the statutory wording in the prescribed form, the notice must give a number of pieces of information, including:

- the name and address of the tenant;
- the name and address of the landlord;
- the address of the demised premises;
- the termination date;
- the landlord's proposals for the new tenancy;
- details of the person to whom correspondence about the notice should be sent; and
- a signature and date

Name and address of tenant

As discussed in section 4.2, this is not as straightforward as it might seem, as the address could be the address of the premises or, if the tenant is a company, its registered office. Also, if the tenancy was granted to a partnership and only one of the original partners remains in occupation there is the question of whether to address the notice to all the partners or just the one in occupation.

Name and address of landlord

The only person legally entitled to give a section 25 notice is the 'competent landlord' as defined by section 44 LTA 1954. However, it is possible for a duly authorised agent to give notice on the landlord's behalf, but the landlord's name and address must still be stated, and the fact that an authorised agent has given the notice on behalf of the landlord should also be stated.

Address of the demised premises

Set out the address of the premises that were let under the current tenancy.

What is the best way of identifying the demised premises in the notice? My tenant only occupies part of a floor in a large office block and doesn't really have a proper postal address.

Identify the premises by a mixture of description and reference to the current tenancy agreement. For example:

'Part 3rd floor, Victoria Towers, Southwark, London as more particularly described in and demised by the lease made on 1 January 2005 between (1) L [the landlord] (2) T [the tenant]'

If there is only one tenancy, even if the tenant occupies different parts of a building, there should only be one notice. If more than one notice is served, in relation to the different parts occupied (such as different floors, for example), each of the notices will be invalid[44].

Names and addresses

In any notice, the competent landlord or tenant's full name and address should be stated and where there are joint landlords or tenants, the name and address of each of them should be stated. If there is an error in the name or address given on the notice, this may invalidate the notice if the recipient could not reasonably have known (from the notice itself or surrounding circumstances) that the notice was being given by the person entitled to give it or that it was being given to the right person(s)[42].

In the case of a company, checks should be made at Companies House to ascertain the correct full name[43]. The address of the company's registered office should always be used on the notice, even if copies of the notice are also going to be served at the demised premises or another address specified in the lease.

Date the current tenancy will end (the 'termination date')

For fixed-term tenancy agreements this date is calculated as follows. Excluding the day of service, the termination date must be:

- not earlier than the last day of the current tenancy (section 25(4) of LTA 1954); and
- not earlier than six months or later than 12 months after the notice is given (section 25(2)).

A section 25 notice that specifies a date of termination that is the last day of the term is valid[45], but it is usually better to choose a date which is a couple of days after this for the avoidance of any doubt.

Assume that it is 1 June 2005 and that T's two year, fixed-term tenancy agreement is due to end on 1 January 2006. L, the landlord, wants to serve a section 25 notice today giving the earliest termination date possible. L calculates that, excluding the day of service, a section 25 notice six months long and served today would have a termination date of 1 December 2005.

However, because T's tenancy agreement does not end until 1 January 2006, using a termination date of 1 December 2005 would invalidate the section 25 notice. L therefore correctly inserts a termination date of 1 January 2006 and serves the section 25 notice. This termination date is valid because it is more than six months after the section 25 notice is given and is not earlier than the last day of T's tenancy agreement.

If T's tenancy agreement had already expired by 1 June 2005 then L's notice would be valid if any termination date between 1 December 2005 and 1 June 2006 inclusive was used.

As discussed in chapter 3 the termination date for periodic tenancies and tenancies with break clauses is calculated slightly differently (section 25(3) of LTA 1954):

- Periodic tenancies normally terminate on expiry of a notice to quit and it is not necessary to serve a notice to quit and a section 25 notice to end a periodic tenancy that is subject to LTA 1954. A section 25 notice alone will be sufficient provided that the termination date specified in that notice is not earlier than:
  - six months nor later than 12 months after the section 25 notice is given; and
  - the date on which the periodic tenancy could have been determined by a common law notice to quit.
- Tenancies with break clauses can be terminated using a section 25 notice so long as the termination date is not earlier than:
  - six months nor later than 12 months after the section 25 notice is given (or, if longer, the period required by the break clause plus six months); and
  - the date the tenancy could have been determined in accordance with the break clause.

For more information on ending periodic tenancies or tenancies that have break clauses with section 25 notices see chapter 3.

Set out the landlord's proposals for the terms of the renewal tenancy

The landlord *must* (under section 25(8) of LTA 1954) specify: the property to be comprised in the renewal tenancy, the new rent, and the other terms of the renewal tenancy, or risk invalidating the notice. The purpose is to give the tenant as much notice as possible of the landlord's intentions and, hopefully, speed up the renewal process.

The proposals are not thought to be binding, indeed the prescribed wording in the section 25 notices states the terms are 'merely suggestions as a basis for negotiation.' However, landlords should act reasonably when setting out their proposals (taking into account the *Code of Practice for Commercial Leases in England and Wales*[46]). As a brief guide:

- *The property to be comprised in the new tenancy* will often simply be the premises demised under the current tenancy agreement. However, sometimes the tenant has sublet part of the premises, or otherwise only occupies part of them, so the landlord must state whether the property to be demised by the new tenancy is to be either the whole or part of the property comprised in the current tenancy (if part only, the landlord should specify which part). If the landlord does not specify anything in relation to the property to be comprised in the new tenancy, the reasonable recipient of the notice would probably understand the landlord to require the tenant to take a new tenancy of the whole of the premises comprised in the tenancy, but it is better to state this expressly if this is the case.
- *The new rent.* The landlord should state the rent it proposes for the new tenancy.
- *Other terms of the renewal tenancy.* The LTA 1954 does not specify what information the landlord should put here, although section 25(8) makes clear the section 25 notice will be invalid if the landlord does not set out its proposals. As the intention is to provide the tenant with as much information as reasonably possible, landlords should include the other basic heads of terms of the new tenancy, such as term length or if there is to be a landlord development break option.

The authors do not believe that a landlord needs to annex a draft lease to the section 25 notice. It is probably enough, provided the proposed demise, rent and term length are specified, that the notice refers to other terms in a general way such as 'and on other terms similar to those contained in the current tenancy agreement'. Landlords are advised to keep any such phrase as wide as possible to permit maximum flexibility.

Details of the person to whom correspondence should be sent

If the landlord is dealing with this matter, his or her own name and correspondence address should be inserted. If an agent (such as a surveyor or solicitor) is representing the landlord, then the agent's name and address should be inserted.

Signature and date

The notice should be signed and dated by the person giving the notice. This can be the landlord, mortgagee (if the mortgagee is in possession of the premises), or their agent (who must be duly authorised to give the notice[47]). The notice will not necessarily be invalid if it is not signed, provided it is reasonably clear who is giving the notice and in what capacity (through use of a covering letter, for example[48]).

Hostile section 25 notices

The section 25 notice opposing the grant of a new tenancy must be in the prescribed form and must contain the same information as a section 25 notice offering a new tenancy, except that it will not contain the landlord's proposals for a new tenancy. Instead, the landlord must specify the ground(s) relied on to oppose the grant of a new tenancy.

These grounds (a) to (g) are set out in section 30(1) of LTA 1954 and are discussed in detail in chapter 7. These are grounds on which the landlord intends to rely at trial – although it is not necessary to be in a position to establish the ground at the time the notice is served. The accompanying notes to the prescribed form describe what each of the grounds of opposition are for the benefit of the tenant.

Details about the landlord's ground of opposition need not be given at this stage, but if the ground relied upon is not specified, the notice is invalid. If the landlord relies on more than one ground, these should all be stated in the same notice. The landlord risks a finding that intentions are unclear if separate notices specifying the grounds individually are served, rendering all of the notices invalid.

Once the notice has been served it cannot be amended, the landlord cannot add any new grounds of opposition.

If the landlord opposes the grant of a new tenancy on a certain ground, the landlord must have an honest belief in the ground stated and do so in good faith[49].

Where vacant possession is obtained from a tenant by means of a misrepresentation or concealment of material facts, compensation is payable under section 37A LTA 1954. It is uncertain whether a notice given in bad faith is invalid, but the authors do not believe that it is. If the notice is valid, the tenant can apply to the court for an order for the grant of a new tenancy, which – presumably – the landlord would have no real prospect of defending. If the notice is invalid, and the tenant does not make an application to the court but moves out, the tenant is protected by a claim for damages in fraud and/or under section 37A LTA 1954 (this is discussed further in chapter 10).

So long as the landlord had an honest belief in relying on the ground at the time the section 25 notice is served, then there is nothing to stop the landlord from later having a change of mind and withdrawing the ground of opposition. This does not mean that the landlord then has to serve a non-hostile section 25 notice. In fact, once one valid section 25 notice has been served, the landlord cannot then serve another as a replacement.

It is important to remember that under section 37 of LTA 1954 if the landlord relies on any one or more of three of the statutory grounds of opposition to the grant of a new tenancy (grounds (e), (f) and (g)), the tenant becomes entitled to statutory compensation. As soon as a landlord serves a section 25 notice relying on one or more of these grounds they become liable to pay the compensation if the tenant then leaves the premises. As the amount of compensation can be significant in some cases, it is vital that the landlord understands this before any section 25 notice specifying one or more of the grounds is served.

I represent a landlord that wants to serve a section 25 notice. My client is thinking of opposing the grant of a new tenancy on ground (f) but is not yet sure of his plans and might later want to change his mind. What should I do?

You must advise your client that he will become liable to pay the tenant the statutory compensation as soon as he serves a section 25 notice relying on ground 'f'. The tenant will become entitled to claim the compensation if he leaves the premises after the section 25 notice has been served. This is so even if your client changes his mind and withdraws his ground 'f' opposition before the tenant decides to leave. Your client could sue you in negligence if you fail to give this advice.

It might be appropriate for your client to serve a non-hostile section 25 notice but include a proposal for a re-development break clause to be inserted into any new tenancy. This avoids the immediate prospect of being liable to pay statutory compensation and gives your client the time to consider his plans in greater detail.

The ground of opposition on which the landlord intends to rely may, in some circumstances, have a bearing on the date of termination chosen:

- If the landlord intends to rely on one of the grounds that would entitle the tenant to compensation, there should be some thought given to the date of termination specified in the notice. The amount of compensation to which a tenant is entitled will double if they or a predecessor in title in the business have been in occupation of the premises for 14 years or more. The relevant period is counted back from the date of termination specified in the notice. It goes without saying that it will be in the landlord's interest (if there is a choice) to specify a date of termination which is less than 14 years since the date on which the tenant or predecessor in title to the business first occupied the premises.
- If a landlord relies on ground (g) (that the landlord wishes to occupy the premises), they have to have owned the premises for at least five years before the date of termination specified in the notice.

- If the landlord would like to rely on ground (f) (for demolition or construction), but plans are not sufficiently advanced, the landlord may nevertheless gain some extra time by relying on section 31(2) of LTA 1954, which provides that the court may decline to order the grant of a new tenancy even if the landlord fails to make out ground (f) if it considers that the landlord would have been able to do so within a period of not more than a year from the termination date specified in the section 25 notice. If there is any prospect that a landlord would like to rely on this section, it is worth specifying the latest termination date in the notice possible.

Once a section 25 notice is given, either the landlord or the tenant can apply to the court for an order for the grant of a new tenancy and a landlord who has served a hostile notice can apply for a termination order.

4.4 Superior landlord's notice to withdraw a section 25 notice

Only the 'competent landlord' (or its mortgagee in possession) can serve a section 25 notice. If that landlord is also a tenant whose tenancy will end within 16 months of the date of the section 25 notice, then that landlord/tenant must serve a copy of the section 25 notice on its superior landlord (this requirement also applies to any section 26 request that the landlord might receive – under paragraph 7 of schedule 6 of LTA 1954). If the superior landlord is also a tenant, it is obliged to serve a copy of the notice on its own landlord, regardless of the length of its own tenancy. This obligation continues right up to the freehold landlord.

If within two months of the section 25 notice being served, a superior landlord becomes the competent landlord it can serve a prescribed form of notice to withdraw the original section 25 notice (paragraph 6 of schedule 6 of LTA 1954 and form 6 of schedule 2 of the *Landlord and Tenant Act 1954 Part 2 (Notices) Regulations* 2004). The superior landlord's withdrawal notice must be served within that same period of two months from the date of the section 25 notice. The section 25 notice then ceases to have effect.

T's tenancy of part of a building is due to expire on 1 December 2006. L (T's landlord) is himself a business tenant whose tenancy of the whole building will expire on 1 January 2007. F is the freeholder and is L's landlord.

On 2 December 2005 L serves a non-hostile section 25 notice on T giving 1 December 2006 as the termination date. Because

L's tenancy has less than 14 months left F is also served with a copy of the section 25 notice. F has decided that it wants to redevelop the premises and so serves a hostile section 25 notice on L – this means that L immediately ceases to be T's competent landlord. F is then entitled to serve notice withdrawing L's original non-hostile section 25 notice, instead serving a hostile notice on T.

4.5 Tenant's section 26 request and landlord's counter-notice

As with section 25 notices, the tenant's section 26 request must be given in the prescribed form (*Landlord and Tenant Act 1954 Part 2 (Notices) Regulations* 2004, form 3 of schedule 2 – see appendix 5). The information the section 26 request must contain is similar to a section 25 notice served where the landlord is offering a renewal tenancy:

- Name and address of landlord – details of the competent landlord must be given. The tenant cannot rely on section 23(2) *Landlord and Tenant Act* 1927 to excuse service of a section 26 request on an old landlord where there has been a change in the identity of the competent landlord. Such notice will be invalid.
- Name and address of tenant.
- Address of the demised premises.
- Start date of the renewal tenancy ('the renewal date') – calculated in a similar way to the termination date, the renewal date must not be

  - less than six months nor more than 12 months after the section 26 request is served; or
  - earlier than the last day of the fixed term of the tenancy.

- Proposals for the terms of the new tenancy – when a landlord serves a hostile section 25 notice, they must have an honest belief that they will rely on the statutory ground of opposition specified. The question arises whether a tenant is under a similar obligation of good faith when they specify proposals for the terms of a new tenancy. The answer appears to be 'no' – the tenant can make any proposals and they need not be genuine ones[50].

Whilst this is the current state of the law, the authors have doubts whether this is correct, since it seems to undermine the point of requiring the tenant to state proposals in the first place, i.e. to give rise to genuine negotiations with the landlord concerning the grant of a new tenancy.

A section 26 request cannot be served if:

- the landlord has already served a section 25 notice (section 26(4));
- the tenant is a periodic tenant (not including a tenant who takes a fixed term which, at the end of that term, is expressed to continue 'from year to year' unless such tenant can only determine a tenancy after the fixed term on giving less than six months or more than 12 months notice to the landlord) or a tenant whose original tenancy was for a fixed term of less than a year (section 26(1));
- the tenant has served a break notice[51] to end a fixed-term or notice under section 27(1) of LTA 1954; or
- the tenant has already served a section 26 request (where, for example, a second notice is served because the tenant did not make an application to the court before expiry of the statutory period following service of the first request[52]).

The landlord's counter-notice

If the landlord (meaning, as before, the competent landlord) wishes to oppose the grant of a new tenancy, then a counter-notice needs to be served stating:

- that the landlord will oppose an application to the court for the grant of a new tenancy; and
- on which of the grounds mentioned in section 30(1) the landlord will oppose the application.

(There is no prescribed form to use but see appendix 6 for a suggested precedent.)

The counter-notice must be served within two months of the tenant making the request (section 26(6) of LTA 1954). If a landlord fails to serve a counter-notice within that period, they then lose the right to do so. The landlord cannot rely on a statutory ground of opposition to defend a claim for a new tenancy or make a claim for a termination order if a counter-notice has not been served and a counter-notice cannot be amended or withdrawn once given.

If a landlord does not oppose the grant of a new tenancy, they need not serve a counter-notice.

4.6 Section 27 notices

As discussed in chapter 3, section 27 notices are served by tenants of protected tenancies to confirm that they do not wish their tenancy to continue. The notices only apply for protected fixed-term tenancies and there are two types of section 27 notice: section 27(1) and section 27(2).

Section 27(1)

Normally section 24(1) of LTA 1954 will continue a fixed term tenancy after the fixed term expires, but if (before then) a tenant of such a tenancy does not want it to continue, then they can serve a section 27(1) notice.

A section 27(1) notice must be at least three months long and must expire on the last day of the contractual tenancy. If the tenant does not have enough time to serve a section 27(1) notice but does not want a new tenancy, there is the possibility to vacate the premises so that LTA 1954 ceases to apply to the tenancy. In such case, the tenancy will end on expiry of the fixed term (section 27(1A)).

The section 27(1) notice cannot be served if the tenant has already served a section 26 request (section 26(4)) and it also cannot be served until the tenant has been in occupation under its tenancy for at least one month.

It is not clear whether the tenant can serve a section 27(1) notice if the landlord has already served a section 25 notice. A tenant might wish to do so where the landlord has served its notice to expire, say, on 31 December 2006 but the tenant's fixed term tenancy expires on 1 June 2006. The authors and other commentators[53] believe that it is possible for a tenant to serve its section 27(1) notice in such a case and end the tenancy earlier than the date of termination in the landlord's section 25 notice.

Section 27(2)

Section 27(2) notices are used where the fixed term has expired and the tenancy is being continued by section 24(1) of LTA 1954. These notices cannot be used in relation to periodic tenancies. The notice must be at least three months long but it can expire on any day. The notice can be served both before and after the last day of the fixed term – meaning that a tenant can decide exactly how long it wants its tenancy to be continued by section 24(1).

As with section 27(1) notices, a section 27(2) notice cannot be served:

- after a section 26 request is served; and
- until the tenant has been in occupation under the tenancy for at least one month.

It is thought that a section 27(2) notice can be served after a section 25 notice is served, to end the tenancy before the date in the section 25 notice.

4.7 Section 40 information requests

Either the landlord or tenant (limited under section 40(3) to those tenants able to serve a section 26 request) can serve a notice under section 40 LTA 1954 requiring the other to provide certain, statutorily required information.

The information that must be provided is useful in establishing who the correct landlord or tenant is for the purposes of serving a section 25 notice or section 26 request or for establishing who is the actual occupier of the premises.

A notice should not be served earlier than two years before the day on which the tenancy could come to an end either by the effluxion of time or by a notice to quit served by the landlord. The response to the notice must be given within one month of the notice being served including the date of service. For example if a landlord serves a section 40 notice on 2 January 2006, the tenant must respond on or before 1 February 2006, not 2 February 2006.

I represent a landlord whose tenant has sublet. She does not know whether the tenant has sublet the whole or only part, and in the circumstances does not know on whom to serve her section 25 notice. The tenancy agreement has more than five years left to run but there is a tenant-only right to break the tenancy that can now be operated. Can my client serve a section 40(1) notice on its tenant?

No. Section 40(6) of LTA 1954 prevents your client from doing so. This is because:

- there are more than two years left before the tenancy agreement comes to an end; and
- the tenancy agreement cannot be brought to an end within the next two years by a notice to quit served by the landlord. The fact that the tenant can now serve a notice to quit (i.e. the break notice) is irrelevant. However, had the break notice been operable by the landlord then your client could have served a section 40(3) notice.

Although the Act is silent on the point, the authors consider that any number of section 40 notices can be served within the relevant period. This might happen where, for example, a section 25 notice is not served immediately after receipt of a tenant's response to a section 40 notice, and when the landlord comes to serve a section 25 notice, another section 40 notice is needed to make sure that there have been no changes in the interim.

The landlord's section 40(1) notice

This notice can be served by any person with a reversionary interest in the premises, whether immediate or not (section 40(1) of LTA 1954), but they must use the prescribed form (*Landlord and Tenant Act 1954 Part 2 (Notices) Regulations* 2004 form 4 of schedule 2 – see appendix 10). The tenant is under a statutory duty to answer the below questions in writing (there is no prescribed form for this) within one month of service:

1   *Do you occupy the premises or any part of them wholly or partly for the purposes of a business that is carried on by you?*
    The tenant must confirm whether it wholly or partly occupies the premises for its business purposes. Also, because of the reference to occupation by the tenant for business purposes in section 23(1B) of LTA 1954, this request also requires the tenant to provide further information as follows:

    –   if the tenant is an individual, the tenant will also have to tell the landlord if a company in which it has a controlling interest is in occupation for business purposes; and
    –   conversely, if the tenant is a company it must tell the landlord if a person (i.e. an individual or another company) that has a controlling interest in it or another company within the same group is in occupation for business purposes.

2   *To the best of your knowledge and belief, does any other person own an interest in reversion in any part of the premises?*
    If the ownership of the tenancy's reversion is split between two or more people, the tenant must confirm the names and addresses of the other owners.

3   *Does your tenancy have effect subject to any subtenancy on which your tenancy is immediately expectant?*
    The tenant must state (either 'yes' or 'no') whether its tenancy is subject to any immediate subtenancies. If the tenant answers 'yes', then it must go on to answer the rest of the questions.

    (a) *What premises are comprised in the subtenancy?*
        If these cannot be easily described, the tenant may attach a plan showing the subdemise(s).
    (b) *For what term does the subtenancy have effect or, if it is terminable by notice, by what notice can it be terminated?*
        The tenant must confirm the subtenancy's term length. If the subtenancy is periodic or if it is subject to a break clause, the tenant must confirm the length of the notice needed to terminate the tenancy and/or provisions of the break clause.
    (c) *What is the rent payable under it?*
    (d) *Who is the subtenant?*
    (e) *To the best of your knowledge and belief, is the subtenant in occupation of the premises or part of the premises comprised in the subtenancy?*

If the tenant answers 'no' to this question, the tenant must provide the landlord with the subtenant's address.

(f) *Is an agreement in force excluding, in relation to the subtenancy, the provisions of sections 24 to 28 of the Landlord and Tenant Act 1954?*

The tenant must state whether the subtenancy is contracted out of the LTA 1954.

(g) *Has a notice been given under section 25 or section 26(6) of that Act, or has a request been made under section 26 of that Act, in relation to the subtenancy?*

If the tenant answers 'yes', it must provide details of the section 25 notice or section 26(6) counter-notice that has been served on the subtenant, or of the section 26 notice that has been served by the subtenant. The simplest way to answer this is to provide the landlord with a copy of the relevant notice.

The tenant's section 40(3) notice

The tenant can serve this notice on its landlord or any superior landlord (all the way up to the freeholder) or on the mortgagee in possession of the landlord or superior landlord's interest (section 40(3) of LTA 1954). The notice must be in the statutorily prescribed form (*Landlord and Tenant Act 1954 Part 2 (Notices) Regulations 2004*, form 5 of schedule 2 – see appendix 11). The recipient is then under a statutory duty to answer in writing (again there is no prescribed form) and provide the following information within one month of service of the notice:

1. *To state in writing whether you are the owner of the fee simple in respect of the premises or any part of them or the mortgagee in possession of such owner.*

   The recipient must confirm whether it is the freehold owner of the premises or any part of them or if it is the mortgagee in possession of such an owner. If the answer is 'no' then the following information must be given, to the best of the recipient's knowledge and belief:

   – *The name and address of the person who is your or, as the case may be, your mortgagor's immediate landlord in respect of the premises or of the part in respect of which you are not, or your mortgagor is not, the owner in fee simple.*

   – *For what term your or your mortgagor's tenancy has effect and what is the earliest date (if any) at which the tenancy is terminable by notice to quit given by the landlord.*

   The landlord must confirm the length of its (or if the recipient is a mortgagee in possession, its mortgagor's) own tenancy of the premises. It must also state whether its tenancy can be determined by a landlord's notice to quit and, if so, the earliest date it could be determined.

- *Whether a notice has been given under section 25 or 26(6) of the Landlord and Tenant Act 1954, or a request has been made under section 26 of that Act, in relation to the tenancy and, if so, details of the notice or request.*
  The landlord must state whether a section 25 notice, a landlord's counter-notice or a section 26 request has been served in relation to its tenancy. If so it must provide details of the notice (the simplest way to do this is to provide a copy to the tenant).

2. *To state in writing, to the best of your knowledge and belief, the name and address of any other person who owns an interest in reversion in any part of the premises.*
   The recipient must state whether any other person owns a reversionary interest in the premises. If so, their name and address must also be given.

3. *If you are a reversioner, to state in writing whether there is a mortgagee in possession of your interest in the premises.*
   If the landlord answers 'yes' it must also provide the name and address of the mortgagee in possession.

Obligation to update replies

If the person who replies to a section 40 notice becomes aware that the facts given in reply have since changed or were incorrect, section 40(5) of LTA 1954 imposes an obligation to update/correct these facts. This obligation applies for a period of six months starting with the date of service of the section 40 notice.

Although the Act is silent on the point, the authors consider that the recipient is under a continuing obligation to update or correct, such that a notice to update/correct must be served whenever there is a relevant change during that period, even if the original information has already been updated or corrected previously.

The recipient has a period of one month (starting with the date on which they became aware of the change/error) to write and update/correct the facts. Failure to do so is a breach of statutory duty and the court can require the update/correction to be provided and/or award damages (section 40B LTA 1954).

On 1 January 2005 L serves a section 40(1) notice on T. On 20 January T replies confirming, amongst other things, that there are no subtenants of the premises. On 30 May 2005 T unlawfully sublets part of the premises to S. Under section 40(5) T must notify L of this change on or before 30 June 2005. If L then suffers any loss as a result of Ts failure to update with notice of the subletting, L will be entitled to seek damages under section 40(B).

Failure to reply

If a recipient fails within one month to reply to the notice, section 40B LTA 1954 authorises the court to order them to do so. The court can also require them to pay damages.

What happens if either party transfers their interest in all or part of the premises during the six-month period?

This depends on whether the party transferring their interest gave or received the section 40 notice.

If the person who gave the section 40 notice has transferred their interest and they (or the person to whom they transferred their interest) give written notice to the recipient of the section 40 notice of:

* the transfer; and
* the name and address of the new owner,

then the recipient of the section 40 notice is required to send a response to the notice/provide any updates/corrections to the new owner. If no notice of the transfer is given, then the section 40 notice recipient can provide the information either to the old or the new owner.

If the person who received the section 40 notice has transferred their interest and they give written notice to the person who served the section 40 notice of:

* the transfer; and
* the name and address of the new owner,

then their obligation to provide the required information/update it ends on the day they give notice of the transfer. If they do not give notice of the transfer then they remain liable to provide the information/update it. In either case, the new owner has no obligation to provide any response to the original section 40 notice. A new section 40 notice must be served.

4.8 Serving notices under LTA 1954

In general terms, if the person giving the notice can prove that it was received and came to the knowledge of the recipient, then the notice will have been properly served no matter what method was used to serve it. However, that is often a lot easier said than done.

Wherever possible it is better to use a method that eliminates the risk of service being disputed or not being effective. Indeed, the LTA 1954 achieves this by incorporating the provisions of section 23 *Landlord and Tenant Act* 1927 (section 66(4) of LTA 1954), which provides three methods of service. If one of the statutory methods is used, service is effected even if it is shown that the notice was never actually received (because, for example, the notice is returned undelivered[54]). As stated above, in all other cases the person giving the notice will need to prove that the person to whom it was given actually received it.

The statutory service methods

Statutory service method		Deemed date of service
Personal service	Can only be used for individuals[55]	Date the notice is given to the individual
Leaving notice at last known place of abodein England and Wales	For individuals, this includes a business address as well as a personal residence.	Date the notice is left[56]
	For companies, this means its registered office. For local or public authorities, statutory companies (one established by an Act of Parliament) or public utility companies (section 25(1) of the *Landlord and Tenant Act* 1927), this means the principle office of such authority or company (addressed to the secretary)	
Sending by post using special or recorded delivery to the last known place of abode in England and Wales		Date the notice is given to the Post Office for sending

The *Landlord and Tenant Act* 1927 refers to 'registered post', but this service has been replaced by the Special Delivery Service, and under the *Recorded Delivery Service Act* 1962 where any Act refers to service by 'registered post', service by 'recorded delivery' is equally valid.

If the notice is not left or sent to 'the last known place of abode in England and Wales', but some other place, service will need to be proved as if the statutory method of service had not been used. As seen from the table above, the 'last known place of abode' is not necessarily the demised premises, although a copy of the notice will usually be sent there as well as to any address for correspondence.

With each of the statutory methods, service on a duly authorised agent will be effective[57], but care should always be taken if there are joint landlords or tenants, as service must be effected on each of them. This may not be difficult if the 'last known place of abode in England and Wales' is the same for each of them but, if different, the notice will need to be served at each of the different places.

Alternative service methods

As explained above, any other method of service can be used. The authors consider that this includes service by fax or by email, although this has yet to be tested in the case of notices served under LTA 1954.

If non-statutory methods of service are used the burden of proving that service was effective falls on the sender unless service is effected pursuant to a method specified in the tenancy agreement which also contains a deemed service provision[58]. That said, the provisions of the tenancy agreement will have to be examined carefully to ensure they actually achieve this result.

With this in mind, the authors recommend that statutory methods of service should always be used.

4.9 Problems with notices

Various problems can arise in the course of preparing and serving notices. As discussed in this chapter errors can be made in the information given in the notice, or the notice served on the wrong person or at the wrong address. If a surveyor is in any doubt about the validity of a notice or whether good service has been effected or not, legal advice should be sought as soon as possible.

Errors in notices can undoubtedly mislead recipients, but sometimes it will be clear that a mistake has been made where, for example, there is a typographical error. Where that mistake is or ought to have been obvious, the notice will be valid. Case law refers to what the 'reasonable recipient' of the notice would have understood[59], making this an objective test.

I have been told that if there is an error in a notice I have served under LTA 1954 this invalidates it. Is this right?

Not necessarily, provided you are the person entitled to give the notice or the duly authorised agent of that person and the notice is properly served.

The courts are taking an increasingly commercial and common-sense approach to errors in notices. The first step is to identify the information that is wrong and the second is to consider whether, notwithstanding the mistake, the reasonable recipient of the notice would have understood what the notice was meant to do.

In approaching this question, the courts consider a range of factors including (but not limited to) whether:

- the incorrect information is a crucial element of the notice: if it is, the error is more likely to lead to the notice being held invalid;
- any other information was given with the notice which would have corrected the error, such as in a covering letter;
- there was anything in the circumstances of the notice being given which would have identified the error and/or made clear what the intention was of the person giving the notice; and
- the recipient of the notice realised the error or ought to have done so had they acted reasonably.

Certain errors cannot be ignored, such as a failure to use the prescribed form or specifying a termination date that is not permitted by section 25 LTA 1954. In all other cases, the concept of the 'reasonable recipient' of the notice becomes relevant.

If there is any doubt, after service, as to the validity of the notice served, a fresh notice can be served provided that it is made clear that the second notice is being served without prejudice to the validity of the first[60]. If the first notice is invalid and the second is valid, the second notice will stand.

This works well if the person serving two notices, one without prejudice to the other, is trying to do the same thing. Where, however, a landlord serves a hostile section 25 notice, followed by a non-hostile section 25 notice stated to be without prejudice to the hostile notice, it is likely that both notices will be invalid. Such notices would be entirely inconsistent with one another, and the reasonable recipient would understandably not know what it was that the landlord was trying to do[61].

Similarly, curing an error in a notice is not the same as serving a second notice inconsistent with and following a change of mind after service of a first notice. The concept of 'reasonable recipient' has no application in such case[62]. Arguments that this was contrary to the *Human Rights Act* 1998 were ventilated in *Pennycook v Shaws*[63] and, whilst the Court of Appeal accepted that article 1 of the First Protocol, which provides that:

'every natural or legal person is entitled to the peaceful enjoyment of his possessions. No one shall be deprived of his possessions except in the public interest and subject to the conditions provided for by law and by the general principles of international law.'

was engaged by the service of notices under section 25, declined to find that entitlement to only 'one bite at the cherry' violated those rights.

5

Court claims and pre-action conduct

The *Landlord and Tenant Act* 1954 (LTA 1954) refers to the grant of a new tenancy being 'opposed' and provides a list of grounds for opposition in section 30(1) of LTA 1954 (these are dealt with in greater detail in chapter 7). But what is the difference between an 'opposed' or 'unopposed' claim?

The *Civil Procedure Rules* (CPR) distinguish between two types of claim:

- an unopposed claim (CPR, 56.3(2)(b)), being a claim under section 24 of LTA 1954 for a new tenancy in circumstances where the landlord does not rely on any of the statutory grounds of opposition. Although it is unclear from the wording used, this must include those claims where the grant of a new tenancy is not opposed, but there is disagreement over what the terms of that tenancy should be (were it otherwise, there would be no dispute for the court to try and the remainder of the provisions in CPR part 56 relating to 'unopposed claims' would be pointless); and
- an opposed claim (CPR, 56.3(2)(c)), being a claim where a landlord:
  - relies on a statutory ground of opposition to oppose the grant of a new tenancy; and/or
  - applies for a termination order.

The CPR do not specifically refer to claims where a defendant challenges the court's jurisdiction to try the claim, but it is likely that this will be treated as an 'opposed claim' by default, since it does not fall within the definition of an 'unopposed claim'.

Comparing the differences between opposed and unopposed claims, this chapter looks at what happens when a business tenancy that is protected by LTA 1954 comes to an end where a claim to the court may be contemplated. It considers:

- the context of a claim (section 5.1);
- pre-action conduct for unopposed claims (section 5,2);
- pre-action conduct for opposed claims (section 5,3);
- preparation for a claim (section 5.4);
- who is entitled to make a claim to the court (section 5.5); and
- the time-limits for such claims (section 5.6).

5.1 The context of a claim

Prior to the contractual expiry date of a business tenancy it is common practice for the parties' representatives to discuss the possibility of the grant of a new tenancy and to negotiate the terms of any such tenancy.

Current best practice is reflected in *the Code of Practice for Commercial Leases in England and Wales*[64], which makes a number of recommendations about the negotiation of particular terms of a business tenancy, but where the parties cannot agree, LTA 1954 gives the court power to determine:

- the property to be comprised in the new tenancy (section 32 LTA 1954);
- the duration of the new tenancy (section 33 LTA 1954);
- the rent payable under the new tenancy (section 34 LTA 1954); and
- any other terms of the tenancy (section 35 LTA 1954).

The prospect of litigation is, however, doubtful, until – at the very least – a landlord has served a section 25 notice or the tenant a section 26 request. Until that time the current tenancy continues, but once a notice has been given, and even if negotiations have not yet begun, it is arguable that litigation is in reasonable contemplation (particularly if it is genuinely believed that negotiations will not result in a consensus).

This is why it is extremely important for any agent of the landlord or tenant to consider the issue of client privilege, even before the negotiations have begun. This may seem strange, but before negotiations begin, the client will often receive a valuation report, which will then form the basis for discussion and instructions going into any negotiation. The question arises as to whether anything can be done to protect from disclosure this and other potentially sensitive documents between client and agent at this early stage.

Communications between a client and agent will be privileged if, but only if, they come into existence for the dominant purpose of obtaining legal advice, or to conduct or aid in the conduct of litigation in reasonable prospect *at the time of its production*[65], which could mean that a successful claim of privilege cannot be guaranteed at this early stage. The chances of success may be enhanced by making it clear in the document that its author believes there may be a dispute within reasonable contemplation to which the document will be relevant.

The following might be sufficient (although it will depend on the particular circumstances of each case):

'In this document, I am dealing with matters which are relevant to the terms of any new tenancy of the property. These will be referred to the court if they cannot be agreed. Since they have not (or not yet) been agreed, I am assuming for these purposes that a claim to the court will be made.'

I am not really sure whether there will be a dispute between the parties or not at some stage in the future, but want to issue my valuation report to my client. Can I ensure that this documents attracts privilege by just copying it to my client's solicitors?

No. Unless a document itself is privileged, merely copying it to a client's solicitors does not make it privileged. Copying it to a solicitor with a request for legal advice to the client is different, but it is difficult to see what legal advice a lawyer might give in relation to the valuation report or matters contained within it.

5.2 Pre-action conduct for unopposed claims

Sections 32, 33, 34 and 35 of LTA 1954 provide that the terms of a new tenancy shall be such 'as may be agreed between the landlord and the tenant'. Whilst this does not appear to impose any statutory duty to negotiate, it is at least incumbent on the parties as a matter of good practice to discuss terms for a new tenancy prior to making any application to the court for a new tenancy[66].

Prior to 1 June 2004, a tenant was forced to make an application to the court for the grant of a new tenancy, even if they were in the process of negotiating with the landlord and there was no real need for the court to intervene. In these circumstances, it was not uncommon for the parties to only really negotiate once proceedings had been issued and the court would grant a number of stays to the parties to facilitate those negotiations, with the majority of cases never getting beyond the directions stage.

Since 1 June 2004, the parties have been able to extend the time limits within which an application to the court must be made (as it can now be by either of them). This amendment is likely to change the way the courts deal with applications under LTA 1954 and they will probably become increasingly reluctant to grant a series of stays for negotiations to continue as opposed to pushing claims through to trial.

If the parties want to negotiate without the court's intervention they can extend the time limits for applying to court (as discussed later in this section) and use that 'extra' time for proper commercial discussions. Where a tenant has served a section 26 request, the parties must in any event wait two months before any claim can be made to the court for a new tenancy. The court will expect them to have used this time productively.

Provisions in the CPR reinforce this as the CPR contain a number of pre-action protocols, which regulate parties' action prior to commencement of proceedings. There is not a specific pre-action protocol for applications under LTA 1954, but the CPR Practice Direction on Pre-Action Protocols applies to all cases.

Paragraph 4.1 of the Practice Direction provides:

'... the court will expect the parties, in accordance with the overriding objective and the matters referred to in CPR 1.1(2)(a), (b) and (c), to act reasonably in exchanging information and documents relevant to the claim and generally in trying to avoid the necessity for the start of proceedings ...'

The Practice Direction further provides in paragraph 4.2 that:

- a potential claimant should write to the potential defendant, giving details of a claim;
- the potential defendant should acknowledge the claim letter promptly;
- the potential defendant should give a detailed response within a reasonable time; and
- the parties should conduct genuine and reasonable negotiations with a view to settling the claim economically and without court proceedings.

In the claim letter, a potential claimant should enclose copies of essential documents which are relied on, ask for any essential documents that are needed, and state whether they wish to enter into mediation or another method of alternative dispute resolution (ADR). At a very early stage, therefore, it is incumbent on any potential claimant to consider whether to use ADR (this is dealt with in greater detail in chapter 11).

These provisions apply whether the claim is opposed or unopposed.

I have received a request for documents that I have, but am nervous about handing these over as I do not want the other side to get any tactical advantage by seeing them at this stage. Can I refuse?

Ask yourself why you are nervous. As paragraph 4.8 of the Practice Direction makes clear such documents are provided on a 'without prejudice' basis and 'may not be used for any purpose other than resolving the dispute, unless the other party agrees.' If the request is ignored, the court has the power to impose costs sanctions (under CPR, 44.3(5)(a) and paragraphs 3.3, 3.4 and 4.3(g) of the Practice Direction).

If the court believes that proceedings could have been avoided if you had handed the documents over and that you are at fault for failing to do so, it can order you to pay the costs of the proceedings on an indemnity basis (even if you are successful on the claim). It can also deprive you of any interest, which you might otherwise have been awarded, or award the other party a greater rate of interest (subject to a cap of 10%), which it might otherwise normally receive.

If, having considered the matter, there remain good reasons not to hand the documents over, you can refuse. The court is unlikely to impose costs sanctions if it agrees with you that there were good reasons for withholding the documents.

Application of the Practice Direction on Pre-Action Protocols to unopposed claims

A section 26 request and a non-hostile section 25 notice served where the landlord does not oppose the grant of a new tenancy must contain the proposed terms of the new tenancy of the party serving it. No counter-notice needs to be served, so where the tenant has served a section 26 request, the landlord is not required to serve a counter-notice if there is no opposition to the grant of a new tenancy.

In these circumstances, the party serving the notice or request could nevertheless request a detailed response from the other party as to the proposals, pursuant to the Practice Direction.

The ability to request documents before proceedings begin is of some tactical importance. For example, if one party believes that the only real issue is the level of rent, the Practice Direction could be used to request disclosure of the other side's valuation file or other relevant documents. In the event that such documents are disclosed, they may provide information relevant to offers to settle.

The parties should, in any event, start negotiating, but how far negotiations are taken depends on what is reasonable in all the circumstances. It plainly makes little sense to attempt to continue negotiation if the parties' positions are entrenched and far apart, or if one of the parties is refusing to negotiate – in good faith or otherwise.

Whilst issuing proceedings will apply pressure to the other side, the claimant should be prepared to follow these through: it is very unlikely that the court will allow a series of stays following the issue of a claim only for negotiations to continue.

The basis on which negotiations should be conducted

Negotiations should always be conducted openly, constructively and considering the views of the other side (taking into account recommendation 1 of the *Code of Practice for Commercial Leases in England and Wales*[67]). Negotiations are often, but not always, conducted on a 'without prejudice' basis and 'subject to contract'. It is important to understand what each of these phrases means.

Without Prejudice

Without prejudice correspondence is 'privileged' from production to the court or third parties. When negotiating to settle a dispute, parties should not be afraid to make admissions or concessions in order to facilitate settlement, although they may not wish those admissions or concessions to come to the court's attention in the event that the dispute proceeds to trial.

The effect of the 'without prejudice' privilege is that neither party can refer the court to matters discussed or correspondence made without prejudice. For example, if a landlord offers, on a without prejudice basis, to grant a new lease at a rent of £4.50 per square foot, even if the landlord asked for £4.75 per square foot in the section 25 notice, the tenant cannot subsequently tell the court that the landlord was prepared to accept less than originally asked for.

This principle is subject to the following limited exceptions:

- The existence of without prejudice negotiations can be referred to explain any delay, where the court is concerned to know the reasons for this (as it might be, for example, if a claim is begun but no steps are taken to progress it for a lengthy period).

- The content of without prejudice negotiations can be referred to if the dispute is whether agreement was reached during those negotiations. An offer made 'without prejudice' is binding once it has been accepted, in the same way that an offer made on an open basis is binding once accepted.
- If correspondence has been referred to as 'without prejudice save as to costs' (such as Calderbank letters, discussed further in chapter 6), it may be referred to once the court has given judgment and is dealing only with the issue of who should pay the costs of any proceedings and how much they should pay.

Without prejudice documents are privileged from production but their existence must be disclosed. It is often thought that such documents can be omitted from a list of documents served on a party who was in fact the recipient or author of such correspondence, but this is incorrect. However, the nature of the documents need only be described in broad terms and as a category, without listing each one particularly.

I have received a letter which is not marked 'without prejudice' which is helpful to my client. Can I show the letter to the court?

If the reason why you want to show the letter to the court is because the writer has made an admission about the case or because the writer is offering to settle, for example, for a shorter term than he has previously asked for, then the answer is 'no'.

A document does not attract 'without prejudice' privilege just because it is so marked. Similarly a document may attract the privilege even if it does not contain the words 'without prejudice'.

If the correspondence or discussions are for the purpose of resolving the dispute and contain admissions, statements touching on the strengths or weaknesses of a party's position or which place a valuation on a party's rights forming part of an attempt to compromise the litigation, then they are 'without prejudice'. If one party wishes to revert to open correspondence after a series of without prejudice correspondence, this needs to be made clear and unambiguous words to this effect should be used.

Subject to contract

Where an offer is made 'subject to contract' (STC), if it is accepted, there will be no binding agreement until that agreement is reduced to writing and signed by the parties.

As a general rule, an offer should only be made STC if, once it is accepted, there are still matters that will need to be agreed before the parties are ready to 'sign up' to their deal. This will be the case where parties are attempting to agree heads of terms, for example. It will not be the case, however, where a landlord is prepared to grant a new tenancy on exactly the same terms as the existing one but wants to vary the rent.

If the landlord makes an offer without making such offer STC and it is accepted there is a binding agreement between the parties that obliges the tenant to take a new lease at the rent offered by the landlord. The landlord would be able to seek specific performance of that agreement if the tenant subsequently changed his or her mind, or refused to sign up. The same would not be true if the landlord's offer had been made 'subject to contract'.

Recording agreement

In principle, any agreement reached during negotiations should be reduced into writing as soon as possible. The only reason for not doing this is where one party wishes to agree all matters before committing to a deal, and not be bound to certain terms in a piecemeal way. If that party does wish there to be a written record of the agreement reached in principle, they should ensure that the record is headed 'subject to contract'.

Extending statutory time-limits

Under LTA 1954 there is a 'statutory period' for making a claim to the court. This is set by section 29A LTA 1954 and expires:

- on the termination date specified in the landlord's section 25 notice; or
- on the date immediately before the commencement date specified in the tenant's section 26 request.

For example if a section 25 notice contains a termination date of 1 June 2006, so the statutory period expires on 1 June 2006; or if a section 26 request contains a commencement date of 1 June 2006, the statutory period expires on 31 May 2006.

Agreement to extend the statutory period

An agreement to extend the statutory period must be:

- between the landlord and the tenant (or their authorised agents);
- made in writing; and
- made before expiry of the statutory period.

Any number of extensions can be made, provided that each extension is agreed in writing before expiry of the current statutory period.

The 'landlord' for these purposes is not necessarily the tenant's immediate landlord, as the person who agrees to the extension must be the 'competent landlord' as defined in section 44 of LTA 1954 (this was discussed in chapter 4).

Where the landlord and tenant act by agents, it is important for the written agreement to record that the agents have authority to bind their clients. At the very least, any agent should sign 'for and on behalf of' their client (a similar approach should be taken where the landlord or tenant is a company or partnership).

There is no specified form of agreement, so an exchange of correspondence will be sufficient, but it is important to show that the extension has been agreed within the relevant period and to date any such agreement. A sample form of words is as follows:

> *Words to evidence agreement under section 29B LTA 1954*
> 31 March 2006
> The parties agree to extend the statutory period referred to in section 29A of Part II of the *Landlord and Tenant Act* to 1 June 2006. An application to the court under section 29 of LTA 1954 may be made by either of them on or before 1 June 2006.

> *Words to evidence further agreement under section 29B of LTA 1954*
> 31 May 2006
> On 31 March 2006, the parties agreed to extend the statutory period referred to in section 29A of Part II of the *Landlord and Tenant Act* to 1 June 2006. The parties have now agreed to further extend the statutory period to 31 July 2006. An application to the court under section 29 of LTA 1954 may be made by either of them on or before 31 July 2006.

Any extension of the time limit for making an application to the court will also have the effect of extending the date of termination in the section 25 notice or date of commencement in the section 26 request similarly.

Thought will need to be given to what is an appropriate time for an extension – it should be long enough to allow the parties to negotiate, but not so long that the impetus to do so is lost. It is not clear whether an extension needs to be for a fixed period or can be referenced back to, for example, a period of 28 days after service of a notice requiring an application to the court to be made.

LTA 1954 refers to a 'specified period' only. Since it is arguable that a period fixed by reference to service of a notice does not fix a specified date for its expiry, clients should be advised to agree extensions to fixed dates only. Such extensions can always be renewed.

Agreeing some terms but not others

During negotiations that contemplate that an application will be made to the court for the grant of a new tenancy if they do not succeed the parties might:

- agree on all four matters dealt with in sections 32 to 35 of LTA 1954; or
- agree on some but not all of those matters; or
- fail to agree on anything.

In the first of these cases, the court will be bound to grant a new tenancy in the terms agreed if the agreement is recorded in writing. This is so even if the usual formal requirements for the grant of a tenancy have not been met (those imposed by the *Law of Property (Miscellaneous Provisions) Act* 1989 – such as the requirement that all terms be included in a single document, signed by both parties).

In such case the court has no jurisdiction to determine those terms itself because there is an 'agreement' for the purposes of LTA 1954 between the landlord and tenant. The court only has power to determine the terms 'in default of' an agreement between the parties.

LTA 1954 only requires that such an agreement be made in writing[68] and an exchange of written correspondence would suffice. An agreement on all points that was not written down would not be sufficient. A court might still give effect to such an oral agreement, on an application for specific performance made within an application for the grant of a new tenancy, but the court would then have a discretion as to whether or not to do so, rather than being required to do so.

In the second of these cases, provided the agreement is made in writing the court will be bound to grant a new tenancy in the terms agreed, even if they are not all agreed. The court will determine those terms that are not agreed. In the third of these cases, the court will determine all of the terms of the new tenancy.

Heads of terms

There is no particular format for heads of terms, but they should be as comprehensive as possible, as they will form the basis of instructions to solicitors to draft the new tenancy agreement. If matters have been missed, the solicitors will revert and this will inevitably delay completion. Other documents and information may be required before the matter can be taken further. Consideration should be given to these at or around the time that heads of terms are being agreed.

Examples include:

- Where the landlord is a head tenant, consider what consents are required from the superior landlord for any new subtenancy;
- If the tenant is a foreign company, does any previous opinion letter cover the proposed new tenancy?
- If there has been a history of default during the current tenancy, should the landlord request any security and, if so, what?
- If a change of user from the current tenancy is proposed, does this need to be authorised by the holder of any charge over the landlord's interest?

5.3 Pre-action conduct in opposed claims

There is little point in the parties negotiating terms of a new tenancy if the landlord is fundamentally opposed to the grant of a new tenancy on one or more of the statutory grounds of opposition. If a landlord is opposed to the grant of a new tenancy, they might try to secure vacant possession by offering the tenant incentives to leave.

There is no reason (although no requirement) why negotiations of this sort ought not to follow the same good practice as that applying to the negotiation of terms of a new tenancy.

Whether or not the landlord attempts to negotiate the tenant's exit from the premises, the provisions of the CPR regulating pre-action conduct are the same. Arguably, the Practice Direction on Pre-Action Protocols is of greater assistance where the grant of a new tenancy is opposed than when such a tenancy is unopposed.

Pre-action protocol: tactics for landlords

A landlord's grounds of opposition might be reasonably strong but a tenant might nevertheless apply to the court for a new tenancy to put the landlord under pressure in the hope that this will force the payment of a premium for vacant possession rather than go through a costly and lengthy litigation process. In these cases, a landlord can protect on costs by sending with the section 25 notice documents any information that is relied on to oppose the grant of a new tenancy.

The landlord is then able to invite the tenant to agree that on the basis of the documents and information supplied, the tenant has no real prospect of successfully challenging the grounds of opposition. If the tenant agrees, the landlord could apply for a termination order and, at the same time as issuing the claim, submit a consent order signed by both the landlord and the tenant providing that the current tenancy be determined without the grant of a new tenancy.

If the tenant does not agree and the landlord subsequently makes out the ground of opposition, the court could order the tenant to pay the landlord's costs on an indemnity basis.

Pre-action protocol: tactics for tenants

Where the grant of a new tenancy is opposed, a landlord must specify this in a section 25 notice or counter-notice to the tenant's section 26 request and state the grounds of opposition.

On receipt of that notice, the tenant should consider asking for further information as shown opposite.

Early access to documents and information should give the tenant a head start in preparing any defence to a claim for a termination order or opposition to the claim for a new tenancy. If documents or information cannot be provided because they are not available, the tenant could expedite the claim for a new tenancy in the hope that the landlord will still not be ready to make out the grounds of opposition at trial.

Where a tenant suspects that the landlord will oppose the grant of a new tenancy, the tenant may have to wait up to two months for the landlord to serve any counter-notice before receiving confirmation of the landlord's position. A tenant should use the Pre-Action Protocol to gain earlier access to documents or information about that position.

5.4 Preparing for court claims

Even if the grant of a new tenancy is unopposed and the parties have been negotiating over its new terms, those negotiations sometimes fail and it becomes necessary to make a claim. Where the grant of a new tenancy is opposed, it should be assumed that the dispute will be litigated, even if there are negotiations to avoid that.

Landlord relies on ground . . .	Information/documents to request
(a) Failure to repair	Schedule of dilapidations showing the condition of the premises, the work required to remedy it and the covenant of which the tenant is allegedly in breach
(b) Persistent rent arrears	Schedule showing the payment history
(c) Other reasons or breaches of covenant	Schedule showing the covenants in respect of which the tenant has been in breach together with particulars of the alleged breaches (date, manner of breach, persons involved etc.)
(d) Offer of alternative accommodation	Description of the alternative accommodation which the landlord intends to provide, on what terms and explanation as to why it is suitable for the tenant's business
(e) Current tenancy created by subletting of part	Level of rent which the landlord considers is obtainable on the letting of the whole and of the individual parts together with an explanation showing when the landlord will obtain vacant possession of the remainder of the building
(f) Demolition and re-construction	Description of the works which the landlord will carry out
	If consents are required, whether they have been obtained and, if not, when they are expected to be obtained
	Confirmation of when the landlord intends to commence works
	If relevant, an explanation as to how the landlord will obtain vacant possession of the remainder of the building to be developed
	Evidence as to the landlord's ability to meet the cost of the works, of necessary internal authorisations or otherwise as to the viability of those works
(g) Own occupation	Description of the business which the landlord intends to carry on at the premises or how the premises will be used as a residence

In each case, parties should take certain steps in relation to documents to protect themselves if and when litigation is commenced.

Collection of relevant documents

When a court claim is in reasonable contemplation, parties should take reasonable steps to ensure that documents relevant to the claim are preserved and collected together for any subsequent investigation into the factual background of the claim and to ensure that disclosure obligations are satisfied.

'Document' in this context means anything in which information of any description is recorded and therefore includes draft documents, manuscript notes, day books, meeting notes, diary entries, computer disks and databases, word processing files, audio/video tapes, voicemail messages, photographs and email. The document collection exercise should include all copy documents as well as originals.

A person should be identified who will take formal responsibility for checking that all originals of the relevant documents have been collected together in one place and that there are no additional documents that have been overlooked. The individual may, in due course, be required to submit a witness statement confirming the steps that were taken to identify and collect the relevant documents. It is therefore important that this exercise be conducted diligently and fully.

It is our firm's policy to destroy documents on file that are over a year old, so that our files remain a manageable size. Can we still do this?

It is entirely reasonable for you to have a document destruction policy in place but, in a case where litigation is a reasonable possibility, the policy should be suspended for the time being. You will not be criticised for having followed your usual policy before litigation was in reasonable contemplation, but run the risk that the other side will say you could have destroyed relevant documents if you continue to pursue any destruction policy once litigation becomes a reasonable possibility.

When documents are collected together originals should usually be sent to a party's solicitors for safekeeping as it is possible that the other side will wish to examine ('inspect') the originals in due course.

Document creation generally

The duty on a party to court proceedings to preserve and disclose relevant documents is an ongoing duty that continues throughout the proceedings, and therefore if new documents are created which are relevant to the issues in LTA 1954 proceedings, these would have to be disclosed in the same way as documents that already existed.

If legal privilege can properly be claimed over a document, that document would not be required to be produced to any other party, but in view of these disclosure duties, it is important that the client takes measures to ensure that the creation of new non-privileged documents is kept to an absolute minimum.

There are a number of practical steps that can be taken to increase the chances of this:

- The client should, where practically possible, **avoid creating any new written communications** that discuss *any* aspect of the claim (including, in particular, emails and manuscript notes). Accordingly, individuals should be instructed not to discuss matters relating to a possible claim in any form of written communications.
- Where it is absolutely necessary to create a document discussing matters relevant to the claim, if possible, **the document should be prepared in a such a way as to attract legal privilege**. Documents should only be prepared at the specific request of the client's solicitors and/or to enable them to provide advice, and the document itself ought to record the fact that it has been prepared at the request of a lawyer (and should be sent or copied to that lawyer). It would be advisable to contact the client's solicitors in advance to discuss how the document could be prepared such that it would attract legal privilege.
- If a document discussing matters relevant to the claim must be created, and it is not possible to attract legal privilege over the document, **the author should be aware that the document may be required to be disclosed** in the course of the proceedings and that he or she could be cross-examined on its contents.

I want to discuss with my client difficulties in continuing to press for a rent that, in my view as a surveyor, is too high. What is the best way to do this?

This is exactly the sort of information that, if recorded in a document, could be highly embarrassing for the client were it to be revealed at a later stage.

If you need to have this sort of discussion, it may be best to do so by telephone or at a meeting face-to-face. The discussion should

Continued

not be recorded in an attendance or meeting note. If it is the note will be considered to be a disclosable document. If you need to create such a note because, for example, you need to record the terms of your advice for the file, it could be sent to the client's lawyer (at the same time as to the client) with a request for advice, for example, on the possibility of settlement in line with the advice that you have given.

5.5 Who can make an application to the court?

The tenant or the landlord can make an application to the court for an order for the grant of a new tenancy and the landlord can also apply for a termination order. The person applying to court will be named as the claimant, and the person responding to the claim will be named as the defendant.

Appropriate parties

In many cases, it will be obvious who the 'tenant' is for the purposes of LTA 1954. But as discussed in chapter 1, this can be complicated if:

- **the tenancy is held on trust.** It is the trustees who are the appropriate parties, not the beneficiaries (even if the latter occupy the premises for business purposes). One trustee can make a claim provided they do so in that capacity and on behalf of the trust[69]. If the trustee refuses to make such an application, the beneficiary can apply to the court for an order compelling him or her to do so under section 14 of the *Trusts of Land and Appointment of Trustees Act* 1996.
- **there are joint tenants.** Each of the joint tenants must apply, or none of them can apply, unless they are former partners and section 41A of LTA 1954 applies. In this latter case, the appropriate parties are those of the previous joint tenants now occupying the premises for business purposes or to those joint tenants and their new partners jointly. If joint tenants apply for the grant of a new tenancy, they will each be named as claimants. If a landlord of property demised to joint tenants applies for the grant of a new tenancy or for a termination order, each of the joint tenants will be named as defendants.

The relevant 'landlord' for making an application may not be the tenant's immediate landlord. As a rule of thumb, if a person has served a section 25 notice or a tenant has served a section 26 request on a person, that person is the 'landlord' entitled to apply to the court (he is the 'competent landlord', as discussed in chapter 4).

If a person serves a section 25 notice on the tenant, the person will be prevented from disputing that they are the competent landlord for the purposes of any claim brought by the tenant, even if the person is not – in fact – the competent landlord[70].

If the land is registered, the identity of the correct persons should be readily identifiable from the Office Copy entry. However, if a claim for a new tenancy is made by the tenant, the person who in relation to the claimant's current tenancy is the competent landlord must be a defendant (under paragraph 3.3 of CPR Practice Direction 56).

Where different people hold reversionary interests in different parts of the property, there can be more than one 'landlord' of the property demised to the tenant. Separate landlords of parts are collectively the 'landlord' for the purposes of LTA 1954, including for the purpose of serving notices or applying for the grant of a new tenancy (section 44(1A) of LTA 1954). As with joint tenants, landlords of parts must act together in order to make a claim for a new tenancy.

What to do if the parties are the wrong ones

If a claim is not made by all joint tenants or by each landlord of separate parts of the demise then the court has no jurisdiction to try it. A defendant cannot agree to confer jurisdiction on the court to deal with the matter, but nothing prevents these parties coming to an arrangement regarding the property without the court's involvement.

Where, however, a claim is started against an incorrect party, it is irregular rather than void. The court can substitute the correct party in order to regularise the claim. If the Claim Form has not yet been served when the mistake is realised, it can be amended without the court's permission.

Where the correct parties change over time (because, for example, the landlord sells the interest in the reversion or the tenant assigns the current tenancy), an application should be made to substitute the correct party under CPR Part 19. This should be fairly straightforward if the statutory period has not yet expired, but if it has expired, the stricter conditions of CPR 19.5 will need to be met.

If the claimant intended to sue the correct party and did not do so because of a mistake, an application to substitute the correct person as a party falls within CPR 19.5(3)(a)[71]. It is worth bearing in mind that where the property demised is registered land a new owner cannot be a party to a claim until their ownership is registered.

Other interested persons

Although they need not be parties to an application, certain persons will be interested (at least potentially) in the outcome, and they must be served with the application once it has been issued.

The interested parties include:

- any person who has an interest in the reversion in the property (whether immediate or in not more than 15 years) on the termination of the current tenancy. This would include, for example, any mortgagee; and
- any other person with a freehold interest in the property. This would include any superior landlord.

Where there is a chain of interests and the duration of a new tenancy granted by the court is longer than the length of the immediate landlord's tenancy, the court can grant such reversionary tenancies as may be required to secure the combined effect of a grant of such a term. If it is likely that a tenant will be asking the court to grant such reversionary tenancies, then the tenant should – as a matter of good practice – include these persons as defendants to the application.

Priority of claims

This is dealt with by sections 24(2A) and (2B) of LTA 1954 and paragraph 3.2 of CPR Practice Direction 56, and in principle, a tenant's claim for the grant of a new tenancy takes precedence over a landlord's claim for the same relief, and a landlord's application for a termination order takes precedence over a tenant's claim for a new tenancy. However, this order of priority does not take effect until applications have been served. It is worthwhile noting the difference between issue of a claim and service of a claim – a claim is issued when the court processes the claim form (and records an issue date on it), but a claim form is not served until it is received by the defendant (or other appropriate person), although service may be deemed rather than actual in some circumstances. (See chapter 6 for more information.)

Claim	Response to claim
Claim for new tenancy served by tenant	The landlord cannot issue an application for a new tenancy. If the application for a new tenancy was already issued and served on the same day, the landlord's claim is stayed until further court order. The landlord cannot otherwise serve any application for a new tenancy or for a termination order already issued without the court's permission.
Claim for new tenancy served by landlord	The tenant cannot issue an application for a new tenancy and cannot serve any application for a new tenancy already issued without the court's permission.
Claim for termination order served by landlord	The tenant cannot issue an application for a new tenancy, and if the application for a new tenancy already issued by tenant and has been served on the same day as the landlord's claim, the tenant's claim is stayed until further court order. If the tenant's claim was not served before the landlord's claim, then the tenant must serve or discontinue its claim within 14 days.

I am a landlord and my tenant has made an application for a new tenancy. I have a leasehold interest in the property, but my head lease requires me to obtain my superior landlord's consent before granting any new under-tenancy. What should I do?

In this case, you need to:

- check that you are the competent landlord for the purpose of the proceedings;
- if so, make sure that your proposals for the terms of the new tenancy take account of any conditions which your superior landlord may impose before giving consent; and
- ensure that the superior landlord is served with a copy of the claim form.

If the court makes an order for the grant of a new tenancy, the authors believe that the landlord can execute a new tenancy in the terms set by the court even if the superior landlord has not consented to it, since following a court order is a lawful excuse for non-performance of a covenant (here, the failure to obtain superior landlord's consent).

The position is different if no court order is made: a landlord and tenant cannot agree between themselves to execute a new tenancy without superior landlord's consent.

5.6 The time limits for making a claim

The earliest time a claim can be made will depend on whether the application follows service of a section 25 notice (by the landlord) or a section 26 request (by the tenant):

- If a section 25 notice has been served, an application can be made immediately after the notice is given (in theory, even on the same day).
- If a section 26 request has been served then under section 29A(3) of LTA 1954 no application can be made until the earlier of:
  - the landlord serving a counter-notice (if the landlord opposes the grant of a new tenancy); or
  - the expiry of the period of two months, beginning on the date of the making of the request (if the landlord does not oppose the grant of a new tenancy).

L served a section 25 notice by recorded delivery, which is received by the Post Office at 10.30am on 1 August 2006. L then issued a claim for a termination order at 3.30pm on that date – the claim is valid. However if L were to serve a section 25 notice by first class post on 1 August 2006 – which according to the lease is deemed served two days after posting – and then L issued a claim for a termination order by close of business on 1 August 2006, such claims would be invalid.

T served a section 26 request by recorded delivery, which is received by the Post Office at 10.30am on 1 August 2006. L does not serve a counter-notice and T then issued a claim for an order for the grant of a new tenancy two months later, on 1 October 2006 – the claim is valid. The claim would also be valid if L served a counter-notice on 8 August 2006 and T issued a claim for an order for the grant of a new tenancy on 9 August 2006.

The latest that an application must be made is before the expiry of the 'statutory period' (section 29A(1) LTA 1954). Proceedings are started when the court issues a claim form at the request of the claimant, and a claim form is issued on the date entered on the form by the court (CPR 7.2).

There are some courts that do not process claim forms themselves. In these circumstances, parties should not expect that claim forms delivered to the court will be issued that day or even within a short period thereafter. If a claim form needs to be issued that day (for example because it is the last day of the statutory period), it should be taken to the court, the position explained, and the person asking for it to be issued should wait whilst the process is completed.

If the statutory period ends on a day when the court office is closed (at the weekends and on Bank Holidays), the last day for making an application will, in practice, be the last day on which the court office is open before the expiry of the statutory period. So, for example if a statutory period ended on Saturday 3 December 2005, then the last day for making an application is Friday 2 December 2005. Days on which the court office will be closed are usually advertised in advance on the Court Service website[72].

In exceptional circumstances, the court may consider that an application has been 'made' (as required by LTA 1954), even if it has not yet been issued, provided the court has taken some positive step to process it. This might be, for example, where the court sends out a letter requesting the claimant to pay the correct fee because the amount tendered is wrong[73].

6

Unopposed claims

As discussed in the previous chapter, an unopposed claim (as defined by *Civil Procedure Rule* (CPR) 56.3(2)(b)) is a claim under section 24 of the *Landlord and Tenant Act* 1954 (LTA 1954) for a new tenancy in circumstances where the landlord does not rely on any of the statutory grounds of opposition.

An unopposed claim will include those claims where the grant of a new tenancy is not opposed, but there is disagreement over what the terms of that tenancy should be.

This chapter looks at unopposed claims for an order for the grant of a new tenancy made to the court. It considers:

- the powers the court has when dealing with unopposed claims for an order for the grant of a new tenancy, in particular:
  - to decide what property will be comprised in the new tenancy (section 6.1);
  - its discretion to decide the length of the new tenancy (section 6.2);
  - its decision over any other terms (section 6.3); and
  - its valuation of the rent to be paid under the new tenancy, including claims for interim rent (sections 6.4 and 6.5).
- the various stages in the litigation process, focussing in particular on those matters in which a surveyor will be most closely involved, such as:
  - starting and responding to an unopposed claim (section 6.6);
  - steps in the litigation process (section 6.7);
    offers to settle and costs (section 6.8); and
  - the court's order for the grant of a new tenancy (section 6.9).

6.1 Deciding what property will be comprised in the new tenancy

LTA 1954 protects, among other things, a tenant's right to occupy premises for business purposes. Accordingly, if a tenant does not occupy all of the land demised for those purposes, there is no need to provide any security of tenure in respect of the part not occupied (this concept of business occupation was dealt with in greater detail in chapter 1).

LTA 1954 calls the part of the premises which the tenant does occupy for business purposes 'the holding' and a tenant can only ask the court to grant a new tenancy of the holding.

T takes a lease of a three-storey building from which T operates a retail business. During the course of the term, T's business scales down such that (by the time the court decides the application for a new tenancy) the business only occupies the ground and first floors of the property. Thus, the holding comprises the ground and first floors only and the court can only grant T a new tenancy of those two floors, even though the previous tenancy was for all the floors in the building.

> **Exceptions for granting a new tenancy of property other than the holding**
>
> In certain circumstances the court will grant a new tenancy of property comprising more or less than the holding:
>
> - If the landlord opposes the grant of a new tenancy on redevelopment grounds, but the tenant establishes that some part of the holding is an economically separable part and that the landlord need not obtain vacant possession of that part in order to redevelop the premises (section 32(1A) of LTA 1954). (This is considered in greater detail in chapter 7.)
> - The landlord can elect that the tenant should take a new tenancy of all of the property that was previously demised (section 32(2) of LTA 1954). In such case, if the court grants a new tenancy at all, it must grant a tenancy of the whole of the premises.
>
> This is particularly useful for landlords where their tenant has sublet part but remains in business occupation of the other part. In this way the landlord does not have to become the subtenant's direct landlord.

The court can also, as part of the property comprised in the new tenancy, include 'rights enjoyed by the tenant in connection with the holding' (section 32(3) of LTA 1954). In order to be included the right must:

- be a right rather than a mere permission;
- attach to the holding itself;
- not be greater than a right previously enjoyed by the tenant under the old tenancy; and
- continue to be necessary for proper use and enjoyment of the holding.

A occupies a timber yard leased from L, who has given A temporary personal permission for trucks taking deliveries from the yard to park on adjacent land. The ability to do so is not a 'right' that the court may grant to A on renewal of the tenancy, since L can withdraw it at any time.

B occupies only the ground and first floors of a four-storey building let by L. The top two floors comprise a self-contained unit that enjoys rights of way to the back of the property over land owned by L. As the holding comprises only the ground and first floors, this right does not attach to the holding, so the court cannot include the right in any new tenancy.

In the above example if B occupied each floor of the four-storey building, but does not use the right of way enjoyed by the self-contained upstairs unit because, during the course of the tenancy, access to that unit was gained by means of adjacent land which B purchased himself, then the court would be unlikely to grant the right of way because even though the right attaches to the holding, B no longer needs it to enjoy the holding.

L let premises to C that contained an option for C to acquire the freehold at a stated price exercisable by notice given not less than three months before expiration of the term. C did not exercise the option and now the court cannot grant, along with the new tenancy, a similar option.

Relevance of date for determination

A tenant may occupy different parts of business premises from time to time and to take account of this, LTA 1954 has fixed the date for deciding which part of the property comprises 'the holding' as being the date on which the court makes an order for the grant of a new tenancy (section 32(1) of LTA 1954).

Technically, therefore, a tenant who does not occupy the whole of premises demised could obtain a new tenancy of the whole of the premises simply by re-occupying the whole of those premises for business purposes before the court makes any order.

At the time of an application to the court for a new tenancy, T only occupies the ground and first floors of the three-storey building. A week before trial, T re-occupies the second and third floors by storing stock there for the purpose of the business operated from the ground and first floors. T continues to occupy all floors for business purposes at the date the court grants a new tenancy, so the holding comprises the entire property.

L appeals against the grant of a new tenancy and T cross-appeals against the new rent set by the judge. Before the appeal is heard, T ceases to occupy the second and third floors again. The appeal court dismisses L's appeal and varies the rent. Even though, at the date of its order, T has ceased to occupy the top two floors of the premises, the appeal court cannot also vary the extent of the property comprised in the new tenancy because 'the holding' is fixed as at the date of the order for the grant of a new tenancy (i.e. by the judge at first instance).

6.2 Setting the length of the new tenancy

When there is no agreement between the parties, section 33 of LTA 1954 provides that:

- the court should grant a new tenancy with a reasonable length in all the circumstances; and
- if the new tenancy is for a fixed period, the court may not order a new grant longer than 15 years, beginning on the coming to an end of the current tenancy (i.e. that which the tenant holds for the time being). Sections 24, 25, 26 and 64 of LTA 1954 determine this date.

The date on which the current tenancy ends depends on:

- the date of termination specified in the section 25 notice served by the landlord (the **termination date**); *or*
- the commencement date of the new tenancy specified in the section 26 request served by the tenant (the **commencement date**); *and*
- the date on which a claim to the court is finally disposed of (the **disposal date**).

The disposal date

Section 64 of LTA 1954 refers to:

'... the earliest date by which the proceedings on the application (including any proceedings on or in consequence of an appeal) have been determined and any time for appealing or further appealing has expired ...'

The following table sets out the final disposal date in different scenarios:

Scenario	Disposal date
Order made by Circuit Judge and not appealed	Fourteen days after the Circuit Judge's order or such other period as the Circuit Judge allows
Order made by High Court Judge on appeal from the Circuit Judge	Fourteen days after the High Court Judge's order
Order made by Court of Appeal on appeal from the circuit judge or on second appeal from the High Court Judge	One month after the Court of Appeal's order or three months if the Court of Appeal gives permission for an appeal
Appeal to the House of Lords	Date of the judgment of the House of Lords

In either case, the current tenancy will end three months from and including the disposal date unless the termination date or the commencement date is more than three months later than the disposal date, in which case the current tenancy will end on the termination date or a day before the commencement date.

L lets premises to T on a fixed term expiring on 31 May 2006. On 1 June 2005, T serves a section 26 request on L, giving 1 June 2006 as the date of commencement of the new tenancy. On 2 August 2005, T applies to the court for a new tenancy. The court determines that application on 2 February 2006, and decides that a new fixed-term tenancy of ten years is reasonable in all the circumstances. L does not appeal and since the disposal date is more than three months earlier than the commencement date, the current tenancy ends on 31 May 2006 and the new tenancy runs from 1 June 2006 to 31 May 2016.

On 1 August 2005, L serves a section 25 notice on T, which gives 1 June 2006 as the date of termination. On 1 April 2006, T applies for a new tenancy. The court determines that application on

1 December 2006, and decides that a new fixed-term tenancy of ten years is reasonable in all the circumstances. L does not appeal and since the disposal date is after the commencement date, the current tenancy continues for three months from the final disposal date (15 December 2006) and the new tenancy runs from 15 March 2007 to 14 March 2017.

In the past, certain courts have ordered the grant of a new tenancy to begin from a given date, but this practice has been disapproved, because the court may get the wrong date (where, for example, the court orders the grant of a new tenancy from the date of termination specified in the section 25 notice, but its order is appealed and the current tenancy in fact extends beyond that date).

In the circumstances, the court should either:

- make an order for the grant of a new tenancy 'from the termination of the current tenancy' without naming a date[74]; or
- make an order for the grant of a new tenancy that is to terminate on a given date.

Decide what is a reasonable length

Each case must be determined on its own merits, but invariably parties will seek to adduce expert evidence of market practice in order to justify the term that they wish the court to set. If the court does not have regard to the prevailing market, its task in other respects (e.g. to determine the rent under section 34 of LTA 1954) becomes that much harder. However, whilst the term, which the holding might be expected to let for in the market, is a significant factor for the court to consider, it is not determinative.

In at least one reported case, the court went against market practice, granting a term of only one year (as requested by the tenant) rather than the much longer term (as requested by the landlord) then prevalent in the market[75]. The primary reason for the difference in term length required by the tenant and the landlord was that the former intended to relocate within a matter of months, but needed some time to complete this. The judge was persuaded by the tenant's argument that:

- the landlord would have effectively 11 months in which to find new tenants;
- the prospect of a void was small;
- the present tenant would be in difficulty in disposing of what would be a 13 year lease;

- the suggested diminution in market value of the reversion was irrelevant as the landlord was not looking to sell or use the property as security for funding; and
- the purpose of LTA 1954 was to protect the tenant, which meant that the tenant should be given the protection needed and no more.

Whether or not that final submission would meet with unquestioned approval today must be doubted, as the identity of property owners has changed considerably in the past 20 years. There are now far more individual landlords who require the court to strike a balance between them and their large corporate tenants.

From 1 June 2004, landlords have been able to apply to the court for an order for the grant of a new tenancy. Whilst the tenant is not obliged to take a new tenancy, this change must signify some shift away from the primary tenant focus under the previous law. Ultimately, the court is involved in a balancing act between the protection to which the tenant is entitled in order to carry on a business and the landlord's interests in dealing with the property as required.

This has always been the law[76] but has, until now, been a principle that has been paid more lip service than given practical effect. A change may be signified by the decision in *Davy's of London (Wine Merchants) Limited v The City of London Corporation* (2004)[77] which, although determined under the previous law, saw the trial Judge's order, that a redevelopment break clause could not be exercised for seven years, reduced to half that time.

6.3 Deciding on other terms

'Other terms' means any term other than as to the property, duration and rent payable under a new tenancy. Those terms attracting most interest usually relate to service charges, use, alienation and repairing obligations.

The court has a discretion as to the terms which it will impose, but this must be exercised 'judicially' – meaning the court should only impose a term if it is necessary for the reasonable operation of the new tenancy and imposition of that term is fair, just and equitable to both parties. The court will make its decisions based on the evidence it receives – inference from other terms of the lease is not necessarily *evidence*, so If a party wants to change a lease term, it is up to them to prove why the court should do that.

In determining these matters, the court must have regard to:

- the terms of the current tenancy;
- all relevant circumstances, including the operation of the provisions of the *Landlord and Tenant (Covenants) Act* 1995.

Whenever the court exercises this or any other discretion, it is important to bear in mind that the prospects of appealing against its decision are very limited. A body of case law exists regarding the exercise of this discretion, but even if the facts of one case are seemingly identical to another, this does not mean that the court is bound (although it is likely) to set the same terms as in the previous case.

The discretion conferred on the court by section 35 of LTA 1954 is effectively a 'catch-all'. Where, for example, the court wanted to confer certain rights on a tenant on the grant of a new tenancy but was unable to hold that such rights fell within section 32(5) of LTA 1954 (such as granting a new tenancy of property other than the holding), it was nevertheless able to confer the rights by exercising its powers under section 35.

Consideration of the *Landlord and Tenant (Covenants) Act* 1995

Prior to 1 January 1996, if a tenant assigned its tenancy to a third party and that assignee defaulted, the original tenant was obliged to make good the default. Where a tenant has entered into an agreement on or after 1 January 1996 (called a 'new lease'), the original tenant will not be liable for any default after an assignment unless an authorised guarantee agreement (AGA) is executed, by which the tenant agrees to guarantee the performance of the assignee.

In order to protect themselves under LTA 1954, landlords will often ask the court to impose a term in the new tenancy that the tenant should not assign the renewal tenancy unless it enters into an AGA. Whilst the matter is discretionary, the court will usually impose a term that the tenancy may not be assigned unless the tenant enters into an AGA where it is reasonable for the tenant to do so[78].

Constraints on the discretion

There are two constraints on the court's discretion:

- Section 1 of the *Costs of Leases Act* 1958 provides that:

    'Notwithstanding any custom to the contrary, a party to a lease shall, unless the parties thereto agree otherwise in writing, be under no obligation to pay the whole or any part of any other party's solicitor's costs of the lease.'

Accordingly, the court cannot in exercising its discretion include a term that requires one party to pay the other's costs of preparing the lease, since this is expressly excluded (absent agreement between the parties) by the 1958 Act[79].

- Where premises are provided under the *Distribution of Industry Acts* 1945 and 1950, the Secretary of State can, under section 60 of LTA 1954, certify that the court should include terms prohibiting assignment, sharing possession and/or change of use in any renewal tenancy. If a certificate is given, the court must include such terms. A similar situation exists in relation to properties let by the Welsh Development Agency (section 32(2) of LTA 1954).

Practice

In practice, the court will grant a new tenancy on exactly the same terms as the existing tenancy. If either party wishes to amend, remove or add a term, the burden of proof is on that party to justify this[80]. The table below gives details of what the landlord or tenant will need to show depending on the change required.

Party wishes to:	Party needs to show that:
amend the terms of the current tenancy	the existing terms are deficient in some respect
	The current tenancy was granted orally, with no particular user being specified (in which case an open user covenant was implied). The landlord shows that the restriction to the retail use currently carried on by the tenant is necessary, in order that the landlord should not breach covenants owed to other tenants in adjoining properties whose leases prohibit office use (and which entitle them to call on the landlord to enforce the same prohibition against other tenants).
remove terms of the current tenancy	the terms sought to be removed are obsolete
	The current tenancy, which is decades old, refers to the landlord providing an electricity supply to the premises. The tenant has long since installed its own electricity generator at the premises and made its own arrangements for the supply of electricity with an external provider. The parties do not intend that the landlord should continue to offer this service.

add terms to the current tenancy	The terms sought are necessary for the reasonable operation of the new tenancy and are fair
	In assessing whether the imposition of a new term is 'fair', the court will consider a range of factors, including: • that the tenant or landlord may be in a weak negotiating position[81]; • any detriment suffered by either party as a result of imposing or not imposing the proposed term; • whether the other party upon whom the proposed term will be imposed will be 'compensated' by other terms of the new tenancy; • the reasons why the imposition of the term is opposed by the other party; • whether imposition of the proposed term will transfer risk to the other party and, if so, whether that risk is disproportionate to their interest in the property; and • whether imposition of the proposed term would affect the protection of the tenant's business that the LTA 1954 is intended to confer.

6.4 Rent

Rent is always the last matter to be determined, since it is necessary for the court to have first established the extent of the new demise, length of the tenancy and all other terms, each of which might have an impact on the rent payable[82].

For these purposes, 'rent' means the basic rent, not any additional rent such as insurance or service charges, even if these are reserved as rent.

If the parties have agreed a basis for payment of rent, for example a turnover rent, then the court need not assess it. In all other cases, however, the court must follow the provisions of section 34 of LTA 1954 which, as the Court of Appeal has said, contains all the essential guidance for determination of the rent, including statutory disregards. Lower courts should be slow to imply any other elements into the section[83].

The valuation formula

Section 34(1) of LTA 1954 provides:

'The rent payable under a tenancy granted by order of the court under this Part of this Act shall be such as may be agreed between the landlord and the tenant or as, in default of such agreement, may be determined by the court to be that at which, having regard to the terms of the tenancy (other than those relating to rent), the holding might reasonably be expected to be let in the open market by a willing lessor, there being disregarded:

(a) any effect on rent of the fact that the tenant has or predecessors in title have been in occupation of the holding;

(b) any goodwill attached to the holding by reason of the carrying on thereat of the business of the tenant (or by a predecessor in that business);

(c) any effect on rent of an improvement to which this paragraph applies; and

(d) in the case of a holding comprising licensed premises, any addition to its value attributable to the licence, if it appears to the court that having regard to the terms of the current tenancy and any other relevant circumstances the benefit of the licence belongs to the tenant.'

Whereas the court has a discretion in setting the duration of the tenancy or its other terms, it must set the rent of a new tenancy at the open market rent (OMR) which it will assess by hearing relevant expert evidence of comparable lettings and valuing OMR accordingly. Evidence of market lettings is the primary yardstick. Whether or not a letting is a proper comparable depends on a comparison of the terms of the comparable and the new tenancy. In *GREA Real Property Investments Limited v Williams* (1979)[84], Forbes J said:

'It is a fundamental aspect of valuation that it proceeds by analogy. The valuer isolates those characteristics of the object to be valued which in his view affect the value and then seeks another object of known, or ascertainable value, possessing some or all of those characteristics with which he may compare the object he is valuing. Where no directly comparable object exists the valuer must make allowances of one kind or another, interpolating or extrapolating from his given data. The less closely analogous the object chosen for comparison, the greater the allowances which have to be made and the greater the opportunity for error.'

Where a comparable transaction carries a headline rent which covers a more complicated deal, the evidence will need to break that deal down in terms of drawing out the evidential value of the transaction in terms of OMR.

Different types of evidence carry different weight, depending on quality and relevance. Leaving relevance aside, the courts have expressed a preference for certain types of evidence over others. The scale (with the most preferred first and the least preferred last) is as follows[85]:

- open market lettings;
- agreements between valuers at arms' length on lease renewal or rent review;
- determinations by an independent expert (where admissible);
- an arbitrator's award (where admissible); and
- determination of terms by the court under LTA 1954 (where admissible).

I am involved in a case in which the subject premises is a hotel and spa. All terms have been agreed, except for rent, but there are no comparable lettings for me to refer to. What can I do?

If there are no appropriate comparables, the court can receive evidence of the general trend in rent levels in the locality. Alternatively, the court can consider any of the following (although the weight to be attached to each may be insignificant):

- an actual offer made for the premises in question by a third party (provided the person making the offer is a bona fide independent third party);
- transactions relating to other property owned by the landlord; and/or
- transactions achieved by tender (where the bid made by the loser might in fact provide the best evidence of actual market practice).

The valuation date

LTA 1954 does not specify the valuation date. In practice, the court will value OMR based on rents prevailing at the date of the hearing, but in theory the proper date should be the date of commencement of the new tenancy[86]. If, therefore, it is likely that something will happen after the hearing but before the new tenancy begins which is likely to significantly affect rentals, the court should take account of this.

Assumptions and disregards

In valuing the rent payable under the new tenancy, the court will make certain assumptions and disregards. Whilst some are expressly stated in LTA 1954, others are sourced from case law.

Assumptions	Disregards
The **user is lawful** (in compliance with the user covenant and not in breach of any statutory or other controls, such as planning)	**Any effect of the tenant's occupation**, e.g. sitting tenant's overbid. This may mean that the valuation assumes vacant possession, unless the actual tenant has sublet, when the valuation takes account of that fact.
The holding is notionally **available to let**	**Any rent-free period** which a hypothetical tenant might hope to receive in the market
There needs to be a **'willing lessor'**. There is no reference in LTA 1954 to a **'willing lessee'**, but in practice one is to be assumed[87]. The circumstances of the actual landlord and tenant are ignored, and any ransom value is therefore excluded, although the fact that they might own adjoining land is not (for example, where property let to a hypothetical tenant would be land-locked because the actual tenant owned all of the adjoining land[88]).

One consequence of this is that the court can (but need not) value the rent assuming a different user, for example, from that actually carried on by the tenant, provided such user would be permitted under the terms of the new tenancy. | **Disrepair** which the tenant is obliged to repair |
| | **Goodwill** attached to the holding |
| | **Improvements**:

• carried out by the person who was the tenant at the time (or by employees, servants or agents);
• other than pursuant to an obligation to the immediate landlord (e.g. pursuant to a repairing covenant or side-letter agreeing to carry out a schedule of works);
• during the current tenancy *or* completed not more than 21 years before the application for a new tenancy *and* at all times since the improvement was completed LTA 1954 has applied to the tenancy. |

Rent review provisions

The court has the express power to include provisions for rent review under section 34(2) of LTA 1954, which in practice it will exercise in all cases where the term of the new tenancy exceeds five years. It has a discretion, however, as to:

- whether to include any rent review provisions at all;
- if so, when during the life of the term those provisions should take effect;
- whether those provisions should be 'upwards only' or 'upwards-and-downwards'; and
- what the rent review provisions should be.

What the court will usually seek to do is follow market practice, in which case expert evidence of that practice will be required. The *Code of Practice for Commercial Leases in England and Wales*[89] recommends that landlords offer alternatives to upwards-only reviews priced on a risk-adjusted basis and that if an alternative is accepted or ordered, the effect of this should be reflected in the initial rent.

If there is disagreement about the actual rent review provisions, the court is likely (but not bound) to follow the valuation formula contained in section 34(1) of LTA 1954, particularly if improvements have been made (which should, therefore, be disregarded on review).

Requirement for a guarantor

The court can impose, as a precondition to the grant of a new tenancy, the requirement for a tenant to provide a guarantee or surety within a particular time. Where section 41A of LTA 1954 applies (that is, where the tenant is a business occupier who was previously a joint tenant of the premises in partnership with others), this discretion is conferred on the court expressly by section 41A(6) of LTA 1954. The purpose of this is to compensate the landlord for the loss of the previous joint tenants, since the court is to have 'regard to the omission of the other joint tenants from the persons who will be the tenant under the new tenancy'.

In all other cases, the discretion is conferred on the court by section 35 of LTA 1954[90]. It is usually exercised where the tenant is an assignee and only recently incorporated. The court can, where circumstances require it, specify the number of individuals required to stand as guarantor and identify who those individuals should be.

6.5 Interim rent

The interim rent is, very broadly speaking, the rent payable for the period between expiry of the current contractual tenancy and execution of a new tenancy. Prior to 1 June 2004 only the landlord was entitled to ask the court to set an interim rent, and the interim rent period ran from the later of the date in the section 25 notice or section 26 request and the date of the landlord's interim rent application.

For renewals where the section 25 notice or section 26 request was served on or after 1 June 2004, the interim rent procedure has changed.

The rules in existence prior to 1 June 2004 encouraged tenants, in a rising market, to delay court proceedings, because the interim rent was usually set at a discount to OMR. The longer the period that the tenant was paying interim rent, the better it was. The authors consider that the object of the changes to the legislation was to minimise the discount that was routinely awarded in previous cases, and attempt to put interim rent on an OMR basis, thereby removing any advantage in delaying court proceedings.

Under the post-1 June 2004 procedure, an application can be made for the court to determine interim rent as soon as a section 25 notice or section 26 request has been served (section 24A(1) of LTA 1954). Either the landlord or the tenant is allowed to apply, provided the other has not already made such an application. In that case, a second application can only be made if the first is withdrawn (section 24A(2) of LTA 1954). The last date for making the interim rent application is six months after the termination of the current tenancy (section 24A(3) of LTA 1954).

L lets premises to T for a term of ten years commencing 1 May 1996. L serves a section 25 notice specifying 1 June 2006 as the date of termination. If T vacated the premises on 10 May 2006 (i.e. after the contractual expiry date) and no application to the court is made, the current tenancy ends on 1 June 2006 (i.e. the expiry of the statutory period). The latest date to apply for an interim rent (payable from 1 May 2006 to 1 June 2006) is 1 December 2006.

However, if, rather than vacating the premises, T applied for a new tenancy, which L opposes on ground (d), the court would try L's ground of statutory opposition as a preliminary issue. Then, say, on 1 September 2007 the court dismisses T's claim for a new tenancy and T does not appeal. The final disposal date of T's proceedings is 14 September 2007 and T's tenancy continues until 13 December 2007. The latest date to apply for an interim rent (payable from 1 May 2006 until 13 December 2007) is 14 June 2008.

What period is the interim rent payable for?

Unlike the position before 1 June 2004, the start date for the interim rent period is:

- the earliest termination date that could have been given in the landlord's section 25 notice; or
- the earliest commencement date for the new tenancy that could have been given in the tenant's section 26 request.

The start date of the interim rent period is known as 'the appropriate date' (section 24B of LTA 1954).

On 1 January 2006 L serves a section 25 notice on T, giving 1 January 2007 as the termination date. The earliest date L could have given as the termination date would have been six months from 1 January (i.e. 1 July 2006), so this is the appropriate date (i.e. the first day that interim rent becomes payable from).

The last day of the interim period is either:

- the day immediately before any renewal tenancy starts; or
- the day on which the current tenancy is lawfully terminated if no renewal tenancy is granted.

I am advising a landlord whose tenant is holding over under LTA 1954 as the fixed term tenancy has expired. The passing rent under the current tenancy is a long way below what I believe is the current market rent. Is there anything I can do to make the tenant liable to pay a higher rent before any renewal lease is granted?

Yes, you should immediately serve a section 25 notice. The interim rent period's 'appropriate date' will be six months after the section 25 notice is served. So long as you make an interim rent application within the time limits, your client will become entitled to a market rent from the 'appropriate date'.

Deciding how much the interim rent should be

If the landlord has not opposed and grants a new tenancy of the whole of the premises comprised in the current tenancy, under section 24C LTA 1954 the interim rent will, in principle, be the same as the initial rent payable under the new tenancy.

There are two exceptions to this rule:

- where either party proves that the interim rent substantially differs from the rent that would have been payable under the new tenancy if it had started on the appropriate date, i.e. at the start of the interim rent period. In this case, the interim rent is deemed to be the rent payable under the new tenancy but valued (using the valuation principles set out in section 34 of LTA 1954) as though its start date was the appropriate date. (This provision is most likely to apply where there has been a long passage of time between the appropriate date and the new tenancy's start date.)
- where either party proves that:

  (1) the terms of the new tenancy are substantially different from those of the current tenancy; and
  (2) the effect of 1) is that there will be a substantial difference between:

  - the rent due at the start of the new tenancy; and
  - the rent the court would set for a tenancy starting on the same day as the new tenancy but whose terms are the same as those in the current tenancy.

  If this exception applies, then the rent is deemed to be the reasonable rent the tenant should pay for the duration of the current tenancy (section 24C(6) of LTA 1954). This 'reasonable rent' is the rent that would be fixed having regard to:

  - the passing rent (as the court must have regard to the passing rent, this should prevent the change between the value of the passing rent and the interim rent being too extreme);
  - the rent of any subtenancy of part of the property demised under the current tenancy (this ensures that any sub-tenancies granted after the section 25 notice or section 26 request was served are taken into account);
  - the valuation provisions in section 34(1) and (2) of LTA 1954; and
  - an assumption that the interim rent valuation is based on a tenancy of equal length to that of the new tenancy.

Unhelpfully, it is not clear what the valuation date should be nor whether the terms of the tenancy being valued are the same as the current or the new tenancy. There is consensus amongst commentators that the valuation date must be the 'appropriate date'. However, some commentators believe that the terms the tenancy should be valued on are those of the current tenancy[91] whilst others believe they should be those of the new tenancy[92].

The authors believe that the first view is correct, so that the valuation is based on the terms of the current tenancy (i.e. as if the tenant were holding over on the existing tenancy), save that the duration should be that of the new tenancy. If it were otherwise, then the interim rent would be entirely based on a tenancy on whose terms neither party had (during the interim rent period) been able to rely.

For example, assume the terms of the current tenancy absolutely prevented any alienation but the new tenancy allowed unrestricted alienation. If the terms of the new tenancy were to be used as the basis of the valuation, the tenant would have to pay an increased interim rent. This would be so even though the tenant was not actually entitled to alienate at all during the interim rent period. Moreover, if the valuation were to be based on the terms of the new tenancy, then the interim rent would be the same as the initial rent payable under that tenancy, which would mean there is no need to make an exception out of circumstances where the terms of the current and new tenancies are substantially different.

Interim rent where the order for a new tenancy has been revoked or not acted on

If an interim rent has been awarded under section 24C but either:

- the tenant decides not to enter into the new tenancy (i.e. the tenant asks the court to revoke the order for the new tenancy under section 36(2) of LTA 1954); or
- the parties agree not to enter into the new tenancy granted by the court,

then either party can apply under section 24D(3) for the interim rent to be re-determined using the valuation principles in section 24D(1) and (2). This ensures that the tenant need not pay an interim rent based on the rent in the new tenancy if the tenant is not actually going to be taking the new tenancy.

Valuing all other cases

All cases not falling within section 24C LTA 1954 are valued under section 24D. These would include, for example, cases where:

- the landlord was opposed to a renewal; or
- at the date of service of the section 25 notice or section 26 request the tenant did not occupy the whole of the property demised under the current tenancy.

Under section 24D LTA 1954 the interim rent is that which it is reasonable for the tenant to pay for the duration of the current tenancy (section 24D(1)).

This 'reasonable rent' is the rent that would be fixed having regard to:

- the passing rent;
- the rent of any subtenancy of part of the property demised under the current tenancy
- the valuation provisions in section 34(1) and (2) of LTA 1954; and
- an assumption that the interim rent valuation is based on a tenancy from year to year.

As with section 24C, it is not clear what terms the tenancy is to be valued on (i.e. those of the current or the new tenancy). The authors (and commentators[93]) agree that the terms to be applied should be those of the current tenancy.

I am advising a landlord where the tenancy is being continued by LTA 1954. The parties have agreed the rent for the new tenancy. The new tenancy will also be on the same terms as (and for the whole of the property that was demised under) the current tenancy. However, we cannot agree what the interim rent should be and the deal is being held up. Can I apply to court for an interim rent to be valued using the principles in section 24C LTA 1954, so that the rent we have agreed for the new tenancy will also be the interim rent?

No. It is important to remember that section 24C only applies if a new tenancy has actually been granted. Assuming a section 25 notice or section 26 request has already been served, you can apply to the court now to set the interim rent level. However, the court will set the interim rent at the level it is reasonable for the tenant to pay under section 24D LTA 1954.

How to make the interim rent application

Bearing in mind that surveyors are generally not allowed to make court applications on behalf of their clients, this will depend on whether a claim for an order for the grant of a new tenancy or termination order has already been commenced. If so, then a claim for interim rent can be made in those proceedings (under paragraph 3.17 of CPR Practice Direction 56):

- by including it in the claim form;
- in the acknowledgement of service or the defence; or
- by an application within the proceedings under CPR Part 23. An application under CPR Part 23 must be made if the applicant wants the court (under section 24D(3) of LTA 1954) to re-determine an interim rent previously set.

If proceedings have not yet been commenced, then a separate interim rent application can be made under CPR Part 8 (paragraph

3.19 of CPR Practice Direction 56). The claim form seeking the determination of an interim rent must include details of:

- the property to which the claim relates;
- the particulars of the current tenancy (including dates, parties, the tenancy's original duration and the passing rent);
- the section 25 notice or section 26 request;
- if the current tenancy has terminated, how and when it terminated; and
- if the current tenancy has terminated and the landlord has granted a new tenancy:
  - particulars of the new tenancy (including start date, duration, parties and rent); and
  - if the claimant believes that section 24C(3) of LTA 1954 applies, details in support of that belief.

6.6 Starting and responding to an unopposed claim

There are certain time limits for litigation specified by LTA 1954 or by the CPR. However, in each case the timetable for a claim, once it is issued and served, is very much subject to the workload of the court dealing with the claim. Where a court has a specialist list, such as the Chancery List in Central London County Court, thought needs to be given to issuing or making an application to transfer a claim to that list, since these are usually able to give shorter waiting times for hearings.

As a rule of thumb, parties can expect their unopposed claims to be dealt with at a final hearing between 12 and 15 months from the issue of the claim form.

Determining if an unopposed claim is the correct course

Care should be taken to ensure that a landlord only applies for the grant of a new tenancy in circumstances where the landlord is committed to that course of action. A landlord may not withdraw such an application unless the tenant consents to its withdrawal (section 29(6) of LTA 1954). If a tenant consents to that withdrawal, it is not then possible for the tenant to make a claim for a new tenancy, so such consent is unlikely to be forthcoming unless the tenant has agreed to vacate the premises.

A landlord's application will, however, be dismissed if the tenant does not want a new tenancy of the premises and informs the court. If the tenant merely informs the landlord, but not the court of that decision, the landlord should apply (on form N244) for an order that the tenant should, within seven days of the date of the order, inform the court and the landlord as to whether it wishes the court to grant a new tenancy.

Sample timeline	
1 March 2006	Claim form issued
10 March 2006	Claim form served
24 March 2006	Acknowledgement of service filed
15 June 2006	Case management conference
29 June 2006	Claimant to send out draft lease to defendant for comments
13 July 2006	Defendant to provide any comments on the draft lease to the claimant
27 July 2006	Claimant to reply to defendant's comments on the draft lease
24 August 2006	Disclosure of documents (if any)
28 September 2006	Exchange of witness statements (if any)
5 November 2006	Exchange of expert reports
13 December 2006	Without prejudice meeting of experts to narrow the issues between them
21 January 2007	Experts to file a joint statement with the court, setting out those issues on which they agree and disagree (with reasons for their disagreement)
28 February 2007	Parties to file listing questionnaires
13 April 2007	Trial

Can a surveyor conduct the claim or represent a client at court?

A party can act by himself or through lawyers, so in principle, a surveyor is not entitled to conduct litigation on behalf of a client or to represent the client at any court hearing (according to Part III of the *Access to Justice Act* 1999, and Part II of the *Courts and Legal Services Act* 1990 (as amended)).

Exceptionally, where a surveyor is an employee of the landlord/tenant company (rather than agent), the surveyor may be entitled to sign documents on its behalf if, and only if, the surveyor holds a 'senior position' within the company (under paragraph 3 of CPR Practice Direction 22 this includes the roles of director, treasurer, secretary, chief executive, manager or other officer of it). The surveyor may also be permitted by the court to represent the company at any hearing, but this is discretionary under CPR 39.6.

If there is any doubt as to whether a party has served a valid section 25 notice or section 26 request, the other can still apply to the court for a new tenancy but should request:

- a declaration that the notice purporting to terminate the tenancy is null and void; and
- (subject to the validity of the purported notice or request) the grant of a new tenancy.

Where to start the claim

CPR 56.2(1) states that the claim must be started in the County Court for the district in which the land is situated. However, if a claim is started in the wrong County Court it is not a nullity. The claim can continue in that court, be transferred to the correct one, or it can be struck out (which would cause problems if the statutory period had then expired, although a strike-out in these circumstances is unlikely).

Exceptionally, a claim can be brought in the High Court (in which case it should be issued in the Chancery Division). A claimant is required to certify why a claim is suitable to be tried there – the sort of case in which this might be appropriate is where the claim raises an important point of law, which it would be appropriate to have tried by a High Court Judge and (possibly) reported in law reports or journals.

How to start a claim

Unopposed claims are made using the CPR Part 8 procedure (56.3(2)), but CPR 8.5 (requiring the claimant to file and serve its evidence in support with the claim form) and 8.6 (the prohibition on relying on evidence not filed and served with the claim form) do not apply.

The Part 8 claim form (and indeed the other forms which are referred to in this chapter) can be found on the Court Service website[94].

A claim is begun by issuing and serving a claim form, which (under paragraph 3.4 of CPR Practice Direction 56) must contain the following details:

- The property to which the claim relates.
- The particulars of the current tenancy (including date, parties and duration), the current rent (if not the original rent) and the date and method of termination.
- Every notice or request given or made under sections 25 or 26 of LTA 1954; and
- The expiry date of:

  - the statutory period under section 29A(2) of LTA 1954; or
  - any extended period agreed under section 29B(1) or 29B(2) of LTA 1954.

The claim form must be verified by a Statement of Truth (CPR Part 22) and must **also** contain the following further information, depending on whether the application for a new tenancy is made by the landlord or the tenant:

Claim started by tenant CPR Practice Direction 56 paragraph 3.5 *(while this paragraph prescribes the content for claim forms where the tenant applies for a new tenancy in both unopposed and opposed claims, the details given here relate only to the content required in unopposed claims. See chapter 8 for more details on opposed claims.)*	The nature of the business carried on at the property.
	Whether the tenant relies on section 23(1A), 41 or 42 of LTA 1954 and, if so, the basis on which the tenant does so.
	Whether any (and if so what part) of the property comprised in the tenancy is occupied neither by the tenant nor by a person employed by the tenant for the purpose of its business.
	The tenant's proposed terms for the new tenancy.
	The name and address of anyone known to the tenant who has an interest in the reversion in the property on the termination of the current tenancy and who is likely to be affected by the grant of a new tenancy *or* if the tenant does not know of any such person, anyone who has a freehold interest in the property.
Claim started by landlord CPR Practice Direction 56 paragraph 3.7	Whether the tenant's tenancy is one to which section 32(2) of LTA 1954 applies and (if so) whether the landlord wants the new tenancy to comprise the whole of the premises let or just that part currently occupied by the tenant.
	The landlord's proposed terms of the new tenancy.
	The name and address of anyone known to the landlord who has an interest in the reversion in the property on the termination of the current tenancy and who is likely to be affected by the grant of a new tenancy *or* if the landlord does not know of any such person, anyone who has a freehold interest in the property.

Care should be taken regarding the terms that are proposed. Although it is possible to amend the proposals at a later stage (by obtaining the defendant's written consent or permission from the court), there is a danger that the claim form contains a contractual offer that, if accepted before the claimant notifies the defendant that it need amending, will be binding. This danger may be short-lived, if the defendant proposes other terms (because this would, in effect, be a counter-offer), but is nevertheless a matter to consider.

It is not fatal if one or more of the matters that should be stated in the claim form are omitted, since this does not render the claim form a nullity. In these circumstances, the defendant is entitled to ask for the missing information and, if it is not forthcoming, to seek an order that the claim be struck out. The court is entitled to make that order of its own volition, even if the defendant has not asked it to, but is unlikely to do so without giving the claimant an opportunity to correct the mistake.

Unless a claimant requests otherwise, the court will serve the claim form. The court will require one copy of the claim form itself, one for the claimant, and enough additional copies to serve each of the defendants and any other person that the claimant has asked the court to serve. A fee must be paid and cheques should be made payable to Her Majesty's Court Service (HMCS) (information about fees is available from the HMCS website[95]). Once the paperwork has been processed, the court should send out a notice to the claimant stating when the form was sent to the defendant and indicating how long there is to respond.

The risk that the court does not serve the claim form in time or at all is on the claimant. In the circumstances, the claimant may ask to serve the claim form, but bear in mind once a claim form has been issued, it must be served within two clear months after the date of issue (CPR 56.3(3)(b)).

Exceptionally, the court can extend this period but only if the court or the claimant has been unable to serve the claim form and the claimant applies promptly to the court for an extension (CPR 7.6[96]). An inability to serve the claim form will include circumstances where the court has failed to send the document to the defendant due to an administrative error, but if there is no good reason for the failure of service and/or the claimant does not apply promptly, the court cannot extend time and cannot just dispense with service of the claim form. Time limits should always be diarised.

A claim form can be served in a number of different ways. If the court is going to serve the claim form, it will invariably do so by first class post. If the claimant wishes to serve instead, there are a number of different ways to do so, such as:

- by leaving it at the defendant's address for service;
- if the defendant is legally represented and solicitors have indicated that they are willing to accept such service, by fax, email or document exchange; or

- in accordance with any provision of the tenancy agreement relating to service of a claim under LTA 1954.

The claim form must be served on the defendant, together with any other person who is identified as having an interest in the proceedings. If a claimant serves the claim form, then they must complete and file a certificate of service (Form N215) at court.

A claim form is served once the defendant receives it. However, if service has been effected under rules in CPR Part 6, service is deemed to have taken place as follows:

Method of service	Deemed day of service
First class post Document exchange	The second day after it was posted. The second day after it was left at the document exchange.
Delivering the document to or leaving it at a permitted address	The day after it was delivered to or left at the permitted address.
Fax	If it is transmitted on a business day before 4p.m., on that day; or
	In any other case, on the business day after the day on which it is transmitted.
Other electronic method	The second day after the day on which it is transmitted.

If a defendant believes that a claimant has issued a claim form but not served it, the defendant can serve a notice on the claimant requiring service of the claim form or discontinuance of the claim within a stated period, which cannot be less than 14 days after service of the notice (CPR 7.7).

Noting the claim at HM Land Registry

Applications to the court pursuant to Section 24 of LTA 1954 are technically registerable as pending land actions against the reversion of the competent landlord for the time being. Where the landlord's title is registered, this can be done by unilateral notice.

The reason for noting the claim is that because LTA 1954 proceedings are 'pending land actions' (though they do not count as overriding interests), a purchaser of the reversion will therefore take free of the tenant if the proceedings are not protected by a unilateral notice. This argument is highly technical and the authors doubt that the court would find favour with it. Further, practitioners are split about whether registration of the proceedings is needed.

The authors would recommend that expert legal advice is taken on this point, particularly as there is currently no decided case law on this point.

If the tenant decides to register its claim the tenant should apply for a unilateral notice by lodging Form UN1 and a statutory declaration setting out details of the pending land action, including:

- particulars of the court (where the claim has been made);
- confirmation that the action is a pending land action;
- the full court reference; and
- the parties.

A copy of the claim form and notice of issue must also be lodged with the notice. The form is available on the Land Registry website[97].

Responding to a claim form: acknowledgement of service

Within 14 days of service of the claim form, the defendant must file an acknowledgement of service (Form N210) at court. The document must also be served on the claimant and any other party, but there is no time limit within which the defendant must do so or stated consequence for failing to do so.

The acknowledgement must contain the following particulars, depending on whether it is the landlord or the tenant who is filing the document:

Landlord filing the acknowledgement PD56 paragraph 3.10	If a new tenancy is granted, whether the landlord objects to any of the terms proposed by the tenant and (if so), to which and what different terms the landlord proposes.
	Whether the landlord is a tenant under a lease having less than 15 years unexpired at the date of termination of the claimant's current tenancy and (if so) the name and address of any person who to the landlord's knowledge has an interest in the reversion in the property expectant.
	The name and address of any person having an interest in the property who is likely to be affected by the grant of a new tenancy.
	Whether the tenant's tenancy is one to which section 32(2) of LTA 1954 applies and (if so) whether the landlord wants the new tenancy to comprise the whole of the premises let or just that part currently occupied by the tenant.

Tenant filing the acknowledgement PD56 paragraph 3.11	Whether any (and if so what part) of the property comprised in the tenancy is occupied neither by the tenant nor by a person employed by the tenant for the purpose of its business.
	The nature of the business carried on at the property.
	Whether the tenant relies on section 23(1A), 41 or 42 of LTA 1954 and, if so, the basis for this.
	The name and address of anyone known to the tenant who has an interest in the reversion in the property on the termination of the current tenancy and who is likely to be affected by the grant of a new tenancy OR if the tenant does not know of any such person, anyone who has a freehold interest in the property.
	If a new tenancy is granted, whether the tenant objects to any of the terms proposed by the landlord and (if so), which terms and what different terms the tenant proposes.

The acknowledgment of service must be verified by a statement of truth.

If the defendant wishes to propose different terms to those put forward by the claimant, then the defendant must state these in the acknowledgement of service. Although the acknowledgement is not a 'statement of case', it can still be amended[98]. As with a claim form, however, there is a danger that the terms proposed by the defendant could be construed as a counter-offer capable of acceptance by the claimant until withdrawn or amended.

If the defendant does not object to any of the terms proposed by the claimant, then the court should proceed to make an order granting a new tenancy in those terms. If some of the terms are agreed, but not others, then the court will proceed to determine only those in issue.

If the defendant fails to file an acknowledgement of service and the period for doing so has expired, the defendant may attend the hearing of the claim but cannot take part in it unless the court gives permission (CPR 8.4). If the acknowledgement of service is late, the claimant cannot apply for default judgment (CPR 12.2(b)) and there will still need to be a hearing, but the defendant can apply for an extension of time. On such an application, the court will consider a number of different factors (CPR 3.9).

6.7 Steps in the litigation process

Directions

On receipt of the acknowledgement of service, the court will set a timetable for the future conduct of the case (CPR 56.3(3)(c)) – quite how the court goes about this varies. In some cases, the District Judge will give directions without a hearing. In others, the court will send out a notice of hearing requiring the parties to attend a case management conference (CMC).

In both cases, the parties should discuss directions at the earliest opportunity. Suggested directions are available at appendix 12.

It is important not to forget an order as to costs. The usual order is 'costs in case', meaning that whichever party wins at the end shall recover its costs associated with corresponding about directions and attendance at any CMC. If the court is not asked to make this order, and makes no order, then these costs may not be recoverable at the end of proceedings.

If agreement is reached between the parties before the court issues its own directions or holds a CMC, they should:

- draft and sign a consent order, and send this to the court with a covering letter inviting the District Judge to approve an order in those terms (and asking for any CMC to be vacated or, if it is imminent, for their attendance to be excused); and
- if the court has listed the claim for a CMC, notify the court's listing office that directions have been agreed and a consent order submitted for the court's approval.

If the court does hold a CMC, prior to the hearing it will expect the parties to have:

- discussed and agreed a timetable if possible;
- considered whether expert evidence is necessary and, if so, whether a joint expert could be appointed rather than separate experts. It might be appropriate to appoint a joint expert, for example, if the difference between the rent proposed by the tenant and the landlord was relatively small;
- brought any other outstanding matters to the court's attention (such as a change of ownership since the claim was started).

The hearings are usually short (30 minutes or so) and conducted by a District Judge. A person who is familiar with the case and who has sufficient authority to agree the timetable should attend, unless the parties have already agreed directions and the court has excused their attendance. These hearings may be conducted by telephone if the court agrees in advance.

The parties have some flexibility and can vary the directions by mutual consent, but they cannot agree to alter the dates set by the court for the following (or put those dates in jeopardy) without the court's permission:

- case management conference;
- return of listing questionnaires;
- pre-trial review; and
- trial or the trial window.

Draft lease

The standard directions in appendix 12 refer to the issue of a draft lease and each side is to comment on the proposed terms before any other steps are taken in the litigation. This can be a very useful exercise in narrowing down the actual dispute between the parties.

Disclosure

A party discloses a document by stating (in a list provided to the other side) that it exists or used to exist. The party need only disclose documents it has or had within its control which are relevant to the claim.

Provided the documents are not privileged from production, the other party can ask for copies (on its undertaking to pay the reasonable copying costs) or inspect the documents in situ. The obligation is on the client, which is party to the litigation, not on the agent and continues for as long as the claim is ongoing. Any new relevant documents that are created or come into the client's possession after providing the original list must also be disclosed.

Disclosure is not always necessary in unopposed claims. Where, for example, the only issue is as to the rent payable under the new tenancy, the matter will be dealt with by expert reports where the expert himself provides evidence of comparables, and the client may not himself have any documents relevant to that issue. The position might be different where, for example, the dispute is focusing on changes to the terms of the new tenancy – the party seeking the change will need to show why it is necessary, and it is very likely that the party will have documents that it wishes to rely on.

A surveyor is likely to become involved in the disclosure process in one or two ways:

- **when involved in the search for documents.** A client is not obliged to search for every last document, but only to make a 'reasonable and proportionate' search. It may be reasonable to decide not to search for documents created before a particular date, or to limit the search to particular places or to documents falling into particular categories; or

- **when asked for copies of documents from their files.** A document is in a client's control (even if it is not in their possession) if the client has a right to:

  - possession of it; or
  - to inspect or take copies of it.

A client may not have control of all of the documents on a surveyor's file (such as working papers or drafts of documents), and such documents need not be disclosed. The client's rights to documents will depend on the terms of any agreement between client and surveyor regarding documents created by the latter in the course of the relationship with the client.

Witness statements

Unless a party is seeking to change a term of the current tenancy in the new tenancy it is unlikely that a party in an unopposed claim will need to serve a written statement of the factual (as opposed to expert) evidence that it intends to adduce at trial.

The purpose of a witness statement is to give the other side advance notice of the evidence that the maker of the statement will be giving. It should be in the witness's own words, and should not include anything that the maker is unable to say or uncomfortable about saying.

Where the content of a statement is uncontroversial, it can be agreed and the party can tender it without the need for the witness to attend court to be cross-examined on what the statement said.

Expert evidence

This is the stage in the litigation process where the surveyor will inevitably be involved (as such this topic merits its own chapter, see chapter 9). In the context of an unopposed claim, certain issues need to be addressed before the court makes directions or holds the CMC.

Expert evidence can only be used with the court's permission, thus it makes little sense to instruct an individual as an expert witness until that permission has been given. The court will nevertheless expect the parties to have identified at an early stage:

- the issues requiring expert evidence;
- the field from which that expert evidence should be drawn; and
- whether a single joint expert would be appropriate, rather than each side appointing their own expert.

The court will usually direct that expert reports be exchanged, that the experts meet on a without prejudice basis to attempt to narrow the issues between them, and that the experts prepare a joint statement indicating those issues on which they agree and disagree (with brief reasons for any disagreement).

Preparation for and attendance at trial

Listing questionnaires allow the parties to inform the court of the readiness of the case to proceed to trial. If there is any reason why an expert or witness cannot attend court on any given day during the trial, they should inform the solicitors acting for the party calling them as soon as possible, as this is one of the matters which needs to be indicated in the questionnaire.

In more complicated cases, the court may hold a pre-trial review and give further directions necessary to bring the case to trial. Experts and witnesses do not attend that hearing.

Preparing to give evidence

It is important for any witness (whether a witness of fact or expert witness) to always re-read his or her report or statement thoroughly before trial. If acting as an expert, it is also advisable to re-read CPR Part 35, Practice Direction 35, any relevant section from the court guide applicable to the court in which trial will take place, and the protocol.

A witness should always check that he knows where and when he should attend to give evidence (a visit to the court is recommended and can usually be arranged if required before he gives evidence to familiarise himself with the layout). The normal court sitting hours are 10am to 4pm.

Expert evidence is usually called after both sides have called their witnesses of fact. Where a trial is estimated to last for a number of days (or even weeks), experts can expect to be called towards the end of that period.

For more information on the procedure for giving oral evidence at trial see chapter 9.

Discontinuance

A tenant can discontinue a claim for an order for the grant of a new tenancy at any time, by serving a notice (N729). If there is more than one claimant (because, for example, there are joint tenants), unless the court orders otherwise, each must consent in writing to the claim being discontinued.

If the landlord makes a claim for an order for the grant of a new tenancy, a tenant can inform the court at any time that they do not want one. There is no prescribed form for this: a letter will suffice. On receipt of such a letter, the court must dismiss the landlord's claim (section 29(5) of LTA 1954).

A landlord cannot withdraw a claim for a new tenancy unless the tenant consents. The reason for this, presumably, is that the landlord might have made a claim (thereby preventing the tenant from doing so), which the landlord might progress until the end of the statutory period, only then to discontinue it at a time when the tenant would be too late to start a new claim.

If the landlord wishes to end a claim, but the tenant has not consented (for whatever reason), the landlord should ask the court to dismiss the claim (by making an application for an order that the claim be dismissed under CPR Part 23). The court is unlikely to do so if the tenant actively objects but may do so, for example, where the tenant has not responded to a request for consent from the landlord, has unreasonably refused to give consent or cannot be traced.

The claim ends on the date on which the notice of discontinuance is given to the defendant or (if applicable) the court makes an order dismissing or discontinuing the claim. Unless the court orders otherwise, the claimant is liable to pay the defendant's costs of the proceedings up to that date (CPR 38.6). It is possible for the defendant to agree not to enforce its entitlement to costs, or to agree to a consent order providing for the claim to be discontinued with no order as to costs. A claimant who wants to discontinue but not pay costs should seek this from the defendant before serving any notice.

The decreasing use of orders for the stay of proceedings

Prior to 1 June 2004, a landlord responding to a request for a new tenancy made by a tenant had a right to request a stay of three months before being required to file an acknowledgement of service. This right is now removed.

The court retains its ability to grant a stay in an appropriate case, but it is thought that it will be much less inclined than it was prior to 1 June 2004 to exercise that power in relation to unopposed claims.

Effective case management requires the court to deal with cases expeditiously and since the parties can delay court proceedings by agreeing to extend the statutory period, once those proceedings have begun, it is likely that they will be pushed to trial in the same way as any other type of claim.

6.8 Offers to settle and costs

Offers to settle

No matter how strongly a party may feel about the merits of its case, there is the risk inherent in every claim that the result may not be as expected. The only way to avoid such risk is to compromise the claim. Moreover, litigation can be (and often is) an expensive and lengthy process and commercially minded clients will often seek to 'do a deal' rather than run through that process to trial. The subject matter of the claim will form the basis for any 'deal', but costs of the litigation should not be forgotten.

Offers to settle are usually made:

- 'without prejudice save as to costs', more normally called *Calderbank offers*; or
- in accordance with the provisions of CPR Part 36, called *Part 36 offers*.

Costs of the proceedings

The usual rule in litigation is that the losing party should pay the costs of the winner ('costs follow the event'), although as the matter is discretionary there is never any entitlement to costs. Working out who has won or lost is often difficult in unopposed claims because the court may not determine that the terms of the new tenancy should be those proposed by one party or the other.

Often, the court will determine a middle-way or agree to some of the terms proposed by the landlord and to some of those proposed by the tenant. In these circumstances, the court can (amongst others) make orders:

- requiring one party to pay a proportion of another party's costs (usually to reflect the number of issues on which that party has succeeded, taking into account the time spent during the claim in dealing with those issues);
- requiring costs to be paid from a certain date (usually to reflect the fact that from the given date the claim could and should have been settled); and/or
- requiring costs incurred before proceedings began to be paid (usually to penalise a party for not following the Practice Direction on Pre-Action Protocols).

Even if the court orders one party to pay the costs of the other, it is unlikely that the amount recovered will be sufficient to cover all of the litigation expenses which that party will have incurred. In large cases, a typical recovery rate is between 60–70 per cent. A party which runs a claim to trial therefore risks not recovering a substantial part of expenses even if the party wins, and might be prepared to settle for less in order to avoid them.

Calderbank offers and 'without prejudice' discussions

If a party wishes to discuss settlement with another, it should do so on a 'without prejudice' basis (this was discussed in greater detail in chapter 5). Such discussions cannot be revealed to the court, unless made 'without prejudice save as to costs'. Offers made on this basis are often called Calderbank offers (after the case in which they were first used[99]). Once the court has determined the subject matter of the claim, such offers can be referred to when (and only when) the court is deciding who should pay the costs of the proceedings.

Offers to settle made in accordance with CPR Part 36 have certain costs consequences (explained in more detail below). Calderbank offers will not attract those consequences unless the court can be persuaded to treat them as if they were Part 36 offers (CPR 36.1(2)). The chances of this will be enhanced if the party making the Calderbank offer follows the requirements of Part 36 as closely as possible.

One of the consequences of making a Part 36 Offer is that if the receiving party accepts, they will be entitled to costs up to the date of acceptance. Where the party wishing to offer to settle does not wish to be liable for those costs or is only prepared to pay for part of them, it should make a Calderbank offer instead.

A party making an offer to settle should ensure that[100]:

- it is made in writing: this avoids the suggestion that something has been said orally which was not;
- the document should be headed 'without prejudice' (or 'without prejudice save as to costs');
- it is clear whether the offer relates to the whole claim or only part of it (relating only to the issue of term, for example, but not to rent); and
- costs are dealt with (if only to say that costs are not included within the offer).

Part 36 offers

An offer made under CPR Part 36 encourages parties to settle by imposing costs consequences on any party who fails to accept a reasonable offer.

Whether or not an offer is one which ought to have been accepted will be determined at trial, by reference to the actual outcome – if the party choosing not to accept the offer has not done any better than that which was offered to him, the following costs consequences apply:

- A **claimant** who only does as well or worse at trial than the defendant had offered will be required to pay the defendant's costs of the proceedings from the latest date on which the offer could have been accepted, unless the court considers that this would be 'unjust'.
- If a **defendant** refuses an offer that the claimant then beats (in the sense that actual outcome is more advantageous to than the offer would have been), the court will order the defendant to pay indemnity costs and interest on those costs at a rate not exceeding ten per cent above base rate (which is not the same as paying absolutely all of the costs incurred), unless such an order would be 'unjust'.

In all cases, a Part 36 offer must be in writing and state that it is a Part 36 offer. It must state whether it relates to the whole or only part of the claim. The offer can just be made in respect of one issue (such as the rent, for example, but not the term), but in such cases, this should be made clear. Finally, the party making it or the legal representative must sign the offer. If the party is a company, a person holding a senior position with the company should sign it (as defined by CPR 36 paragraph 5.6).

If the offer is made more than 21 days before the start of the trial, it must also be expressed to remain open for acceptance for 21 days from the date it is made and provide that after 21 days the party receiving it may only accept it if either the parties agree the liability for costs or the court gives permission. A Part 36 offer made **less than 21 days** before the start of trial must state that the offeree may only accept it if either the parties agree the liability for costs or the court gives permission (CPR 36.5(7)).

A Part 36 offer is deemed made when the party to whom it is made receives it[101]. Once an offer is made, the party receiving it may:

- accept it, provided it has not already been withdrawn by the party making it[102] and acceptance is given within 21 days of the offer being made or the court gives its permission. An offer can be accepted after the 21 days if, for example, there has been a change of circumstances justifying an application for permission[103];
- reject it; or
- request clarification (which must be within seven days of receipt).

If clarification is sought, it must be provided within seven days. If it is not, the receiving party can seek an order from the court compelling it to be provided. If no clarification is provided, the court can take into account the fact that the offer was unclear when deciding what costs order to make. It is an essential part of the scheme under Part 36 that parties should understand and have the information they need to assess whether or not to accept a Part 36 offer.

Acceptance takes place when the party making the offer receives the notice of acceptance (CPR 36.8). A Part 36 offer or payment can be 'improved' by a subsequent offer or payment complying with the requirements of CPR 36.5 (according to CPR 36.8(3)). Time for acceptance will then run from the date details are received by the receiving party. Any notice of acceptance of a Part 36 offer must also be in writing, state the claim number and the title of the proceedings, be filed with the court (as well as sent to the party making the offer), identify the offer to which it relates and be signed by the party to whom the offer was made or the legal representative.

6.9 The court's order for the grant of a new tenancy

If the court grants a new tenancy the current tenancy comes to an end on the date provided for by LTA 1954. Until then, the tenant remains liable under the current tenancy, although if a claim has been made for an interim rent which has been set by the court, that interim rent will be payable until the current tenancy ends rather than the passing rent.

The effect of the court's order

The court does not actually grant a new tenancy. Section 36(1) of LTA 1954 provides that the court makes an order that the landlord shall execute and the tenant shall accept and execute a counterpart of a tenancy in the terms ordered by the court.

However, LTA 1954 is silent on what should happen in a number of important respects:

- *When the new tenancy should be executed.* LTA 1954 specifies no time by which the new tenancy should be executed. The new tenancy cannot take effect until the current tenancy ends, but nothing prevents the parties from executing a new tenancy (stated to commence immediately after the current tenancy ends) before then. Once the current tenancy ends, the new tenancy will take effect in equity even if no formal documents have by then been executed.
- *What should happen regarding any necessary consents.* A landlord does not need the consent of any mortgagee to the grant of a new tenancy (under section 36(4) of LTA 1954), but may require other consents (from a superior landlord, for example). Alternatively, the landlord can seek to join the superior landlord as a party to the proceedings, so that the latter is bound by any final order. The superior landlord may ask the court, in

exercising its discretion under section 35 of LTA 1954, to impose a term in the new tenancy to the effect that the new tenancy should not take effect until such time as consent to it is given.

- *How either party can force the other to execute the new tenancy.* A couple of options appear to be open:

    - If the court's order has specified a date by which the new tenancy should be executed and that date has passed, the party seeking to execute the lease could apply for committal of the other by reason of its deliberate breach of the court's order. The ordinary penalties for contempt are prison, fine and/or sequestration of assets.

    - In all cases, under section 39 of the *Supreme Court Act 1981*, the party seeking to execute the new tenancy can apply to the appropriate officer of the High Court to execute the lease or counterpart in the name of the party refusing to do so.

Agreement not to execute a new tenancy

LTA 1954 requires such an agreement to be in writing. If the new tenancy has already arisen in equity, that interest will need to be surrendered. For this purpose, any agreement would – additionally – need to comply with the provisions of section 2 of the *Law of Property (Miscellaneous Provisions) Act* 1989.

Tenant's change of mind: application to revoke the order

Within 14 days of the court making an order for the grant of a new tenancy, the tenant can apply for that order to be revoked (section 36(2) of LTA 1954). The landlord has no such right. This allows a tenant who considers that the new terms determined by the court are too onerous to withdraw.

Although the court cannot refuse to revoke its order, it can determine how long the current tenancy should continue for so that the landlord has a reasonable opportunity to re-let or otherwise dispose of the property that would have been comprised in the new tenancy. In such case, the current tenancy may not end on a date three months and 14 days from the date of the order for the grant of a new tenancy, but on a later date. The court will need to hear evidence as to the period that the landlord reasonably requires, and cannot set a date arbitrarily.

I want to appeal against the court's order, because the terms it has set are too onerous, and I am only willing to take the new tenancy if my appeal succeeds. What should I do?

You should apply to have the order revoked within 14 days of the order for the grant of a new tenancy being made and file an

Continued

appellant's notice. You should ask the court to adjourn the application to revoke its order pending determination of your appeal. If the appeal is successful, you can ask the court to make no order on your application to revoke its previous order. If the appeal is unsuccessful, the court must make a revocation order and you will not be obliged to take the new tenancy.

7

Grounds of opposition to a new tenancy

The *Landlord and Tenant Act* 1954 (LTA 1954) provides a list of grounds of opposition to a new tenancy. Some of the grounds are 'mandatory' – meaning if the landlord establishes the ground then the court must refuse the new tenancy or grant a termination order – while the others are 'discretionary' – meaning even if the landlord establishes the ground the court still has a discretion as to whether to grant the new tenancy.

This chapter looks at the seven different statutory grounds that a landlord can rely on to oppose the grant of a new tenancy.

The grounds of opposition are listed in section 30(1) of LTA 1954. The letter of each ground relates to the relevant subparagraph in section 30(1):

- (a) Failure to repair (discretionary) (section 7.1)
- (b) Persistent delay in paying rent (discretionary) (section 7.2)
- (c) Some other material breach or reason (discretionary) (section 7.3)
- (d) Suitable alternative accommodation (mandatory) (section 7.4)
- (e) Current tenancy created by subletting of part (discretionary) (section 7.5)
- (f) Demolition and re-construction (mandatory) (section 7.6)
- (g) Landlord's own occupation (mandatory) (section 7.7)

Discretionary grounds of opposition

Of the seven grounds under section 30(1) of LTA 1954, four are discretionary. In other words, even if the landlord can establish that any of these four grounds are made out, the court still has a discretion whether or not to grant the tenant a new tenancy.

The four discretionary grounds are:

- ground (a): the tenant has failed to comply with its repairing obligations;
- ground (b): the tenant has been in persistent arrears of rent;
- ground (c): there are other reasons or other substantial tenancy breaches which show that the tenant ought not to be granted a new tenancy; and
- ground (e): the tenancy was created by a subletting of part, substantially greater rents could be obtained by letting the property as a whole and the landlord requires possession of the holding to let or dispose of the property as a whole.

If the court refuses a new tenancy on any of grounds (a), (b) or (c) then the tenant is not entitled to statutory compensation on quitting the holding. However, it is entitled to compensation if the new tenancy is refused solely on ground (e) (for more information see chapter 10).

Mandatory grounds of opposition

A landlord is entitled to a termination order, alternatively to an order dismissing a claim for the grant of a new tenancy, if the landlord establishes:

- ground (d): the tenant has been offered suitable alternative accommodation elsewhere; and/or
- ground (f): the landlord intends to demolish, reconstruct or carry out substantial construction on that part of the demised premises occupied by the tenant or a substantial part of it; and/or
- ground (g): the landlord intends to reoccupy the demised premises on the termination of the current tenancy.

It is always important for a landlord to have considered well in advance what his or her plans are for a property before any current tenancy comes to an end. However, planning is particularly important if relying on grounds (f) or (g) because this brings statutory compensation into play. Compensation is not payable if the landlord makes out ground (d).

7.1 Failure to repair – ground (a)

Section 30(1)(a) of LTA 1954 states a landlord can seek a termination order/oppose a claim for a new tenancy:

'Where under the current tenancy the tenant has any obligations as respects the repair and maintenance of the holding, that the tenant ought not to be granted a new tenancy in view of the state of repair of the holding, being a state resulting from the tenant's failure to comply with the said obligations.'

To prove ground (a) the landlord must therefore show that:

- the tenant has obligations to repair and maintain the holding;
- the holding is in a state of disrepair and/or lack of maintenance; and
- the poor condition of the holding is due to the tenant's failure to comply with obligations in the tenancy agreement.

If the landlord can prove all three points then the court must exercise its discretion on whether to grant a renewal tenancy.

Obligations to repair and maintain the holding

The landlord must show that the tenant has a repairing and/or maintenance obligation. This could be either an express obligation in the tenancy agreement itself or one that can be implied into the tenancy.

The LTA 1954 defines 'repairs' to include 'maintenance, decoration or restoration' under section 69(1). Therefore not only are the usual repairing obligations included but also any covenants to redecorate.

However, ground (a) only relates to repairing obligations affecting the holding. It therefore does not apply to premises that the tenant does not occupy for its business purposes. This is so even if they actually form part of the tenant's demise under the tenancy agreement (however, the landlord might be able to rely on ground (c)).

I act for a tenant whose tenancy has expired and who has been holding over for the last six years under section 24 LTA 1954. Under the tenancy agreement my client had to redecorate 'in every other year of the Term.' My client has not redecorated at all in the last six years. The landlord is now using this as a reason to rely on ground (a). Can he?

It depends. The obligation to redecorate is to do so in every other year of 'the Term', i.e. in every other year of the contractually fixed length of the tenancy. As the tenancy has expired, the 'Term' has probably also expired.

Continued

There might not be an ongoing obligation to redecorate during the continuation tenancy. However, 'the Term' could be specifically defined in the tenancy agreement. You need to check this. If 'the Term' is defined as 'the term created by this agreement and any statutory continuation of it' (or something similar) then your client should still be redecorating every other year and the landlord could then rely on ground (a).

A state of disrepair and/or lack of maintenance

The landlord will need to show that a serious state of disrepair existed at the premises. It is not strictly necessary that serious disrepair exists at the time the landlord first relies on ground (a) (i.e. when serving the section 25 notice or counter-notice to the tenant's section 26 request). However, in reality a court will not favourably view reliance on ground (a) if the only instance of serious disrepair was one that the tenant remedied years before the court hearing, or if only trivial problems still remain.

The landlord will need to produce evidence of the state of disrepair. This is best achieved by the landlord having instructed an expert surveyor to prepare and serve a costed schedule of dilapidations on the tenant.

As with all grounds of opposition, the court must decide whether at the date of the hearing the landlord has established ground (a).

The state of disrepair is the tenant's fault

This should be obvious: the holding is in a serious state of disrepair and the tenant has done little or nothing to remedy this. Assuming that there is an ongoing obligation to repair, the tenant will be in breach of this obligation.

I am representing a landlord whose tenant has a tenancy of mixed use premises: ground floor shop with a residential flat above. The flat has been in a terrible state for years. Can I advise my client to rely on ground (a) to oppose a renewal of the tenancy?

Maybe. It will depend on whether the flat forms part of the 'holding'. If your client's tenant has sublet the flat it is unlikely to form part of the holding (but see chapter 1 for more details). In these circumstances so long as the shop premises have been kept in good repair then ground (a) will not apply. However, if the flat is used as part of the business (e.g. it is let on a service occupancy to the tenant's employee shopkeeper) then it is likely to form part of the holding. The flat's state of repair can then be used as evidence to oppose a renewal claim under ground (a).

The court's discretion

Once the landlord has proved that ground (a) applies, the court must then exercise its discretion as to whether to grant a renewal tenancy. The court is entitled to look at all of the circumstances surrounding the tenant's repairing breaches. The court will also take into account the tenant's past and proposed future conduct.

The tenant's past and proposed future conduct is often an important factor in the court's exercise of its discretion. The tenant could show that it has been taking proper steps to remedy the breaches. Alternatively, the tenant could undertake to carry out the repairs by a specified time. However, neither of these steps provides a guarantee that the court will exercise its discretion in the tenant's favour. If the landlord can show that it would be unfair for a renewal tenancy to be granted bearing in mind the tenant's past conduct, the court will tend to exercise its discretion against the tenant.

Tactically, a landlord should ensure a dilapidations schedule is served on the tenant well in advance of the tenancy's expiry. The longer the tenant has to remedy the repairs, the more likely that its continuing failure to do so will weigh heavily against it when the court comes to exercise its discretion. Also, if the landlord can prove that the tenant cannot fund the required works this will assist the landlord's case.

From the tenant's perspective, the tenant's expert surveyor should carefully scrutinise the dilapidations schedule. Are all of the alleged items of disrepair actually breaches of the tenant's repairing obligations? Are they items that actually materially affect the value of the landlord's reversion? Alternatively, are they simply minor items that any reasonable tenant would tolerate?

In exercising its discretion, the court can impose conditions in any renewal tenancy to deal with the landlord's complaint. Examples could be: the repairs must be completed by a certain date and the insertion of a landlord's right to forfeit if the specified works are not undertaken.

7.2 Persistent arrears – ground (b)

Section 30(1)(b) of LTA 1954 states a landlord can seek a termination order/oppose a claim for a new tenancy on the ground:

> 'That the tenant ought not to be granted a new tenancy in view of his persistent delay in paying rent which has become due.'

To prove ground (b) the landlord must therefore show that:

- rent has become due; and
- the tenant has persistently delayed paying the rent.

If the landlord can prove both points then the court must exercise its discretion as to whether to grant a renewal tenancy.

Rent has become due

At first glance this seems relatively straightforward: the ground applies to rent that has become due. However, what about other monies that the tenant must pay under the agreement? Can ground (b) be used in relation to, say, service charges and insurance costs?

Whether other monies can be included within the meaning of 'rent' in ground (b) will depend on the tenancy agreement. If the tenancy agreement specifically reserves, say, the service charges as 'rent', then it is likely that this will be 'rent' for ground (b) purposes. Equally, if the tenancy agreement states that insurance costs, service charges etc. 'shall be deemed to be sums due by way of additional rent and shall be recoverable by the landlord as such' (or something similar), then they will probably be 'rent' for ground (b) purposes[104].

The ground concerns rent that has already become due. It does not matter whether the landlord has failed to chase the tenant for the arrears or otherwise seek recovery of them, although this might affect the court's exercise of its discretion.

Tenant's persistent delay

'Persistent delay' does not only mean that the tenant must be in arrears at the date of the court hearing. The landlord can still rely on ground (b) even if there are no arrears at the date of the hearing.

Examples of 'persistent delay' can include:

- a long history of ongoing rent arrears;
- the landlord having to continually chase the tenant for late payment (even if the payment was then made) ;
- a quarter's rent remaining unpaid for a number of years;
- a tenant taking advantage of an 'interest grace period' (i.e. an obligation to pay interest on rent if it remains unpaid for, say, 7 or 14 days) but paying just before the landlord's right to forfeit for non-payment accrues[105].

A good method of evidencing persistent delay is for the landlord to prepare a detailed schedule of the arrears history. This should include:

- rent due and payment dates;
- the number of days each payment has been late;
- and the dates that payment reminders were sent to the tenant.

The schedule should be supported by documentary evidence, including the detailed rent account, copies of the rent demands and chasers.

The court's discretion

As with ground (a), the landlord needs to show that it would be unfair for a renewal tenancy to be granted bearing in mind the tenant's past conduct. For example, if the landlord was financially dependent upon the tenant's rental stream, the persistently delayed payment would be particularly significant. Also, if the court felt the tenant had paid rent late to gain some financial advantage of its own this is likely to weigh heavily against the tenant.

However, if the landlord has historically accepted the rent a few days late without complaining then the court is more likely to find in the tenant's favour[106].

Where the landlord relies on ground (b) the tenant should make every effort to ensure that it pays its rent on time. It needs to convince the court that it will pay the rent on time if it were granted a renewal tenancy. In addition the tenant should consider:

- producing evidence of financial ability to pay the rent;
- offering a rent deposit or guarantor; and
- agreeing to stricter rent-related covenants, for example interest immediately accruing if the rent is not paid on the due date.

It is certainly the case that in recent years the courts have tended to exercise their discretion in the tenants' favour. However, it is important to note that the court will view each case on its own merits. Just because a rent deposit or guarantee is offered this does not mean that a tenant with a history of persistent payment delays will escape with a renewal tenancy.

7.3 Other reason or substantial breach – ground (c)

Section 30(1)(c) of LTA 1954 states that a landlord can seek a termination order/oppose a claim for a new tenancy on the ground:

'That the tenant ought not to be granted a new tenancy in view of other substantial breaches by him of his obligations under the current tenancy, or for any other reason connected with the tenant's use or management of the holding'

To prove ground (c) the landlord must therefore show that:

- the tenant substantially breached its other tenancy obligation(s); or
- there is some other reason concerning the tenant's use or manage- ment of the holding why a renewal tenancy should not be granted.

If the landlord can prove either of these points then the court must exercise its discretion as to whether to grant a renewal tenancy.

Substantial breach of other tenancy obligation

Ground (c) does not relate to breaches of repairing or rent payment obligations. The statutory wording makes clear that it relates to 'other substantial breaches'. Also, any breach the landlord complains of must be 'substantial', not minor or trivial.

Importantly, the substantial breach need not relate to the holding itself. So, ground (c) can apply to a substantial breach by the tenant of an obligation concerning part of the demised premises that are not occupied by the tenant for its business purposes.

I am representing a landlord whose tenant has a tenancy of mixed use premises: ground floor shop with a sublet residential flat above. The flat has been in a terrible state for years. Should I advise my client to rely on ground (a) or (c) to oppose a renewal of the tenancy?

Ground (c). If your client's tenant has sublet the flat it is unlikely to form part of the holding. In these circumstances so long as the shop premises have been kept in good repair then ground (a) will not apply. However, a 'substantial breach' under ground (c) does not have to apply to the holding. The flat's state of repair can then be used as evidence to oppose a renewal claim on ground (c).

The substantial breach does not have to be one that remains actionable by the landlord by forfeiture or other means (such as an injunction or an order for specific performance). This can be important in instances where a landlord has, through no fault of his or her own, lost the right to forfeit the tenancy.

The breach need not exist at the time of the hearing or the section 25 notice/counter-notice to the section 26 request. However, the court will consider matters as they stand at the date of the hearing[107]. Events that have taken place between the breach and up to the hearing will therefore be relevant. However, if the landlord has acquiesced in the breach for some time then it is more likely that the court will exercise its discretion in the tenant's favour.

Other reasons

This second limb of ground (c) allows the landlord to complain about issues that do not relate to obligations under the tenancy. In other words, the landlord can rely on ground (c) even if the tenant is not in breach of its tenancy obligations. 'Other reasons' relied on by landlords are often that the tenant is using the premises for a purpose that is illegal, immoral or contrary to public policy.

L informally grants a tenancy of premises to T. Due to the informality, there are no user restrictions or obligations on T to comply with planning law, and T uses the premises to run an unlicensed striptease bar even though the premises have no planning consent for that type of user.

L is not able to forfeit the lease or obtain an injunction against T for the use of the premises and L cannot rely on any provisions in the tenancy that prevent the use of the premises in this way. However, L can serve a section 25 notice opposing renewal of T's tenancy on ground (c). L can complain that T's use or management of the holding is contrary to law and public policy for the failure to obtain the proper licence and planning consent.

Unlike the 'substantial breaches' part of ground (c), the 'other reasons' must be connected in some way to the tenant's use or management of the holding.

L lets premises to T and then the day before the tenancy expires, T unlawfully sublets them to S who buys T's business and continues to run it from the premises. L only discovers the unlawful subletting after Ts tenancy has expired and so cannot forfeit T's tenancy and S's tenancy even though unlawful is protected by LTA 1954 (See chapter 1 for more information).

L is able to serve a section 25 notice on S opposing the tenancy's renewal on ground (c). L argues that S's unlawful occupation is a 'reason connected with her use or management of the holding' that justifies the court refusing to renew her tenancy.

Whilst the issues complained of do not need to take place actually on the holding, they must be somehow linked to it. For example in *Beard v Williams*[108], the tenant operated a greyhound breeding business from the holding. This required the tenant to reside either on or very close to the holding, so he lived in a van that was parked illegally near to the holding. The Court of Appeal held that the precarious nature of the tenant's living accommodation had a direct effect on his ability to use and manage the holding. If the tenant were forced to move this would quickly have a serious detrimental effect on the tenant's business. The tenant would then not be allowed by the authorities to run his business, which would then eventually fold with clear negative ramifications for the landlord.

The court's discretion

As with grounds (a) and (b), the landlord will need to show that the grant of a renewal tenancy would be unfair given the tenant's conduct. The landlord will need to show that the grant of a renewal tenancy would unfairly prejudice it, for example by harming the value of its reversionary interest in the premises.

Tactically, the tenant will need to be able to explain its conduct to the court. It will also need to convince the court that such conduct will not continue under any renewal tenancy. The court might accept an undertaking from the tenant that it will not repeat the conduct the landlord complained of. Alternatively, the court might impose conditions in the renewal tenancy that prevented the tenant from using the holding in a certain way.

7.4 Offer of alternative accommodation – ground (d)

Section 30(1)(d) of LTA 1954 provides that a landlord may oppose the grant of a new tenancy if:

- he has offered and is willing to provide or secure alternative accommodation to the tenant;
- the alternative accommodation is available on reasonable terms;
- the accommodation is suitable for the tenant's requirements; and
- the time at which the accommodation will be available will be suitable for the tenant's requirements.

Until a landlord has made an offer of alternative accommodation, it is not possible to make out this ground of opposition. However there is no clear authority on the latest time by which the landlord can make such an offer. The authors' view is that the landlord must have made an offer by the date on which his or her statement of case is filed (whether particulars of claim, when applying for a termination order, or defence if defending the tenant's claim for an order for the grant of a new tenancy).

Whilst the landlord must specify grounds of opposition in a section 25 notice or counter-notice where the tenant has served a section 26 request, in each case the notice refers to the ground of opposition on which the landlord 'will' rely. This leaves open the possibility that the landlord might yet rely on a ground at trial the basis for which has not yet (as at the date of the notice) been established.

This contrasts with the requirements, however, for the statement of case: if the landlord intends to rely on a ground of opposition, it is not only necessary to specify what that ground is but also (crucially) to give 'full details of those grounds of opposition' (this falls under paragraph 3.9 of CPR Practice Direction 56 where the landlord claims a termination order; or paragraph 3.12(2)(b) where the landlord defends the tenant's claim for the grant of a new tenancy). A landlord could not give the required details unless an offer had actually been made (since one of the elements of the ground is that the landlord has '*offered*' alternative accommodation).

Withdrawing or amending an offer

There is County Court authority which suggests that once an offer has been made, it 'must be kept open from the time made and throughout and must not be withdrawn'[109]. The authors doubt this is correct (as do others[110]). If it were, then the final part of the requirement that the landlord 'has offered *and is willing*' to provide or secure alternative accommodation would be unnecessary. Viscount Simonds drew this distinction in *Betty's Cafes Ltd v Phillips Furnishing Stores Ltd*[111], saying:

> 'Here the perfect and the present tense are used. Leave out the perfect and look only at the present tense: 'the landlord is willing'. It would be a hardship and worse on the tenant, if the relevant date were any other than that of the hearing; it is to his advantage that the opportunity of accepting an offer of alternative accommodation should be open to the last moment ... nor would it be reasonable to reduce the time within which the landlord should have the opportunity of finding and offering alternative accommodation. If the tenant complains that he has had too little time to consider its suitability, his grievance can be met by an appropriate adjournment ...'

If this is correct, then the landlord can amend an offer or substitute an earlier offer with a new one. This interpretation would assist in circumstances where the landlord has offered certain alternative premises to the tenant, but for reasons out of control, they cease to be available. The landlord can then find a further alternative property. What the landlord cannot do, however, is make an offer then withdraw it and continue to rely on the ground of opposition. In such case, the landlord would not be 'willing' to provide alternative accommodation, as is necessary at the time of trial.

It is not necessary for the alternative accommodation to be available at the time of trial, because in determining the suitability of alternative premises the court is directed to consider whether 'the time at which it *will* be available' is suitable for the tenant's requirements. Once a claim for a termination order or order for the grant of a new tenancy is finally disposed of, the current tenancy will continue in accordance with section 64 of LTA 1954.

The probable intention behind this provision is that the court should consider whether the premises proposed will be suitable for the tenant to move into at the end of its current tenancy. If so, no new tenancy of the present premises should be granted. Nothing prevents the court from assessing the suitability of the proposed premises if they are available as at the date of trial, but the ground also appears to catch circumstances where the landlord offers alternative accommodation which, although not available for the tenant to move into as at the date of trial, will be available in the near future.

Deciding if the terms are reasonable or the alternative accommodation suitable

In order to determine whether the alternative accommodation is offered on reasonable terms, the court will look at the terms of the current tenancy and 'all other relevant circumstances'. The suitability of the alternative premises will depend on:

- what the tenant's requirements are (including the requirement to preserve goodwill, i.e. a local customer base);
- the nature and class of the tenant's business; and
- the situation and extent of the facilities afforded by that part of the premises currently occupied by the tenant.

The court will undertake an objective comparison of the terms of the current tenancy and those of any tenancy of the proposed alternative premises, and consider whether – overall – such terms are reasonable. It will not necessarily undertake a 'like by like' comparison, but where an isolated clause of the tenancy of the proposed alternative premises is markedly different from that of the current tenancy or where that tenancy would impose new obligations on the tenant, this will undoubtedly affect the court's conclusion as to whether such terms are reasonable.

The court is directed to consider not only the terms of the current tenancy but also 'all relevant circumstances'. If the alternative premises were being offered at a high rent but with an initial rent-free period, for example, this would be something that the court would be entitled to take into account.

Similarly, the assessment of suitability is objective. A tenant's subjective view that alternative premises are unsuitable may be ignored. It is important to remember that the tenant need not be offered premises which are exactly the same as those which are currently occupied, and whilst it is possible to be offered something better, the tenant cannot complain if offered something which is no better, even if the nature and class of the business would otherwise require it.

After the hearing if the landlord establishes the ground

The offer made by the landlord should be one that the tenant is able to accept. Since the landlord has to remain willing to offer the alternative accommodation at trial, it must follow that the tenant can accept the offer in the event that the court decides that the landlord has established the ground of opposition. There is nothing to prevent the landlord, however, from withdrawing the offer once the court has determined the claim.

7.5 Current tenancy created by subletting of part – ground (e)

Section 30(1)(e) of LTA 1954 states that a landlord can seek a termination order/oppose a claim for a new tenancy:

> 'Where the current tenancy was created by the subletting of part only of the property comprised in a superior tenancy and the landlord is the owner of an interest in reversion expectant on the determination of that superior tenancy, that the aggregate of the rents reasonably obtainable on separate lettings of the holding and the remainder of that property would be substantially less than the rent reasonably obtainable on a letting of that property as a whole, that on the termination of the current tenancy the landlord requires possession of the holding for the purpose of letting or otherwise disposing of the said property as a whole, and that in view thereof the tenant ought not to be granted a new tenancy ...'

To prove ground (e) the landlord must satisfy each of these four conditions:

- the current tenancy is a subletting of part of premises comprised in a superior tenancy;
- the landlord is the landlord of that superior tenancy;
- the total rents achievable on separate lettings of the holding and the rest of the property are substantially less than could be achieved on a letting of the property as a whole; and
- the landlord requires possession to let or dispose of the property as a whole.

If the landlord can satisfy all four conditions then the court must exercise its discretion as to whether to grant a renewal tenancy.

Subletting of part

The current tenancy must be a subletting of part that has been carved out of a superior tenancy.

L holds a 99 year tenancy of a three storey office building and grants a five year tenancy of the entire building to T who then grants a subtenancy of the first floor of the building to S. S's tenancy satisfies the subletting of part condition.

Landlord must be the superior landlord

The statutory wording for the second condition states:

> '... the landlord is the owner of an interest in reversion expectant on the determination of that superior tenancy...'.

So, both at the time of the service of the notice/counter-notice relying on ground (e) and the eventual court hearing the competent landlord (as discussed in chapter 3) must also be the superior landlord of the tenancy that was created by the subletting of part.

In the example given above, L is the person who meets this condition, but if the day before the hearing L accepts a surrender of T's tenancy, L will become S's direct landlord and will no longer be the 'superior landlord' of S's subtenancy. As a result, the superior landlord condition is no longer satisfied and L could no longer rely on this ground.

Rental value

To satisfy the third condition the landlord will need to produce expert valuation evidence dealing with the following three valuation questions:

(1) What is the rent reasonably obtainable on a separate letting of the premises comprised in the holding? *Using the example above, this would be a valuation of the premises comprised in S's subletting of part.*

(2) What is the rent reasonably obtainable on a separate letting of the rest of premises comprised in the superior tenancy? *Using the example above this would be a valuation of the premises comprised in Ts tenancy of the whole, but excluding the premises occupied by S.*

(3) What is the rent reasonably obtainable on a letting of the whole of the premises comprised in the superior tenancy? *Using the example above, this would be a valuation of the premises comprised in T's tenancy as though there had been no subletting to S.*

In each case the valuation date would be the date of the court hearing.

If the aggregate of the rental valuations achieved for questions 1) and 2) was substantially less than that of 3), the rental value condition would be satisfied.

S's holding is valued at £10,000 pa. T's tenancy (excluding S's premises) is valued at £40,000. The aggregate of the two lettings is therefore £50,000. If a letting of S and T's premises as a whole achieved a rent of, say, £100,000 the rental value condition would have been satisfied.

The landlord's requirement for possession

To satisfy this condition the landlord has to prove that:

- there is a genuine intention to let or dispose of the premises as a whole; and
- that it will be possible to do so once the current tenancy (i.e. the subletting of part) is determined.

The 'genuine intention' will need to be evidenced in much the same way as the landlord's intention in a ground (f) or (g) claim.

Proving the second limb of this condition is more straightforward. It will depend on whether the landlord can actually regain vacant possession of the whole of the premises once the current tenancy ends. So if the superior tenancy has, say, LTA 1954 protection and the landlord cannot prove it can oppose renewal, then it will not prove the second limb. Equally, if the superior tenancy has no protection (e.g. it is contracted out of LTA 1954) then the landlord is likely to be able to prove the second limb of this condition.

The court's discretion

Even once the landlord has satisfied the four conditions, it is still necessary to convince the court to exercise the discretion in the landlord's favour. However, unlike grounds (a), (b) and (c) the tenant has not breached its tenancy obligations or acted improperly in relation to its holding. The court can therefore only really balance the landlord's potential financial loss from having two separate lettings of its premises against the tenant's loss of its renewal tenancy.

7.6 Demolition, reconstruction or substantial construction – ground (f)

Section 30(1)(f) of LTA 1954 provides that a landlord may oppose the grant of a new tenancy if on the termination of the current tenancy the intention is to:

- demolish that part of the demised premises[112] currently occupied by the tenant or a substantial part of it. (This is the physical premises comprised in the tenancy and is capable of including tenant's fixtures);
- reconstruct that part of the demised premises currently occupied by the tenant or a substantial part of it; or
- carry out substantial work of construction on that part of the demised premises currently occupied by the tenant or a part of it; and that
- the landlord could not reasonably do so without obtaining vacant possession.

This is often referred to as the 'redevelopment ground', although 'redevelopment' is not actually referred to.

The landlord's intention

'Intention' is a question of fact in each case and comprises two elements, both of which must be satisfied[113]:

- *The subjective element:* has the landlord reached a firm and settled view, unlikely to be changed, that has 'moved out of the zone of contemplation into the valley of decision'[114]?
- *The objective element:* assuming that the landlord is able to obtain possession of the holding[115], is what the landlord would like to do practicable and not subject to so many hurdles that it could be said that the landlord could not reasonably intend to do it?

It is not necessary to establish the subjective and then the objective element. If, for example, there is no real prospect of the landlord carrying out works, then it is not necessary to consider whether, subjectively, the landlord intends to do so.

The 'landlord' for these purposes is the competent landlord, as identified by section 44 of LTA 1954[116] (discussed in chapter 4). Provided the landlord adduces sufficient evidence of intention, the motive for carrying out the works (to thwart the claim for a new tenancy, for example) is irrelevant[117].

The subjective element

Where the landlord is a single individual, there should be no difficulty in establishing subjective intention by providing a witness statement and being examined on it.

However, in other cases:

- Where the tenant is a company or other corporate body, evidence of the intention of the person or persons who are the 'directing mind and will'[118] of the company as far as the works are concerned should be provided. This may be a sole director (if there is only one), the board of directors (whose intention can be demonstrated by a resolution of the board) or a single director authorised to take the relevant decision on behalf of the company.
- If there is more than one landlord, the intention must be that of them together, save that only one of them is required to give evidence on behalf of each of the others[119]. This would include a partnership.
- If the landlord is a trust, the relevant intention is that of the trustees, rather than the beneficiaries.

Provided the 'landlord' has the required intention, it does not matter that someone else has the same intention when, for example, the redevelopment will be carried out in partnership or joint venture with third parties.

The objective element: practicability

The court might consider a number of factors to determine whether the landlord is able to bring about what is planned. These include:

- whether the landlord has obtained **required approvals and consents** (or, if not, what the likelihood is of obtaining them). This includes both internal and external approvals. The landlord may be a company whose internal procedures require authorisation for any development works or capital expenditure by a particular committee, for example. Similarly, works will almost always require planning permission and other consents for development (such as conservation area or listed building consent). If any approval or consent is conditional, there must be evidence as to the likelihood that the conditions will be satisfied;
- whether the landlord has **sufficient financial resources** to carry out the intention. It is not necessary to go on to show that the redevelopment will be a financial success[120], although clearly a scheme which is not financially viable may cast doubt on the landlord's subjective intention, particularly if the landlord is a company answerable to shareholders;
- whether the proposals are **sufficiently thought through**: evidence of prior discussion and involvement of different professionals (such as architects, building contractors, surveyors) will assist, as will evidence of any preparation for implementing the scheme and consideration of any risks involved. The fact that a landlord is considering a number of different options and has not yet settled on a final scheme is not necessarily fatal provided there is an intention (whatever scheme is ultimately adopted) to carry out relevant works of some kind[121].

147

- whether the landlord has taken other steps to facilitate the proposals (such as co-ordinated lettings if the building is in multiple occupation, with the different terms expiring at or around the same time as the current tenancy).

Effect of an undertaking to the court

An undertaking is a binding promise to the court to do (or not do) something, which the court can enforce by treating any breach of the promise as a contempt of court. If the landlord undertakes to carry out works to the holding, this is very strong evidence of intention to do so, but it is not conclusive[122].

The issue of whether the landlord has the required intention is assessed as at the date of trial[123], whereas the planned works must be intended to commence on or shortly after the termination of the current tenancy.

Where a company seeks to rely on a resolution of its board of directors as evidence of its intention, the court has permitted such resolution to be made during the course of the hearing, although permission to adduce evidence at this late stage was within the court's discretion.

Relevant works

As mentioned, the landlord must intend to:

- demolish the whole of the holding (which is that part of the demised premises currently occupied by the tenant for business purposes); or
- demolish a substantial part of the holding; and/or
- reconstruct the whole of the holding; or
- reconstruct a substantial part of the holding; and/or
- carry out substantial construction on the holding or part of it.

Will the works be considered to be substantial?

This is a question of fact and degree in each case. A useful starting point is to compare the results on the premises of carrying out the proposed work with the condition and state of the premises before the work was done[124].

Care needs to be taken where the tenancy is of bare land. If the tenant has introduced fixtures (such as temporary cabins), the tenant is entitled to remove these at the end of the tenancy. The landlord should be careful not to seek to or assert an intention to demolish these fixtures, because in the usual case where there is no suggestion that the tenant will not remove them, a landlord will generally be unable to show that they will ever be in a position to demolish those fixtures[125].

The proposed works will be looked at as a whole, such that preparatory and ancillary works are relevant and (in particular) will be considered if the court is required to determine whether the landlord's intended works (taken as a whole) are substantial. As previously stated, if a landlord is considering a number of different options, depending on which will be most profitable once implemented, the fact that the final scheme has not yet been chosen is not important, provided that in each scenario the landlord can establish that there will be some works of demolition, reconstruction and/or substantial construction[126].

The landlord must be the one to carry out the works, but this includes work carried out by employees, servants or agents. The issue is whether the landlord has sufficient control over the work intended to be carried out that it can be said to be the landlord's work. Where independent contractors are involved, the court will identify whether the works will be done with the landlord's approval and under his or her ultimate inspection[127].

Only certain works will count for the purposes of establishing ground (f). The following will not be taken into account:

- works to any part of the demised premises not occupied by the tenant (i.e. outside the holding). Where the works comprise demolition and/or reconstruction and are not to the whole of the holding or partly to the holding and partly to another part of the demised premises, they will be ignored unless a substantial part of the holding is involved. This is a question of fact and degree in each case – In *Atkinson v Bettison*[128], for example, the court held that where a tenant occupied three floors of a building but only demolition and reconstruction of the entrance and a back wall on the ground floor were proposed, the works were not to a substantial part of the holding.
- works which a landlord intends to carry out to remedy disrepair, for which they or the tenant are responsible under the current tenancy, or to reinstate alterations that the landlord can require the tenant to do under a licence for alteration[129].
- works that the landlord has a right under the lease to enter the demised premises and carry out[130]. In such case, the landlord does not need vacant possession of the premises in order to carry out the works.

Defining 'reconstruction' and 'construction'

'**Reconstruction**' includes rebuilding works involving a substantial interference with the structure of the building, usually involving its prior demolition. For these purposes, 'structure' is not confined to outside or load-bearing walls, floors or ceilings[131]. It follows that where the demised premises are only an eggshell, they are nevertheless capable of being demolished and reconstructed. It also follows that works to partitions (provided they are not demountable partitions) could also qualify as 'reconstruction' (so long as those works involved gutting the whole interior of an area and rebuilding the interior, rather than simply altering the layout[132].

'**Construction**' means some form of building upon the premises that involves the structure of it, but does not necessarily require the building of a structure above the site. Where, for example, an area is covered in concrete in order to provide a turning point for lorries, this is an act of construction[133]. 'Construction' is different from 'installation', however, of fixtures such as new toilets, pipes or cables for example.

Requirement for vacant possession

The landlord is required to show that in order to carry out proposed works, vacant possession of the holding is needed. This is a question of fact, but in two cases the court is precluded by section 31A of LTA 1954 from finding that the landlord requires vacant possession, if:

- the tenant agrees to terms in the new tenancy permitting the landlord reasonable access to carry out the works intended, provided the works would not interfere with the use of the holding to a substantial extent or for a substantial time. The tenant cannot agree to such terms if the effect of the works would be that the holding no longer existed or the premises otherwise became unusable indefinitely for the purpose of the tenant's business[134]. Whether or not interference would be substantial is a question of fact and degree. In every case the court will consider not only the disruption caused by the landlord's works, but also the extent and timing of any interference caused by additional works that the tenant would then have to do (after the landlord had finished) to make the premises suitable for continued occupation by him; or
- the tenant is willing to take a tenancy of an 'economically separable part' of the holding and:
  - the tenant would take a tenancy of that part including terms permitting the landlord reasonable access to carry out the work intended, provided the works would not interfere with the use of that part to a substantial extent or for a substantial time; or

— possession of the remainder of the holding would be reasonably sufficient to enable the landlord to carry out the work intended.

Whether or not there is such a part depends (assuming the landlord carries out proposed works) on a comparison of the rent that the landlord might get if letting the whole of the demised premises against the aggregate of the rents that are possible if the premises were separated into different units. There is only an 'economically separable part' if the latter is *'not substantially less'* than the former (section 31A(2) of LTA 1954).

The tenant must elect whether or not to rely on section 31A of LTA 1954 and if making a claim for a new tenancy, must state whether they are relying on the section in the claim form (in order to comply with paragraph 3.5(3) of CPR Practice Direction 56). If defending a claim for a termination order, the tenant must state if relying on the section in their defence (paragraph 3.13(2)(b) of CPR Practice Direction 56).

If the tenant agrees to the insertion of terms permitting the landlord access, and the court finds that the works will not cause substantial interference, the landlord will not be able to make good the ground of opposition. The court will – absent any other ground – grant a new tenancy. If the tenant is willing to accept a tenancy of an 'economically separable part', then the court will only grant a new tenancy of that part.

7.7 Own occupation – ground (g)

Section 30(1)(g) of LTA 1954 provides that a landlord may oppose the grant of a new tenancy if on the termination of the current tenancy the landlord:

- intends to occupy the holding for the purposes (or partly for the purposes) of a business carried on by him or her there; or
- intends to occupy the holding as a residence.

Additionally, if the landlord acquired the interest in the holding after the grant of the tenancy vested in the current tenant, the landlord must show that the interest was purchased or created at least five years before the date of termination (meaning the date of termination in the section 25 notice[135] or day before the date of commencement in the section 26 request) unless:

- at some point within that period, LTA 1954 has ceased to apply to the current or previous tenancy (because the tenant has ceased to occupy for business purposes, for example); or

- the landlord (who has held an interest in the holding for five years or more) has a 'controlling interest' in a company and it is intended that that company will occupy the holding.

If the landlord is a company and acquired its interest in the premises from another company in the same group, then that acquisition does not count for the purposes of applying the five-year rule (under section 42(3)(b) of LTA 1954).

The landlord's intention

The meaning of the word 'intends' is the same as for ground (f) and a landlord will often offer an undertaking to the court (in terms that the landlord will not use the demised premises for a specified period other than as a business or a residence) as very strong evidence of intention. If the landlord does so, but the plans later change whilst the undertaking is in effect the landlord must either:

- apply to the court to be released from the undertaking; or
- grant a new tenancy of the demised premises to the tenant, which will have the same effect[136].

Occupation

Whether or not the landlord will occupy the holding is a question of fact and in deciding whether the landlord will be occupying the premises for the purpose of establishing ground (g) the court will look at similar details to those discussed in chapter 1 for determining whether the tenant occupies the demised premises for business purposes.

The court will consider a range of factors including (but not limited to):

- whether the landlord will be physically present or not;
- what control the landlord will exercise over the premises;
- what use the landlord will make of the premises (i.e. whether the landlord actually needs to be present on the premises in order to use them in the way proposed); and
- how much time the landlord will spend in the relevant activity at the premises (be that carrying on a business or living there as a residence).

Occupation for business purposes or as a residence

If a landlord intends to occupy the holding (or a substantial part of it) as a residence, they cannot put the holding to mixed use. 'Residence' is not defined by LTA 1954. If the landlord is an individual, the question is whether the holding is going to be used as a home. This is an issue of fact and a question of degree as a person may have more than one 'residence'.

Meaning of 'holding'

Section 23(3) of LTA 1954 provides that 'holding' means

'the property comprised in the tenancy, there being excluded any part thereof which is occupied neither by the tenant nor by a person employed by the tenant and so employed for the purposes of a business by reason of which the tenancy is one to which this Part of this Act applies.'

The landlord must intend to occupy the whole of the holding or a substantial part of it[137]. The relevant date for establishing the extent of the holding is the date of the court's order.

The meaning of 'business' was considered in chapter 1, but for the purposes of opposing the grant of a new tenancy on ground (g), if the landlord intends to occupy the holding (or a substantial part of it) for business purposes:

- the landlord can still put the holding to mixed use, as the requirement is only to use the holding 'partly' for business purposes; but
- the landlord must intend to carry on a business in or on the holding. If the business will be carried on elsewhere, then the landlord will not make out this ground[138].

The landlord is also able to occupy the holding through a partner, agent, manager, employee or group company.

Companies

If the landlord is an individual who has a 'controlling interest' (for more details see chapter 1) in a company, then it is possible to rely on ground (g) if the landlord intends to occupy the holding or if the company intends to do so.

If the landlord is a company, then it may rely on ground (g) if it intends to occupy the holding, or if a company in the same group (as determined by section 42(3) of LTA 1954) or a person with a controlling interest in the landlord company intends to do so.

Partnerships

Nothing prevents a landlord from relying on ground (g) if the intention is to occupy the holding with others where, for example, they operate a business in partnership. It is important, however, that the landlord should establish that occupation would not just be by a partner even if the business were to be run for the account of them both[139].

One of several persons constituting the landlord

The landlord can comprise more than one person, if more than one person holds the reversionary interest or freehold of the demised premises, or if there are separate landlords of different parts of the demised premises.

If there is a single landlord's interest held jointly by more than one person, the interest will be held on trust for the benefit of each of them. Section 41(2) of LTA 1954 provides that 'landlord' will include any of the beneficiaries. Therefore, it would be sufficient for any one or more of the joint landlords to intend to occupy the holding.

If there are multiple landlord's interests, those holding the interest in the property comprising the holding must each intend to occupy the holding (or a substantial part of it), because references to 'landlord' mean 'a reference to all those persons collectively' (under section 44(1A) of LTA 1954).

When must the landlord intend to occupy?

The landlord must intend to occupy the holding 'on termination of the current tenancy', but this includes a reasonable time thereafter[140].

LTA 1954 does not specify how long the landlord must remain in occupation, but the authors consider that the landlord must intend to occupy the holding for a reasonable time, and what is reasonable will depend on all the circumstances of the individual case.

In *Willis v Association of Universities*[141], Lord Denning suggested that if the landlord intended to occupy and then pass on the business to a family member, six months might be sufficient whereas if the landlord intended to sell the business on to a third party, the same period might not be.

The five-year bar

LTA 1954 prohibits speculators from exploiting sitting tenants, because if a landlord acquires the interest after the grant of the current tenancy (or any previous business tenancy vested in the current tenant), then it is not possible to rely on ground (g) if the landlord has not held the interest in the holding for the period of five years or more from the date of termination. This rule does not apply if:

- at any time during the five-year period the holding has not comprised a tenancy to which LTA 1954 applies; and/or
- the landlord (having held an interest in the holding for five years) has a controlling interest in a company that intends to occupy the holding on termination of the current tenancy.

T took a lease of premises commencing 31 May 2000 for a term of seven years. If by the end of the seven years the property had been acquired by L, then L would be able to rely on ground (g) as a response to a section 26 request if L:

- *purchased the landlord's interest on 15 January 2002 because L's interest in the premises was purchased or created before 1 June 2002;*
- *bought the freehold of the property and exchanged contracts on 30 May 2002. Even if completion did not take place until 15 June 2002, for the purposes of LTA 1954 the 'purchase' takes place at the date of exchange, not completion;*
- *bought the freehold of the property, and exchanged contracts and completed on 15 June 2002, so long as T ceased to occupy the premises for business purposes at some point between 15 June 2002 and the date of the section 26 request. Although L's interest was purchased less than five years before the commencement date specified in T's section 26 request, LTA 1954 ceased to apply to the tenancy of the premises for a time during that period.*

The following table includes a number of examples for different situations that a landlord might come across when wanting to use ground (g)

Situation	Example
What happens if the landlord creates a trust?	*L would not be barred from relying on ground (g) if he executed a deed of trust, for example, declaring that he held the premises on trust for himself and his wife. So long as he had acquired the premises more than five years before the commencement date specified in T's section 26 request the creation of the trust does not bar L from using ground (g) (nor would a change in the identity of the trustee or beneficiaries).*
What happens when dealing with an assigned lease?	*An interest is not created when it is assigned. Where L takes an assignment of an interest from A on 1 June 2006 and the date of termination specified in his hostile section 25 notice is 1 May 2007, L can rely on ground (g) provided A's interest was created or purchased on or before 1 May 2002.*
What happens if the landlord acquires a company less than five years before the termination date?	*L let premises to T on 31 May 1982 for a term of 25 years. On 1 December 2005, L acquired a controlling interest in Newco Limited. T serves a section 26 request giving 1 June 2007 as the commencement date for the new tenancy.*

	L intends that Newco Limited should occupy the holding on termination of the current tenancy and can rely on ground (g), even though L has held an interest in the company which is intended to occupy the premises for less than five years before the termination date.
What happens if L transfers the interest to a company he or she has a controlling interest in?	L let premises to T on 31 May 1982 for a term of 25 years. On 1 December 2005, L acquired a controlling interest in Newco Limited and transferred his interest in the demised premises to that company the following day. Newco Limited intends to occupy the holding on termination of the current tenancy with L in actual occupation running the business, but Newco Limited cannot rely on ground (g) because its interest in the holding has not been held for the required five years or more.
What happens with an intra-group sale and purchase of the landlord's interest?	L lets premises to T on 1 January 2000 for a term of seven years. On 1 January 2001, L sells the interest to Company X. On 1 January 2005, Company X assigns its interest to Company Y (which is in the same group). Company Y intends to occupy the holding on termination of the current tenancy and can rely on ground (g), even though it obtained its interest less than five years before the termination date, because it did so from a company in the same group. The company group from whom the landlord (Company Y) obtained its interest acquired that interest from a third party more than five years before the termination date, which satisfies the rule.

8

Opposed claims and contentious applications

An 'opposed claim' is one in which a landlord relies on one or more of the statutory grounds in section 30(1) of LTA 1954 to oppose the grant of a new tenancy. This can be either by way of defence to a claim made by the tenant for a renewal tenancy or as the basis for a claim for a termination order.

In the context of both opposed and unopposed claims, the court may also be asked to deal with disputes about its jurisdiction to try a claim, as well as other applications aimed at short-circuiting the proceedings or ensuring compliance with court rules or orders.

This chapter considers:

- the court procedure common to all types of opposed claims (section 8.1), including:

  - issuing/serving a claim form (section 8.2);
  - responding to the claim (section 8.3); and
  - final statements of case and allocation (section 8.4).

- contentious applications that might be made during the course of both opposed and unopposed claims (section 8.5).

Acting for the tenant
A tenant can make a claim for a new tenancy, notwithstanding that the landlord opposes it, provided the landlord has not already issued and served a claim for a termination order (as detailed in chapter 5). Practically, the only reasons for a tenant to make a claim are that:

- the tenant believes that the landlord's opposition is not bona fide; and/or

- the tenant wants to rush the hearing of the claim because of a belief that the landlord may not be able to establish the ground(s) of opposition by the time of the relevant hearing. This is usually the case where the landlord opposes on ground (f) but plans are not significantly advanced such that it would be difficult for to establish an intention to carry out relevant works 'on termination of the current tenancy'.

A landlord may 'chance his arm' by indicating opposition in the section 25 notice or counter-notice to a section 26 request, hoping that this will encourage the tenant to leave the demised premises rather than make a claim to court. If the tenant does just that, there is an issue as to whether the tenant will be entitled to compensation under 37A of the Act. (This is dealt with in greater detail in chapter 10.)

If the tenant suspects that the landlord has no real intention to rely on the specified ground(s) of opposition, the tenant can issue a claim. The landlord is not bound to defend that claim just because the notice or counter-notice opposes the grant of a new tenancy, and if 'chancing his arm' the landlord may prefer not to fight the matter through to trial of a preliminary issue but instead deal with the claim as if, in fact, it were unopposed.

Acting for the landlord

It is obvious that if a landlord requires vacant possession of the holding, a statutory ground of opposition must be relied on. The landlord might prefer to do this by applying for a termination order rather than defending a claim for a new tenancy where timing is important for future plans. Regard should always be had to the effect of section 64 of the Act (see chapter 6). Even if a landlord succeeds in making out a statutory ground(s) of opposition, the current tenancy will usually continue for three months after the final disposal of court proceedings.

Whilst it may be desirable for a landlord to apply for a termination order, this is only possible if:

- a valid section 25 notice or counter-notice to a section 26 request has been served stating that the landlord is opposed to the grant of a new tenancy. This means, for example, that if the landlord's counter-notice is served late or does not contain a statement of which of the statutory grounds of opposition are relied on, the landlord will not be able to apply for a termination order; and
- neither the landlord nor the tenant has made an application for an order for the grant of a new tenancy. There may be situations in which claims are issued on the same date and the order of priority of such claims was discussed in chapter 5.

On determining the landlord's claim for a termination order, section 29(4) of LTA 1954 says the court must:

- make an order for the termination of the current tenancy in accordance with section 64 LTA 1954 without the grant of a new tenancy, if the landlord establishes any one or more of the statutory grounds of opposition to the court's satisfaction; or
- make an order for the grant of a new tenancy. Section 29(4) of LTA 1954 is stated to be 'subject to the provisions of this Act' and the authors consider, therefore, that the requirement that the court should order the grant of a new tenancy is always subject to its ability to make a declaration under section 31(2) of LTA 1954 and not to make such an order, where the landlord has only 'near-missed' making out the statutory ground(s) of opposition.

As detailed in chapter 7, certain of the statutory grounds of opposition are discretionary, others are mandatory. Where the discretionary grounds are concerned, the landlord will not establish the grounds of opposition unless the court, in addition to finding for example that there has been persistent delay in paying rent, also finds that the tenant ought not to be granted a new tenancy in view of that fact.

Even if a landlord is able to apply for a termination order, they must be prepared to follow those proceedings through. If not, and the termination order is unsuccessful, the court must (subject to section 31(2) of LTA 1954) order the grant of a new tenancy. It follows that if the landlord is not convinced of the merits of the ground(s) of opposition, it would be preferable not to apply for a termination order, because in doing so the landlord exposes himself to the costs of dealing with those grounds.

If the court is going to make an order for the grant of a new tenancy anyway, the landlord has to ask himself whether the potential costs are justified by the prospects of success. Moreover, under section 29(6) of LTA 1954 the landlord cannot withdraw a claim for a termination order unless the tenant agrees.

A well-advised tenant may only consent to the withdrawal of a speculative claim for a termination order if the landlord agrees to pay costs. If the landlord does not agree, then the tenant could refuse consent to the withdrawal, and push the landlord to trial of the statutory ground(s) of opposition in the hope that the landlord will lose and the tenant will be awarded costs in any event. A landlord also runs the risk that an application for a termination order will be struck out as an abuse of process if it is applied for at a time when the landlord has already decided, for example, not to redevelop the premises[142].

8.1 Common procedure for 'opposed claims'

No claim can be started until a section 25 notice has been served by the landlord, or a section 26 request served by the tenant and counter-notice given by the landlord (or the time for giving one has expired). It will be apparent from the notice or counter-notice, before any proceedings are started, whether the claim will be opposed or unopposed.

If the landlord serves a **section 25 notice**, he or she must state if they oppose the grant of a new tenancy and, if so, what ground(s) of opposition are relied on. If this is not done, the notice will be invalid. A claim can be issued immediately after the notice is given.

If the tenant serves a **section 26 request**, and the landlord opposes the grant of a new tenancy, he or she must serve a counter-notice within two months of the request being given, specifying the same details. Where the tenant serves a section 26 request, he or she cannot issue a claim for a new tenancy until the landlord serves a counter-notice or (if later) the period of two months has expired (in which case the landlord will lose the right to oppose the grant of a new tenancy if the landlord has served no counter-notice).

Elements in common with unopposed claims

Although unopposed claims are made using the *Civil Procedure Rules* (CPR) Part 8 procedure, rather than the CPR Part 7 procedure which applies to opposed claims, there is a degree of overlap between the two, including:

- who the 'landlord' and the 'tenant' are for the purpose of identifying who can make a claim, what to do if the parties are the wrong ones, and identifying other interested persons who must be notified of any proceedings;
- where both landlord and tenant issue claims, the priority of those claims;
- the time limits for making claims;
- which court claims should be started in;
- whether the surveyor can conduct the litigation or represent a client at court;
- service of proceedings;
- noting claims at H.M. Land Registry on behalf of the tenant;
- directions and the case management conference;
- the surveyor's involvement in disclosure, preparation of witness statements, expert evidence, preparation for and attendance at trial;
- discontinuance; and
- offers to settle.

(For more details on any of the above please refer to chapters 5 and 6)

Trial of a preliminary issue

If the tenant issues a claim for a new tenancy, the landlord will raise the statutory ground(s) of opposition by way of defence. If the landlord issues a claim for a termination order then the statutory ground(s) are put immediately in issue.

In either case, the landlord's entitlement to rely on the statutory ground(s) of opposition will be tried as a preliminary issue unless it is unreasonable to do so (paragraph 3.16 of CPR Practice Direction 56).

If the landlord succeeds, the court will not go on to consider what the terms of a new tenancy should have been; if the landlord fails, the court will only then go on to consider those terms.

Outline of procedure

As already stated, opposed claims are made using the CPR Part 7 procedure (CPR 56.3(4)). This procedure begins as follows:

Step	Party taking step	Timing
Issue claim form	Claimant	(latest time for = last day of the statutory period) **DAY 1**
Serve claim form	Claimant (if not the court)	(latest time for under CPR 56.3(4)(b)) **+ 2 months**
Serve particulars of claim	Claimant	(latest time for unless extension agreed) **+ 14 days**
Serve acknowledgment of service	Defendant	(latest time for unless extension agreed) **+14 days**
File and serve defence	Defendant	(latest time for unless extension [of not more than 28 days] agreed) **+14 days**
File allocation questionnaire	Both parties	Date for filing allocation questionnaire (set by the court)
File and serve a reply (if any)	Claimant	

8.2 Stage 1 – Claim form

The claimant must use form N1 (available through HM Court Service website[143]), and must give certain prescribed particulars as follows. These can be given in the claim form or in a separate document called particulars of claim.

Tenant's claim for a new tenancy – PD56 paragraphs 3.4 and 3.5	Landlord's claim for a termination order – PD56 paragraphs 3.4 and 3.9
The property to which the claim relates.	
The particulars of the current tenancy (including date, parties and duration), the current rent (if not the original rent) and the date and method of termination.	
Every notice or request given or made under sections 25 or 26 of the Act; and the expiry date of: • The statutory period under section 29A(2) of the Act; or • Any agreed extended period made under section 29B(1) or 29B(2) of the Act.	
The nature of the business carried on at the property;	The claimant's grounds of opposition.
Whether the tenant relies on section 23(1A), 41 or 42 of the Act and, if so, the basis on which it is relied	Full details of the grounds of opposition.
Whether any (and if so what part) of the property comprised in the tenancy is occupied neither by the tenant nor by a person employed by the tenant for the purpose of its business.	The terms of a new tenancy that the claimant proposes in the event that the claim fails
The tenant's proposed terms of the new tenancy.	
The name and address of anyone known to the tenant who has an interest in the reversion in the property on the termination of the current tenancy and who is likely to be affected by the grant of a new tenancy *or* if the tenant does not know of any such person, anyone who has a freehold interest in the property.	

The claimant must pay a fee on issue of the claim. (The fee payable should always be checked in advance. Information is provided on HM Courts Service website[144]). The claim form must be served within two months of issue (under CPR 56.3(4)(b)). If a claimant serves the claim form himself (rather than leaving the court to do so), they must include:

- a Response Pack (Form N9), which includes an acknowledgment of service form;
- a form for defending the claim (Form N9D); and
- a form for admitting the claim (Form N9C).

It may also be worthwhile including *Notes for Defendants* (Form EX303), which is referred to in the Response Pack.

What level of detail does the landlord need to go into about redevelopment plans in the claim form? Do they need to serve a witness statement at the same time, giving further details?

There is no requirement to serve a witness statement with the claim form, but a bare statement that the landlord requires vacant possession because on termination of the current tenancy he or she intends to carry out relevant works will be insufficient. CPR Practice Direction 56 requires the landlord to give 'full details' of the ground(s) of opposition. Moreover, a tenant must have sufficient details to enable them to put in a meaningful defence. The minimum details that a landlord should give in the claim form are as follows:

- What works will be carried out (in order to satisfy the requirement that the works comprise demolition, reconstruction or substantial construction).
- Where the works will be carried out (in order to satisfy the requirement that the works be carried out to the holding or a substantial part of them).
- Details about when works will be started (in order to satisfy the requirement that the landlord intends to redevelop 'on termination of the current tenancy').
- Details (if it is not obvious from the description of works) about the requirement for vacant possession.

If a bare statement only is given, the landlord runs the risk that the tenant will apply to strike out the claim (for failure to comply with the requirements of CPR Practice Direction 56) or the tenant will alternatively serve a request for further Information under CPR Part 18.

Continued

The bare statement can be remedied by the provision of further details, but if the landlord is working to a tight timetable to obtain vacant possession before works begin, delay in dealing with such an application or request (which could have been avoided by giving sufficient detail in the first place) could have a significant adverse effect.

8.3 Stage 2 – Responding to the claim

Within 14 days of being served with particulars of claim (or, more typically, the claim form if separate particulars are not served), the landlord must:

- serve an acknowledgment of service; or
- file a defence.

Acknowledgment of service

The acknowledgment of service (Form N9) requires the defendant to indicate whether he or she admits the claim, defends part of it or defends all of it. A landlord who has served a hostile section 25 notice may, for example, decide there is no real prospect of succeeding on the ground(s) of opposition previously referred to.

In responding to the tenant's claim for a new tenancy, therefore, the landlord might admit the claim or (if wanting to challenge the tenant's proposals for terms of the new tenancy) indicate an intention to defend part of it. If, despite the limited prospects of success, the landlord still wished to oppose an order for the grant of a new tenancy, then the landlord should indicate an intention to defend all of the claim.

The acknowledgment of service must be filed at court. There is no requirement to serve the acknowledgment on the claimant, since the court will notify if any acknowledgment has been filed. However, the defendant should do so as a matter of good practice.

Defence

If an acknowledgment of service is filed, the defendant has 28 days from the date of service of the particulars of claim to file a defence, which must set out the defendant's version of events, if different to that set out by the claimant in the claim form or particulars of claim.

If the claimant has made any factual errors, or certain facts need proving, the defendant should say so. If not, and it is not clear from the defence that there is a contrary case, it is taken that the defendant admits what the claimant has said according to CPR 16.5.

There are certain additional prescribed matters that the defence must include, depending on whether the claim is one for an order for the grant of a new tenancy or for a termination order.

Claim for an order for the grant of a new tenancy – Landlord's defence PD56 paragraph 3.12	Claim for a termination order – Tenant's defence PD56 paragraph 3.13
The landlord's grounds of opposition with full details.	Whether the tenant relies on section 23(1A), 41 or 42 of the Act and, if so, the basis of its reliance.
Whether, if a new tenancy is granted, the landlord objects to any of the terms proposed by the tenant and if so: • the terms that are objected to; and • the terms that are proposed in so far as they differ from those proposed by the tenant.	Whether the tenant relies on section 31A of the Act and, if so, the basis of its reliance.
Whether the tenant is a tenant under a lease having less than 15 years unexpired at the date of termination of the current tenancy and, if so, the name and address of any person who (to the knowledge of the landlord) has an interest in the reversion in the property expectant (whether immediately or in not more than 15 years from that date) on the termination of the tenant's tenancy.	The terms of the new tenancy that the defendant would propose in the event that the landlord's claim to terminate the current tenancy fails.
The name and address of any person having an interest in the property who is likely to be affected by the grant of a new tenancy.	
If the tenant's tenancy is one to which section 32(2) of the Act applies, whether the landlord requires that any new tenancy shall be a tenancy of the whole of the property comprised in the tenant's current tenancy.	

Default judgment

If no acknowledgment of service or defence is filed within 14 days of service of the particulars of claim, the claimant can obtain default judgment under CPR Part 12 by making an application under CPR Part 23. On hearing of that application, the court would still need to consider:

- on a claim for a termination order: the statutory ground(s) of opposition relied upon by the landlord; or
- on a claim for a new tenancy: what the terms of the new tenancy should be.

If the defendant does not respond or participate the court is likely, in practice, to make an order as sought by the claimant.

It should be noted that default judgment is *only* available in the case of opposed claims. It is not available in the case of unopposed claims, because CPR Part 12 does not apply to claims made under CPR Part 8.

8.4 Stage 3 – Final statements of case and allocation

Before allocation of the case takes place, the defendant may raise in the defence new matters that were not covered in the claim form or particulars of claim. If so, the claimant can file a further statement of case called a reply. A reply is unlikely to be necessary in applications made under the Act, but if the claimant does want one it must be served and filed at the same time as the allocation questionnaire (under CPR 15.8).

The allocation questionnaire (form N150) contains questions to assist the court in deciding which 'track' to allocate the claim to (small claims, fast track or multi-track). The usual track for opposed claims will be the multi-track, unless the value of the dispute is equal to or less than £15,000 and the matters in dispute are likely to be capable of disposal within one day of court time, in which case the fast track is more appropriate – the fast track is subject to fixed legal costs at trial.

The allocation questionnaire (form N150) includes a section (F) requesting the parties to suggest directions. A specimen is set of directions for use in opposed claims is contained in appendix 13, which provide a useful starting point for those considering what directions would be appropriate for inclusion with the allocation questionnaire.

The landlord must file evidence first (paragraph 3.15 of CPR Practice Direction 56). It would appear that the court does not have the power to order simultaneous exchange, but must now order sequential exchange of witness statements and expert reports.

Once the allocation questionnaire is filed and the allocation fee paid by the claimant, the court will allocate the claim and (usually) give directions. If directions are not given, the court will list the claim for a case management conference and then make the appropriate order.

If the County Court in which the claim has been made is not a Civil Trial Centre, the claim is likely to be transferred to such a centre and that court will give directions or hear any case management conference (CMC). This can cause delay.

Trial of a preliminary issue will usually be held within six to eight months of the claim form being issued, although this can take longer – particularly if the court requires the assistance of expert evidence to decide whether the landlord is entitled to rely on the statutory ground(s) of opposition.

Example timeline	
1 March 2006	Claim form issued
10 March 2006	Claim form served
24 March 2006	Particulars of claim served
7 April 2006	Acknowledgment of service filed
21 April 2006	Defence filed
19 May 2006	Allocation questionnaire filed Reply filed (if any)
10 July 2006	Case management conference. Order for trial of a preliminary issue. Directions given.
21 August 2006	Disclosure of documents (limited to the preliminary issue)
18 September 2006	Landlord serves witness statements (limited to the preliminary issue)
2 October 2006	Tenant serves witness statements (limited to the preliminary issue)
30 October 2006	Trial of preliminary issue

8.5   Contentious applications

Contentious applications may be made in unopposed as well as opposed claims. Where, for example, the court gives directions for the parties to comment on a draft tenancy agreement in an unopposed claim, one way of applying pressure to a defaulting party is to apply for an order that the court strike out that party's statement of case and grant a new tenancy in the terms of the current draft unless the defaulting party provides comments within a specified, short time-period.

Tactics should be left to a party's legal advisors, but surveyors should be aware of the types of applications that can and might be made, as follows:

- application for a declaration that the court does not have jurisdiction to try the claim (CPR Part 11);
- application to strike-out a statement of case (CPR 3.4);
- application for an 'unless' order (CPR Part 3);
- application for summary judgment (CPR Part 24); or
- application for expedition of the trial of the preliminary issue.

The procedure for making applications is contained in CPR Part 23. The party making an application is called the 'applicant' and the other party or parties the 'respondent(s)'.

An application is made by issuing an application notice (Form N244) on payment of a fee. The applicant must state what order the court is being asked to make and briefly, set out reasons for doing so. Applications must normally be supported by evidence and if the matter is quite straightforward, this can be included in Part C of the application notice. In more complicated cases, a witness statement will be required.

When deciding whether or not to make an application, the following questions will be relevant:

- Does the court have a discretion whether to order what I am asking for or not?
- Is there any other order that the court could make on my application?
- Can the other side make their own application for an order to remedy the matter I am complaining about?
- What is the likelihood that the court could make some other order (to regularise an error of procedure, for example)?
- What are the likely costs involved in making the application? What might the other side's costs be?
- Do my chances of success justify the costs involved?

In many cases, the applicant may be relying on a technical point and in some cases, the court must allow the application, whatever the underlying merits of the situation. Where, for example, a tenant issues a claim for an order for the grant of a new tenancy a day late, the court cannot accept jurisdiction to try the claim, and must dismiss the claim notwithstanding that this may have a devastating impact on the tenant's business whereas the landlord would have suffered little prejudice if a new tenancy had been ordered.

In other cases, the claimant will be able to remedy the error or the court will be able to make an order that cures any defect of procedure. This would be the case where, for example, the claim form does not contain all of the required prescribed particulars – these can be added by way of amendment. In these situations, an application may be successful, but ultimately the respondent to the application will be able to cure the defect or start again.

The only circumstances where it might be advisable not to make an application are where the respondent has spotted the error and made (or indicated that it will make) an application for an order to cure that defect. If the applicant is invited to consent to that application, there will be a risk on costs if it makes an application, for example, challenging the jurisdiction or to strike-out. That risk will be proportionate to the applicant's chances of success.

Type of application	What do I need to show?	Examples of situations when the application might be made
Declaration that the court does not have jurisdiction to try the claim	As a matter of law, the court does not have jurisdiction to try the claim	Section 25 notice or section 26 request is invalid (e.g. not validly served, given by or to the wrong person, date of termination or commencement date earlier than six months or later than 12 months from date of service of the notice)
		Proceedings issued too early (e.g. after service of section 26 request and before landlord's counter-notice or two months have expired)
		Proceedings issued too late (e.g. a day after expiry of the statutory period)
		Proceedings served too late (e.g. a day after two months from the date of issue)
		Wrong parties (e.g. landlord defendant to a claim for an order for the grant of a new tenancy not the competent landlord)

Strike-out	The statement of case: • discloses no reasonable grounds for bringing or defending the claim; • is an abuse of process or otherwise likely to obstruct the just disposal of the proceedings; or • there has been a failure to comply with a rule, practice direction or court order.	The landlord opposes an order for the grant of a new tenancy on a ground that is not specified in section 30(1) of LTA 1954
		The tenant maintains a claim for a new tenancy, notwithstanding that LTA 1954 ceases to apply to the current tenancy. It is a continuing condition of the right to a new tenancy that LTA 1954 should continue to apply at all times after the contractual tenancy determines. In such circumstances, the claim is an abuse of process.
		The landlord applies for a termination order purely to avoid paying statutory compensation to the tenant and not because it wants or can obtain such an order.
		The claimant seeks an order for the grant of a new tenancy, but has failed to specify the prescribed particulars in Practice Direction 56 paragraphs 3.5 (if the claimant is the tenant) or 3.7 (if the claimant is the landlord).
Summary judgment	• The claimant has no real prospect of succeeding on the claim or issue; or • the defendant has no real prospect of defending the claim or issue; and • there is no other compelling reason why the case or issue should be disposed of at a trial	The landlord relies on ground (g)
		The landlord relies on ground (f), plans are advanced and there are no further obstacles to overcome before the re-development can begin
Unless order	That unless the court makes the order sought the mischief that it is intended to punish or prevent will happen again or continue	A party stops complying with directions and refuses to answer correspondence to address the matter

9

Acting as an expert

In many cases, parties will rely on the evidence of an expert. In unopposed claims this usually involves evidence concerning the rent payable under the new tenancy and in opposed claims expert evidence may be used to substantiate or resist the landlord's grounds of opposition.

An expert involved in claims under LTA 1954 may act in three different capacities or, over a period of time, a combination of them:

- **As an expert witness**: instructed for the purpose of giving or preparing evidence for use in proceedings. The parties may appoint such an expert separately, jointly or the court may appoint the expert.
- **As an adviser**: instructed by the parties for any other purpose.
- **As a 'shadow expert'**: instructed to review and comment upon the evidence given or prepared by an expert witness, particularly used by one or other of the parties if the court has appointed a single joint expert.

This chapter deals with acting as an expert and considers:

- the difference between acting as an expert witness and as an adviser (section 9.1);
- expert evidence: what it is, how it is regulated and when it is used (sections 9.2 to 9.4);
- the various stages involved in acting as an expert witness in court claims (section 9.5), including:

  - acceptance of instructions (section 9.6);
  - the relationship with the client, instructing solicitor and counsel (section 9.7); and
  - the written report (section 9.8); as well as

- giving evidence at trial (section 9.9); and
- single joint experts (section 9.10).

9.1 The difference between an adviser and an expert witness

The distinction, between expert witness on the one hand, and adviser (including shadow experts) on the other is important, as demonstrated by the table below.

	Expert witness	**Adviser**
Regulation	CPR Part 35 and Practice Direction 35 Civil Justice Council Protocol RICS practice statement, *Surveyors Acting as Expert Witnesses* Chancery Guide (if applicable)	No regulation of the adviser. If an adviser is subsequently appointed as an expert witness, the costs of his acting as an adviser may be disallowed if any of the *Civil Procedure Rule* provisions were blatantly ignored or contravened, even though t heywere not applicable at the time he so acted.
Privilege	The court has powers to order the disclosure of specific documents or to permit questioning in relation to instructions and the other side is entitled to copies of any document mentioned and relied upon in the expert report	Documents created by the adviser, or recording any advice, are likely to be the subject of litigation privilege. As such, they need not be disclosed to the other side or any third party.
Primary duty	To the court	To the party instructing him
Immunity from suit	Arguable	None

An adviser can subsequently be instructed as an expert witness and is then subject to the regulation referred to above. Care must be taken to ensure that the change in capacity is properly marked. Fresh instructions should be issued and documents provided, as if the expert were being instructed from the beginning and the surveyor should not refer to previous instructions received in the capacity as adviser. This will not guarantee that instructions previously given to a surveyor in the capacity as an adviser will remain privileged, but it does improve the prospects that any privilege will be maintained.

9.2 Expert evidence

Experts give evidence of opinion, based on, but to be contrasted with, evidence of fact. When a surveyor produces a report on rent for the purpose of assisting the court under section 34 of LTA 1954, the report should contain details of comparable lettings (factual evidence) but also the surveyor's view on what the new rent should be, based on assessment of those comparables (opinion evidence).

Sometimes, the distinction between factual and opinion evidence can be blurred. For example, an expert might be required to explain to the court a particular practice such as the predominance of turnover rents in the hotel sector. Describing a particular practice may involve a predominantly factual report, but if the expert is expressing opinion as to whether that practice does or should apply in the instant case, then this is properly called expert evidence.

An expert is not only someone who can and does express an opinion on a relevant issue, but must be someone with:

- up-to-date expertise relevant to that issue and a high degree of skill and knowledge in the particular subject matter; and
- experience and training appropriate to the value, complexity and importance of the case. This includes, presumably, sufficient education and communication skills to produce a clear written report on the issues and to provide helpful oral evidence to the court.

9.3 The regulatory framework

Before a claim is issued

The *Civil Procedure Rules* (CPR) Practice Direction on Pre-Action Protocols contains provisions that the parties should follow in the event that they require expert assistance before a claim is issued. It states that:

- they should seek advice from a joint expert if possible (paragraph 4.9 of the CPR Practice Direction; and
- the cost of expert advice may not be recoverable or the use of expert evidence allowed if proceedings are in fact started (paragraph 4.10 of the CPR Practice Direction).

The *Protocol for the Instruction of Experts to give Evidence in Civil Claims* (June 2005) (the Protocol) refers to paragraph 1.4 of the Practice Direction and applies to any steps taken for the purpose of civil proceedings by experts or those instructing them on or after 5 September 2005.

The Protocol replaces the previous *Codes of Guidance* issued by the Academy of Experts and Expert Witness Institute and is available from the Civil Justice Council website[145]. It requires the parties to bear in mind the following objectives:

- to encourage the exchange of early and full information about the expert issues involved in a prospective legal claim;
- to enable the parties to avoid or reduce the scope of litigation by agreeing the whole or any part of an expert issue before proceedings are commenced; and
- to support the efficient management of proceedings where litigation cannot be avoided.

Professional guidance

RICS has issued a practice statement on *Surveyors Acting as Expert Witnesses*, which is accompanied by a guidance note. The practice statement is a code of best practice for surveyors who agree or are required to provide expert evidence (whether oral or in writing) that may be relied upon in court proceedings.

The practice statement and guidance note were first published together in 2001. This chapter takes into account changes in the third edition (early 2006).

It does not apply where a surveyor is giving advice, particularly where that advice is being given to assist the client in deciding whether or not to start a claim. However, if the surveyor accepts instructions for the purpose of court proceedings, then it is important to notify the client in writing

> 'if advice or investigations would fall short of that necessary to enable evidence complying with this practice statement to be given ... '

Once a claim is issued

Ultimately, the court decides whether expert evidence can be used at all and, if so, how and to what extent it will be used. CPR Part 35 and Practice Direction 35 apply to any expert who has been instructed to prepare or to give evidence for the purpose of court proceedings.

Key to these provisions is that the expert owes a duty to the court to help it with matters within his or her expertise, and this overrides any duty owed to the party or parties instructing or paying the expert (CPR 35.3).

Practice Direction 35 further provides that:

- expert evidence should be the independent product of the expert. As suggested by paragraph 4.3 of the Protocol, a useful test of 'independence' is that the expert would express the same opinion if given the same instructions by an opposing party;
- an expert should assist the court by providing objective, unbiased opinion on matters within his or her expertise, and should not assume the role of an advocate;
- an expert should consider all material facts, including those which might detract from his or her position;
- an expert should make it clear:
  - when a question or issue falls outside his or her expertise; and
  - when he or she is not able to reach a definite opinion, for example because of insufficient information; and
- if, after producing a report, an expert changes views on any material matter, such change of view should be communicated to all the parties without delay, and when appropriate to the court.

Exceptionally, where a claim is proceeding in the High Court, paragraphs 4.6–4.19 of the Chancery Guide also apply. Expert witnesses should have further regard to the Protocol, which contains provisions relevant to the conduct of an expert both before and after a claim has begun.

The RICS practice statement takes effect once a claim has been issued and the surveyor is instructed to provide expert evidence. Under RICS Bye-law 19(5) every member of RICS is under a duty to comply with the practice statement, unless there are special circumstances that make it inappropriate or impractical for the surveyor to undertake the assignment wholly in accordance with the practice statement. The Protocol expressly requires surveyors to comply with relevant professional codes of conduct.

It is vitally important that any person proposing to or actually acting as an expert is aware of the rules regulating his or her conduct. If not, the expert runs the risk that evidence may be ignored or discounted[146], or that a costs order will be made against him or her personally (CPR 48.2[147]). If this means that the client suffers a loss (including a situation where the client is debarred from recovering the expert's costs from the other party), the expert may be the subject of a claim for professional negligence.

The Protocol states that the court may take into account any failure to comply with its terms when making particular orders (unless such failure is reasonable where, for example, there is urgency because a claim is about to become time-barred). If a surveyor fails to comply with the RICS practice statement they might be guilty of professional misconduct.

Surveyors cannot rely on their client's lawyers to provide them with the information they need: that information should always be asked for if it is not forthcoming.

9.4 When is expert evidence used?

Expert evidence should not be used unless it is reasonably necessary to:

- define or explain any of the issues in dispute;
- assist in evaluating the merits of a party's case by reference to those issues;
- help quantify or assess any sum in dispute (such as rent in an unopposed claim); or
- provide an understanding of the other party's case sufficient to permit reasonable attempts at settlement.

The court will enforce this rule, either by refusing permission to adduce expert evidence or by limiting the expert evidence that can be adduced. After the event, the court may disallow the costs of any expert evidence that was called but ultimately unnecessary. The parties should assist the court by not asking for permission to use such evidence unless it is reasonably required to resolve the issues.

L relies on ground (f) (demolition and reconstruction) in support of an application for a termination order in respect of T's tenancy. L submitted a planning application some time ago and has obtained a witness statement from the planning officer dealing with the application stating that the application meets the local authority's criteria, that the officer will not recommend that any conditions be attached to the grant of permission and will recommend that the application be approved by the planning committee. Expert evidence from a planning surveyor as to the likelihood that L will obtain planning permission is unlikely to assist the court.

If L had not yet submitted an application for planning permission, expert evidence from a planning surveyor as to the likelihood that L will obtain planning permission would assist the court.

In giving its permission to the parties to adduce expert evidence, the court should:

- identify the field of expertise from which the expert should be drawn;
- identify the issues in respect of which the parties have permission to adduce expert evidence;

- confirm the number of experts from whom each party can adduce evidence; and
- if appropriate, name the individual(s) to be appointed as expert(s).

The court may also set a limit on the fees of any expert used, which the party being given permission can recover from the other.

> **I have been appointed as an expert to provide a written report as to whether my client (a landlord) could obtain more by letting her building as a whole than by taking an aggregate of the rents of lettings of different parts of it. She is relying on ground (e) to oppose the grant of a new tenancy to her tenant. Since my appointment, I have discovered a conflict of interest, which prevents me from continuing to act for my client. Can a colleague in my firm act instead of me?**
>
> Subject to confirmation that your colleague has no similar conflict of interest and you are able to erect a sufficient information barrier between you to protect any confidential information, much depends on the court's order. If you have been named in the order giving your client permission to adduce expert evidence, your client will need to seek the court's permission for the new appointment. If the order only specifies a field of expertise, provided your colleague is in the same field as you they should be able to act without the need to refer back to the court[148].

9.5 Acting as an expert witness

The duties and responsibilities of expert witnesses in civil cases were first summarised by Creswell J in the *Ikarian Reefer* case, a landmark case from 1985.

The Ikarian Reefer was a vessel that ran aground on shoals off the Sierra Leone coastline. When the ship's owners attempted to claim under their insurance policy the underwriters alleged that the owners had deliberately set fire to the vessel after it had run aground. When the case went to court, expert evidence was adduced to assess the causes of the fire and after a long drawn out trial Creswell J conveyed his belief that:

'... a misunderstanding on the part of certain expert witnesses ... as to their duties and responsibilities contributed to the length of the trial ...'

He then set down some guidelines for expert witnesses that included the following:

'1. Expert evidence presented to the court should be, and should be seen to be, the independent product of the expert uninfluenced as to form or content by the exigencies of litigation (Lord Wilberforce in *Whitehouse v Jordan*, [1981] 1 WLR 246).

2. An expert witness should provide independent assistance to the court by way of objective unbiased opinion in relation to matters within his expertise (Mr Justice Garland in *Polivitte Ltd v Commercial Union Assurance Co. Plc.* [1987] 1 Lloyd's Rep. 379; and Mr. Justice Cazalet in *Re J* [1990] F.C.R. 193). An expert witness in the High Court should never assume the role of an advocate.

3. An expert witness should state the facts or assumption upon which his opinion is based. He should not omit to consider material facts that could detract from his concluded opinion (as in *Re J* above).

4. An expert witness should make it clear when a particular question or issue falls outside his expertise.

5. If an expert's opinion is not properly researched because he considers that insufficient data is available, then this must be stated with an indication that the opinion is no more than a provisional one (as in *Re J* above). In cases where an expert witness who has prepared a report could not assert that the report contained the truth, the whole truth and nothing but the truth without some qualification, that qualification should be stated in the report (Lord Justice Staughton in *Derby & Co. Ltd. and Others v Weldon and Others*, The Times, 9 November 1990).

6. If, after exchange of reports, an expert witness changes his view on a material matter having read the other side's expert's report or for any other reason, such change of view should be communicated (through legal representatives) to the other side without delay and when appropriate to the court.

7. Where expert evidence refers to photographs, plans, calculations, analyses, measurements, survey reports or other similar documents, these must be provided to the opposite party at the same time as the exchange of reports (15.5 of the *Guide to Commercial Court Practice*[149])'.

These duties were expanded in CPR Part 35:

- The duty of the expert is to help the court on matters within his or her expertise, and this duty overrides any obligation to the person from whom the expert has received instructions or remuneration.
- An expert report must comply with the requirements set out in Practice Direction 35, and an expert must sign a statement that they understand the duty to the court and have complied with it.
- Under Practice Direction 35 a separate statement of truth is required that the expert's opinions are made from his or her own knowledge, that he or she believes them to be true and that the opinions expressed represent his or her true and complete professional opinion.
- If an expert is in any doubt as to what must be done it is possible to, independently of a retainer, file a written request for directions from the court to assist in carrying out the functions

Pre-eminence of the duty to the court

An expert witness may have a change of mind or make concessions to the case put forward by the other side. Reasons for doing so may be various – the expert may, for example, feel compelled by the duties owed to the court to recognise a mistake in advice previously given or views previously expressed.

In previous cases, surveyors acting as expert witnesses have been found to be immune from claims against them relating to their preparation for and conduct at trial. In *Stanton v Callaghan* (2000)[150] the immunity was held to extend to giving evidence in court and to any report produced with a view to giving evidence (even if it was not ultimately given in evidence).

The rationale behind this immunity was that since experts owed duties to the court they should be free to have full and frank discussions with any counterpart instructed by the other party, and should not feel constrained to hold a particular view or be unwilling to make concessions just because that might be inconsistent with advice previously given to their client. Moreover, if experts were to be challenged about their views or advice relating to a certain piece of litigation in any claim for negligence against them, the court could effectively be required to re-open the claim in which the surveyor had acted as expert witness that was undesirable.

These considerations had previously justified similar immunity from suit for advocates, but that has since been removed[151]. In the authors' view, it is likely that the immunity from suit enjoyed by surveyors acting as expert witnesses will also eventually be removed. There is no reason why an expert should be treated differently to any other professional involved in the trial process if their conduct falls short of duties owed to the court and to the client. Leading counsel made this submission in *Phillips v Symes* and, whilst Peter Smith J did not rule on it, he appears to have tacitly approved it.[152]

The practical effect of any removal of immunity should be considered, therefore:

- if an expert has a change of mind or advice in order to comply with duties to the court, the expert could not be held negligent for the change. This leaves open the possibility that the expert could have been negligent in providing the earlier advice and where, for example, that earlier advice led to the litigation (in the sense that a claim would not have been brought if the surveyor had not expressed such a view in the first place), the expert could be liable for any unrecovered costs incurred by the client which would not have been otherwise incurred; or
- if an expert fails to comply with duties to the court and, for example, the court discounts or ignores his or her evidence, the surveyor could be liable to the client for any losses caused by this. The RICS practice statement imposes an obligation on surveyors to comply with the CPR and to make themselves aware of the need to comply as a matter of professional conduct. In the scenario where a client loses a claim, he or she might seek to recover from the expert the value of the lost chance of success if they can establish that it was more likely than not that he or she would have won had the expert complied with the duties to the court.

Acting as an advocate

A surveyor cannot appear as an advocate on a client's behalf before the County and High Courts. Surveyors are expressly prohibited, when acting as an expert witness, from advancing any particular case on behalf of a client[153].

9.6 Acceptance of instructions

A surveyor should only accept instructions to act as an expert witness in court proceedings if the client has instructed solicitors, or the matter arises from direct access to the Bar. The following guidance derives from the RICS practice statement and the *Protocol for the Instruction of Experts to give Evidence in Civil Claims.*

Before accepting any instructions to act as an expert witness, a surveyor should ensure that there is no conflict of interest in acting for that party. There is no prima facie (obvious) conflict between a surveyor acting as an expert witness for his or her employer but the fact that an expert may be an employee of one of the parties may affect the weight to be given to their evidence and this fact should be brought to the employer's attention.

If the surveyor has any doubt about a possible conflict of interest, he or she should advise the potential client in writing to consider obtaining legal advice as to whether the surveyor should decline the instructions. This is especially important if the surveyor believes that the court might attach less or no weight to his or her evidence as a result.

The obligation to advise the client on conflicts is a continuing one, and operates both before and after the surveyor is instructed.

The surveyor must advise a potential client in writing that the RICS practice statement and CPR will apply (and should supply a copy of the practice statement for the client's information). The surveyor must also ascertain whether the court has given permission to the parties to rely on expert evidence and, if so, inform the potential client that if instructed the surveyor would have the ability to seek directions from the court directly and may have to answer questions directly from the other side.

The surveyor will also need a brief overview of the dispute between the parties, in order to confirm that he or she has the relevant expertise necessary to assist both the party and the court. The surveyor should not accept instructions without:

- sufficient impartiality for the assignment, and in particular should have no conflict of interest;
- knowledge, experience, qualifications and training appropriate for the assignment;
- sufficient instructions for the assignment; and
- the resources to complete the assignment within the timescales and to the standard required, including the ability to comply with any orders made by the court.

The CPR does not prescribe the content of instructions, although paragraph 8.1 of the Protocol states that instructions should be clear and gives a list of matters that should be included. Ideally any instructions should contain the following:

- confirmation of the parties to the dispute and that the surveyor has no conflict of interest in acting;
- a summary of the dispute, the issues for determination, and (briefly) the position of each party;
- a list of any other documents provided with the instructions. If the expert is in any doubt that he or she has received all relevant documents, confirmation needs to be sought and, if necessary, the expert will need to ask to inspect the client's files to satisfy that this is correct;
- A list of the questions which the surveyor is asked to consider in the written report;

- An indication of the timetable set by the court for:
  - the exchange of expert reports;
  - provision of questions from the other side;
  - any without prejudice meeting with the expert appointed by the other side; and
  - filing of the joint statement at court.

  The instructions should also notify the expert of the date set for trial, or trial window, together with an estimate of when (within that window) he or she might be expected to give evidence; and

- an indication (where appropriate) as to whether the instructions or documents in them are confidential and, if so, how that confidentiality is expected to be maintained.

From the outset, an expert witness should also ensure that certain matters are agreed as between himself and the person instructing him, namely:

- the basis for charges, including any disbursements (although contingency fees are unacceptable – as per the RICS practice statement and paragraph 7.6 of the Protocol). Payment of fees can be delayed until after conclusion of the case provided that the fee does not depend on the outcome;
- an estimate of the time involved in preparing a report (which should include an allowance for working through various drafts and, often, meeting with a party's solicitors and counsel to discuss);
- a time for delivery of the report; and
- the expert's rates for attending court and provisions for payment if the case settles before trial and attendance is no longer required.

The easiest way to record agreement is for each of these matters to be set out in the letter of instruction, which the expert should then be asked to sign and return. Alternatively, sample terms of engagement are appended to the RICS practice statement. Acceptance of instructions must be given in writing and should, if applicable, attach the surveyor's standard terms of engagement.

9.7 Relationship with client, instructing solicitor and counsel

Prior to the introduction of the CPR, all communications with an expert witness were subject to litigation privilege. Since then, the court has had limited powers to order disclosure of:

- documents mentioned in the expert's report (under CPR 31.14(2)); and
- material instructions given to the expert (whether in writing or given orally), but only if the court has reasonable grounds to believe that the summary of those instructions given by the expert is inaccurate or incomplete (under CPR 35.10(4)).

This power does not extend to disclosure of draft reports or earlier versions of the report that is ultimately exchanged or used in proceedings[154].

For this purpose, however, 'instructions' means the information being supplied by the party instructing the expert and all the material which a solicitor places in front of the expert in order to gain advice (*Lucas v Barking, Havering & Redbridge Hospitals NHS Trust*[155], disapproving Morland J in *Taylor v Bolton Heath Health Authority*[156] who had held that 'instructions' only covered what the expert was told to do).

If a solicitor comments on a draft report, therefore, in order to assist or improve that report, it is likely that the comments will be 'instructions' to the expert. Whether or not the content of the comments needs to be mentioned by the expert depends on whether they are 'material' to the report. Even if the comments do need to be mentioned by him, they should be summarised and need not be set out verbatim.

A surveyor must keep a written record of any changes to instructions. It is worth bearing in mind that such a record might be disclosable to the court and to the other side.

If the surveyor is passed papers which are expressed to be 'privileged' and it is not clear to whether the client has waived that privilege, it is worthwhile checking the status of the papers with those instructing the client without reading them, or return them unread with an explanation as to why not. This protects the client, so far as possible, from the possibility of disclosure of otherwise privileged material.

9.8 The written report

It is possible to distil several requirements regarding the content of an expert's report from CPR Practice Direction 35, the Protocol and the RICS practice statement. Any report must:

- be addressed to the court;
- give details of the expert's qualifications;
- give details of any literature or other material which the expert has relied upon in preparing the written report;
- state the substance of all material instructions (whether written or oral) and basis on which any report is given. Written instructions can be (but need not be) annexed to the report.;
- state the date or dates on which the subject-matter property was inspected and state the extent of such access as was obtained;

- summarise the range of opinion on the matters dealt with in the report and give reasons for his or her own opinion. If the opinion is provisional or the surveyor cannot express a final and unqualified opinion, the report needs to say so and provide an explanation;
- state all assumed and known facts upon which opinion is based, identifying differences from the facts and assumptions made by his or her counterpart instructed by the other party;
- contain a summary of the conclusions reached;
- be presented in an organised and referenced way with brevity, distinguishing between matters of plain fact, expert observations and expert inferences;
- use plain language and explain any technical terms;
- be personally signed and dated;
- be verified with the following statement (statement of truth):

    'I confirm that insofar as the facts stated in my report are within my own knowledge I have made clear which they are and I believe them to be true, and that the opinions I have expressed represent my true and complete professional opinion.'

    This statement is prescribed and mandatory and should not be modified (paragraph 13.5 of the Protocol); and
- contain the following declarations:

    - That the report includes all facts that the surveyor regards as being relevant to the opinion that he or she has expressed and that the court's attention has been drawn to any matter that would affect the validity of those opinions.
    - That the report complies with the requirements of RICS, as set down in its practice statement.
    - That the expert understands the duty to the court and has complied with it.

Provided that the report satisfies each of the above requirements, the expert has free rein to organise and write the report as he or she wishes. A suggested skeleton for an expert report, which might be used in an unopposed claim where the parties have not agreed the rent, is at appendix 14.

Difficulties can sometimes arise where the position of the parties is radically different. In such cases, the surveyor should not attempt to pre-judge the outcome and provide expert evidence based on that assumed outcome. If facts are known to be in dispute, the surveyor should clearly express any effect on his or her opinion of every set of facts in dispute. Unless the surveyor considers one set of facts as improbable or less probable (in which rare case the surveyor can express that view) he or she should therefore either prepare the written report on alternative bases or seek directions from the court as to the basis on which the report should be prepared.

Use of documents

Documents will invariably provide the factual basis for the report, but the client need not supply those documents that the surveyor already has. Similarly, the surveyor may obtain documents from third parties. However, in each case, where the expert intends to rely on any such documents, it is necessary to:

- discuss them with the client's solicitors. The other side may require them to be authenticated (see below); and
- append such documents to the written report, where practicable. If the number of appendices is large, or unwieldy, they should be kept in a file separately from the main report.

Where one party has access to information that is not readily available to the other party, the court may direct the party who has access to the information to prepare, file and copy to the other party a document recording it (CPR 35.9). If experts require such information and it has not been disclosed, they should discuss the position with those instructing them without delay. Unless a document is essential, some regard should be had to whether the cost and time involved in producing or providing it would be proportionate (paragraph 12.2 of the Protocol).

Hearsay and comparable transactions

Hearsay is evidence given by a witness in court of a statement made by some other person out of court (whether orally or, importantly, in writing) that the person giving evidence asserts is true. Essentially it involves asserting that something about which one has only second-hand knowledge is true.

In unopposed claims, an expert report will invariably refer to matters that are outside the expert's immediate knowledge such as, for example, the terms of comparable transactions in which he or she was not personally involved. Prior to the passing of the *Civil Evidence Act* 1995, such evidence could be adduced but only by following a particular procedure. Since then, the expert can refer freely to such matters, and the court has to decide what weight to give them under the *Civil Evidence Act* 1995.

Usually experts will try to agree the comparables they wish to rely upon. If they cannot be agreed the party wishing to rely on a particular comparable can:

- disclose a document containing its terms, such as the tenancy agreement. If the other side wishes to challenge the authenticity of the document, they must (according to CPR 32.19) serve a notice requiring it to be proved at trial within seven days of disclosure or

- serve a notice to admit facts, not less than 21 days before trial under CPR 32.18. If the other side does not admit the facts contained in the notice, and the party serving that notice successfully proves them at trial, the costs of proving those facts will usually have to be paid by the party receiving the notice – whatever the ultimate outcome; or
- adduce evidence from someone who does have first-hand knowledge of the transaction(s) concerned (by serving a witness summons under CPR Part 34 if necessary).

It is also worth noting that if a particular document is included in a trial bundle that has been agreed, its authenticity cannot be challenged unless the court permits that or the party seeking to challenge the document has previously objected in writing to its inclusion (paragraph 27.2 of CPR Practice Direction 32).

Amendment of a report

A report can be amended at any time, and must be amended if the expert's view as expressed in the report has significantly altered (for example as the result of receiving new evidence) or if a material inaccuracy is discovered.

The amendment can sometimes be conveniently recorded in a memorandum. Where the amendment is wholesale, large or significant and justifies the expense, an amended report should include the reason(s) for the amendment and be re-verified with a new statement of truth.

The surveyor should notify the client, the other side and the court of the need to amend the written report as soon as possible. If timing is short, the surveyor can avoid this by applying to the court for directions.

Requesting directions from the court

An expert can seek directions directly from the court under CPR 35.14, but this should only usually be done as a last resort. If the expert is unsure about something, it is best to first refer back to those instructing him or her.

It may be that the matter can be dealt with by agreement between the parties. If this is not possible, the client may itself apply to the court for directions. In exceptional circumstances, the expert may apply to the court without notifying the client. An example of those circumstances, given in the Academy of Experts' *Code of*

Guidance, is where there has been an attempt to bribe or intimidate the expert.

A direct application for directions is made by letter (on notice of at least seven days to the party instructing the expert and at least four days to the other party, where appropriate – in accordance with paragraph 11.1 of the *Protocol for the Instruction of Experts to give Evidence in Civil Claims*), which should contain:

- the title and number of the claim;
- the expert's full name and name of the party by whom he or she is instructed;
- the directions sought and an explanation as to why they are necessary;
- copies of any relevant documentation; and
- an explanation (where appropriate) of the reasons why he or she seeks permission to deal with the matter without notifying the parties.

The court will deal with the application on paper unless it decides otherwise. If a surveyor is in a position where he or she is considering withdrawing from a case, it is worth deciding whether withdrawal could be avoided by first applying to the court for directions.

Effect of exchange of a report

Once a report has been served by one party on another:

- any party in the proceedings, not just the party on whose behalf it was produced, can use it under (CPR 35.11). Any privilege which previously attached to the report is extinguished, which prevents a party from seeking to withhold unfavourable expert evidence from the court by simply not calling the expert author of that report;
- the party on whom it is served may apply to the court for inspection of any document mentioned in it (CPR 31.14); and
- the party on whom it is served may also apply to the court for an order for specific disclosure of the expert's instructions if there are reasonable grounds to believe that the statement in the report relating to them is inaccurate or incomplete.

If a report has not been disclosed to the other party, it cannot be relied upon unless the court gives permission (CPR 35.13). It is important to remember that the expert report can *only* be used in the proceedings that it relates to (unless all of the parties in those proceedings agree otherwise). It cannot, for example, be used as evidence in a different rent review arbitration.

Dealing with questions from the opposing party

When a party serves an expert report, the receiving party has 28 days within which to put questions to the expert author to clarify what has been written (CPR 35.6(2)). Questions that go wider than clarification are only allowed if the court permits them or the party instructing the expert being questioned agrees.

The expert's response to those questions, which should be given within 28 days of being asked, will be treated as part of the report and accordingly, the RICS practice statement, the CPR and the Protocol apply to their preparation.

The expert is obliged to answer all proper questions (unless directions have been sought from the court and the court has said not to) and if the expert fails to answer, the party instructing him or her may not be able to rely on the written report and/or may not recover the fees or expenses of the expert from the other side (CPR 35.6(4)).

Questions should only be asked once. There cannot be several rounds of questioning to seek, for example, clarification of a response to a request for clarification, unless the parties agree or the court permits this.

I have prepared a report for a tenant in an unopposed claim dealing with rent valuation. I understand from my client's solicitors that my report was served on the landlord over six weeks ago, but I have just received a request for clarification of aspects of my report. What should I do?

The request is out of time. You should refer back to your client's solicitors, who may be able to agree with the landlord's representatives that you should answer the questions put.

Is there any basis for arguing that the questions you have been asked go further than seeking clarification? If so, this is also something that you should discuss with your client's solicitors.

If no agreement can be reached, the landlord may apply to the court for permission to ask a question out of time. If you still think that the questions asked are improper, your client should raise this with the court on the hearing of that application. The court will ultimately direct whether you should answer the questions put and, if so, whether they should be limited so that they do seek clarification of your report only.

Meetings between experts

The court can direct the parties' experts to meet at any time (including a meeting between any shadow experts and a single joint expert), but usually requires them to do so only once their reports have been exchanged. If it is possible (or likely) that a meeting between experts might lead to shorter reports in the first place, some consideration should be given to holding the meeting before exchange. A meeting can take place by telephone or exchange of letters in simpler cases.

The purpose of any meeting is to agree facts or issues and, if that is impossible, to identify those facts or issues which remain in dispute and the reasons for differences in opinion. Meetings can also be useful to identify what action, if any, can be taken to resolve any outstanding issues between the parties. The court may (and usually will) require the experts to prepare a joint statement following their meeting.

Meetings are often stated to be 'without prejudice'. CPR 35.12(4) and (5) make clear that:

* the content of the discussion between the experts at any meeting between them shall not be referred to at trial unless the parties agree; and
* if the experts reach agreement on an issue during their meeting, their clients shall not be bound by that agreement unless they expressly agree to be bound. Save in circumstances where the agreement is unreasonable, it is difficult to envisage in what circumstances a client would not agree to be bound by an expert's view on a particular issue.

Before a meeting takes place, the claimant's expert should prepare and agree an agenda with the defendant's expert. The parties' solicitors may agree a list of questions for the experts to consider and/or respond to. Whilst experts should liaise with their clients closely in preparing and agreeing this beforehand, they should not agree any instructions to limit the discussion or not to make concessions if appropriate. Solicitors and clients do not normally attend the experts' meeting (solicitors, in particular, should not attend unless all parties agree or the court so orders – in accordance with paragraph 18.8 of the Protocol).

The joint statement of issues for the court

The statement should be prepared as soon as possible after the meeting. Whilst its content is not prescribed, it should include:

- a list of issues which are agreed; and
- a list of issues that are not agreed. The experts should give brief reasons for their disagreement, but should not give substantial details of the discussions between them at their meeting (since these should not be disclosed to the court).

Surveyors will be familiar with Scott Schedules, and joint statements invariably follow that format. The statement is addressed to the court, not to the parties (although it may be copied to them), and is prepared for the court's benefit. It should be signed by each of the experts present at the meeting.

Notwithstanding that the experts may have agreed certain issues, the parties instructing them are still permitted to disagree as to those issues. The cases in which they will do so will be rare. The court will, particularly when it comes to consider costs, look unfavourably on a party who seeks to argue a particular issue when that party's expert had agreed it with his or her counterpart unless there are significant and compelling reasons for doing so.

9.9 Giving evidence at trial

An expert is a witness like any other and, as discussed in chapter 6, it is important for any witness to always re-read the written report or statement thoroughly before trial. If acting as an expert, it is worthwhile re-reading CPR Part 35, Practice Direction 35, and any relevant section from the court guide applicable to the court in which trial will take place.

The procedure when giving oral evidence at trial is:

1. Counsel for the party calling the witness will formally call them up to the 'box' to give evidence. The expert will be given a 'holy book of preference' (e.g. the Bible) by the court usher and asked to swear (or affirm) to tell the truth.
2. Next to or in the box will be a number of bundles – these are the trial bundles and the witness will be referred to these whilst giving evidence. Someone will be sitting near to pass the appropriate bundle. The witness should not take any notes or annotated documents into the witness box.
3. The witness will asked to look at a copy of the witness statement or report in the trial bundle. counsel will ask the witness to

confirm his or her name, address and that the copy of the report or witness statement found in the trial bundles is a true copy of the report or statement he or she has signed in the proceedings. The witness will also be asked whether they want to change any part of the report or statement and to confirm that it remains accurate and true. There will be an opportunity to make any corrections.

4. The witness' report or statement will then stand as evidence in chief in the proceedings (i.e. the witness will not normally be asked to repeat any part of it to the court). Counsel may ask a few questions if there are points arising from the report or statements that require correction or clarification.

5. The other side's counsel will then start to cross-examine him. Where there is more than one opposing party each is entitled to cross-examine the witness in turn, provided they do not duplicate the cross-examination that has gone before.

6. After the cross-examination has finished counsel for the party calling the witness will have an opportunity to re-examine on points where the counsel thinks the witness needs to explain further.

7. The judge may also ask the witness questions. If the witness wants to address the judge he or she should be addressed as 'Your Honour' (assuming, as is normal, that the claim is proceeding in the County Court. If in the High Court, the judge is referred to as 'My Lord' or 'My Lady'). Counsel should be addressed as 'Mr/Ms/Mrs'.

8. If there is a break in the witness giving evidence, for instance for lunch or overnight, then the witness is not allowed to discuss the case or evidence with anybody (including the party calling him or her and the legal advisers) until they have finished giving evidence.

Practical guidance for giving evidence

Always direct your replies to the judge.

Take your time answering each question – do not be rushed.

Think about the question before answering.

Answer the actual question asked (and only that question). If you are unclear, ask for the question to be repeated or explained. You should always be specific in the way you answer the question: do not generalise.

Answer the question fully but do not volunteer information. If counsel needs more information, they will ask for it.

If you do not know the answer to a question or you cannot remember a detail or fact **do not speculate**. Say so or give an indication of how certain you are.

If you think you have made a mistake, **correct yourself** even if it is later in your evidence when you realise it.

You should only have to give evidence as to matters within your own expertise or knowledge – **if an issue is outside your area of expertise or knowledge, say so**.

Do not let yourself be irritated by cross-examination questions. **Never lose your temper** – be polite but firm at all times. Do not make any comments other than the answers to the questions put to you.

Avoid jargon and technical terms where possible.

Do not try to memorise answers to possible questions in advance as the answer may appear rehearsed.

Speak clearly and simply. If necessary, repeat a previous answer by way of explanation.

If you need to consult a document, ask for it.

If you are shown a document, read it even if you think you are familiar with it. Do not assume you know what questions will follow.

Remember that the examiner might try to bore and tire you. **Be alert**, particularly towards the end of the examination. If you require a short break, ask for one.

9.10   Single joint experts

Originally hailed as a means of significantly decreasing the cost of litigation, the reality is that single joint experts (SJE) are rarely used. The court has the power to impose the use of a SJE on the parties (under CPR 35.7(1)), but where multi-track cases are concerned will do so only in exceptional cases.

In unopposed claims, for example, where rent is in issue, valuation is a more subjective exercise than – say – medical diagnosis in a personal injury claim. This is probably reflected by the court's unwillingness to impose SJEs on the parties in claims under LTA 1954 whereas in other types of claim it encourages their use.

The only type of case in which it might be appropriate to use a SJE is where the difference between the parties' positions is relatively small, but the size of any dispute will need to be put into context.

L lets premises to T and the passing rent is £250,000 per annum. T has made an unopposed claim, but the level of rent is in issue. L has asked for £255,000 per annum, whereas T has asked for £245,000. It might be appropriate for the court to impose the use of a SJE.

Whereas, if the passing rent is £25,000 per annum and L had asked for £30,000 per annum, and T £25,000. It is unlikely that the court should impose the use of a SJE unless the parties agree.

In the rare cases in which a SJE is imposed, the parties invariably instruct their own shadow expert to comment on the evidence given by the SJE, such that costs are in fact increased.

In *Daniels v Walker* (2000)[157], the Court of Appeal said that the correct approach was to regard a joint instruction as the first step in obtaining expert evidence on a particular issue which, whilst it might be hoped to be the final step, need not be if there were good reasons for seeking further advice and/or to challenge the views of the SJE.

The court retains a discretion to allow evidence from a shadow expert: it may not exercise that discretion if the costs involved were disproportionate, and should not normally do so in any event unless the SJE and the shadow expert have met to see whether they can reach agreement.

The duties of single joint experts

The duties and responsibilities of a SJE are the same as for any other expert witness, although arguably the evidence (if no shadow expert is called) will have greater significance for the proceedings as a whole. As such, the parties may place greater reliance on acting fairly than they might if they were adducing evidence from their own separate expert.

Appointment of a single joint expert

The parties appoint a SJE jointly, but if the parties cannot agree on who should be instructed by them, the court may select someone from a list prepared by the parties and give further directions as to their instruction (under CPR 35.7(3)).

Each party can send instructions to the expert, provided they are copied to the other party (in accordance with CPR 35.8(1) and (3)) and unless the court orders otherwise, the parties will be jointly and severally liable for the expert's fees (under CPR 35.8(5)).

10

The tenant's right to statutory compensation

Under section 37 of the *Landlord and Tenant Act* 1954 (LTA 1954) a tenant is usually entitled to statutory compensation on vacating its premises if the landlord has opposed the grant of a new tenancy solely on one or more of the following grounds:

(e) subletting of part;
(f) demolition and reconstruction;
(g) landlord's own re-occupation.

This chapter looks at the statutory compensation that a business tenant might be entitled to if its landlord opposes renewal of the tenancy.

It is worth noting that a business tenant might also be entitled to statutory compensation under the *Landlord and Tenant Act* 1927 for any improvements it has made to the holding, but this topic is outside the scope of this book and the reader is directed to other landlord and tenant books[158].

In short, statutory compensation will be paid to a tenant where:

- the landlord's section 25 notice or counter-notice contains *only* grounds (e),(f) and/or (g); and
- the landlord's section 25 notice/counter-notice contains grounds (e), (f) and/or (g) and any other ground, but the landlord later cease to rely on the other ground so only (e), (f) and/or (g) remain; or
- the landlord only successfully opposes renewal/obtains a termination order solely on grounds (e), (f) and/or (g); and
- one of three 'compensation cases' applies:

  1. either the tenant does not apply for a new tenancy or the landlord does not apply for a termination order; or

2. the tenant's application for a new tenancy or the landlord's application for a termination order is withdrawn; or
3. the tenant's application for a new tenancy is dismissed or the landlord's application for a termination order succeeds solely on grounds (e), (f) and/or (g); and

- the tenant quits the holding; and
- the right to compensation has not been properly excluded under the tenancy agreement.

This chapter examines:

- when compensation is available (section 10.1);
- when it becomes payable (section 10.2);
- how much can be claimed (section 10.3);
- contracting out of the right to compensation (section 10.4); and
- compensation for landlord's misrepresentation (section 10.5).

10.1   When compensation is available

The landlord must have first served either a section 25 notice or a counter-notice opposing renewal on one or more of grounds (e), (f) and (g). There are then three 'compensation cases' when the right to compensation arises (although the situation is different if the landlord has relied on other grounds *as well as* any of grounds (e)–(g) – see later in this chapter for more details):

- **Where no application for a new tenancy/termination order is made** – As soon as a landlord serves notice relying on any of grounds (e)–(g), the tenant becomes entitled to compensation if he or she later quits the holding. This is so even if the landlord later withdraws the grounds of opposition (it is possible for a superior landlord to withdraw a section 25 notice in certain circumstances, see chapter 4). If the tenant then leaves the premises once the section 25/26 notice expires, the compensation must be paid. However, the situation might be different if the tenant vacates before the section 25/26 notice expires. Also, if the landlord has included grounds other than (e), (f), or (g) then compensation is not due unless the landlord ceases to rely on the other grounds.
- **Where the tenant withdraws its renewal proceedings or the landlord withdraws its application for a termination order** – If the tenant applies for a new tenancy but later withdraws ('discontinues') the renewal proceedings, the tenant remains entitled to compensation. If the landlord has included grounds other than (e), (f), or (g) then compensation is not payable unless the landlord has ceased to rely on those other grounds.
- **Where the tenant's renewal proceedings are dismissed or the landlord's termination proceedings are successful** – In either of these cases, the tenant is entitled to compensation if the landlord has succeeded solely on grounds (e), (f) and/or (g).

I am advising a landlord who is thinking about redeveloping his premises. The landlord has said he might later change his mind and not proceed with the development but he wants to keep his options open for now. I have advised that he should consider serving a section 25 notice opposing renewal, relying on ground (f). Issues of proving the necessary intention aside, is there anything else I should be advising my client?

Yes. You must warn your client that as soon as he serves the notice he may become liable to pay statutory compensation if the tenant leaves. If he later decides not to redevelop but the tenant vacates the premises without being granted a new tenancy, compensation must still be paid. In some cases this can be hundreds of thousands of pounds. If you have not advised your client about this possibility then you will probably have been negligent and you might then have to reimburse your client the entire compensation amount.

Traps for tenants

The last two scenarios (opposite) contain traps for the unwary tenant, as the entitlement to compensation only exists if:

- the tenant withdraws its application or the landlord withdraws its application for a termination order;
- the tenant's application is dismissed by the court; or
- the landlord's application for a termination order succeeds; and
- in each case the tenant quits the holding.

Were the tenant to cease business occupation of the premises before any of the above events then he or she could arguably lose the right to compensation.

T is the business tenant of a shop unit. The landlord, L, serves a section 25 notice opposing a new tenancy on ground (f) and then applies for a termination order from the court to end the tenancy. T's solicitors review L's claim and decides that L is able to prove the necessary intention to carry out substantial construction works. They advise T that there is no point wasting money opposing the claim.

L's solicitors make an offer that if T immediately surrenders the tenancy then they will not seek the cost of the proceedings. T's solicitors advise her to agree, which T does and then vacates the shop and returns the keys to L, effecting a surrender of the tenancy by operation of law.

T's solicitors then ask L's to arrange for payment of the statutory compensation, but they correctly refuse as T's surrender does not fit any of the compensation scenarios set out in section 37 of the LTA 1954. After all, T has not vacated the premises as a result of L's termination application succeeding and T has therefore lost the right to compensation (although T might have a claim in negligence against the solicitors for poor advice).

A tenant might not be entitled to compensation even on quitting the premises if the right to compensation is specifically excluded in the tenancy agreement.

Relying on other grounds as well as (e), (f) or (g)

A tenant is entitled to compensation if the landlord only relies successfully on grounds (e), (f) and/or (g). If the landlord also relies successfully on any of the other statutory grounds of opposition, then the tenant has no right to compensation (section 37(1A) and (1B) of LTA 1954).

A tenant will only be entitled to compensation if either:

- the landlord withdraws the other grounds of opposition; or
- the landlord successfully opposes the grant of a new tenancy only on grounds (e), (f) and/or (g) and not on any other ground.

So, how does this affect the compensation cases detailed at the start of this section? Assuming that the landlord has served a notice/counter-notice relying on ground (e), (f) and/or (g) and any of the other grounds:

- **Where no application for a new tenancy or a termination order is made** – The tenant will not be entitled to any compensation if it simply vacates its premises once the section 25/26 notice expires.
- **Where the tenant withdraws its renewal proceedings** – The tenant will not be entitled to any compensation.
- **Where the tenant's renewal proceedings are dismissed or the landlord's termination proceedings are successful** – The tenant will not be entitled to any compensation if the landlord successfully relied on one of the other grounds of opposition. This is so even if the landlord also successfully relied on any of grounds (e)–(g).

L serves a section 25 notice on tenant, T, opposing renewal of the tenancy and relies on grounds (b) (persistent delay in paying rent), (f) and (g) in the notice. T subsequently vacates the premises once the notice expires and will not be entitled to any compensation, even though grounds (f) and (g) were relied on in the notice.

If T had applied to court for a new tenancy there would still be no entitlement to compensation if the court finds that T has persistently delayed paying rent even if it also decides that L has proved grounds (f) and (g). However, if the court had decided that ground (b) had not been proved, then T would have been entitled to compensation. This is because T's application was dismissed due to grounds (f) and/or (g).

Where a landlord has relied on various grounds but only succeeded on any of grounds (e)–(g), the tenant can ask the court to issue a certificate confirming this under section 37(4) LTA 1954.

A tactic for landlords

If a landlord intends to rely on any of grounds (e)–(g), then it is worthwhile deciding whether it is possible to properly rely on any of the other statutory grounds of opposition. If the landlord can, then it will be possible to oppose the grant of a new tenancy without having to pay any compensation. However, if a landlord does not have a truthful and honest belief in any of the grounds specified in its notice/counter-notice then he or she runs the risk of having the notice declared invalid (see chapter 4 for further details).

10.2   When does the compensation become payable?

Section 37(1) of LTA 1954 states that the tenant is entitled to be paid the compensation 'on quitting the holding'. In other words, once the tenant gives up vacant possession of the premises it occupies for business purposes it is then entitled to receive its compensation. However, tenants still need to be careful even at this stage of the compensation process.

Tenancy agreements often contain clauses excluding the right to compensation. These will be valid *unless* the tenant (or its predecessor in the business) has occupied the holding for five years or more (whether under the current tenancy or a succession of tenancies).

However, if a tenant permanently moves out of the premises before the fixed term expires (or if periodic, before the periodic tenancy has been brought to an end) the tenant will no longer occupy them for business purposes and the tenancy will then no longer be one to which Part II LTA 1954 applies. Accordingly, even if the tenant has occupied for five years or more the exclusion clause is valid and so the tenant loses its right to the compensation.

T is a periodic business tenant of office premises and has occupied them for 15 years. T's tenancy agreement contains a clause excluding the right to compensation under LTA 1954. The landlord, L, serves a section 25 notice relying on ground (f) to end the tenancy on 31 December 2006. T decides not to renew her tenancy and does not make a court application and nor does L, so accordingly the date on which T is to quit the premises will be 31 December 2006. If T quits on 3 December 2006 (and not earlier) T will be entitled to compensation.

However, if T decides to leave the premises as soon as possible and vacates them on 1 September 2006, ceasing to occupy them for business purposes. As a result the tenancy is no longer one to which Part II of LTA 1954 applies. The exclusion clause then becomes effective meaning T is prevented from claiming compensation.

So, where a tenancy agreement excludes the compensation provisions of LTA 1954, a tenant who would otherwise be entitled to compensation (because they or their business predecessors occupied the premises for five years or more) must obtain the landlord's written agreement that the tenant will still be paid its statutory compensation if it quits the premises early.

There are cases where a tenant has vacated shortly before the date in the section 25/26 notice but the court has held that the business occupation has nevertheless continued. In *Bacchiocchi v Academic Agency Ltd*[159] when the tenant quit the premises 12 days before the expiry of the three month period after the final disposal of its renewal proceedings. The court held that the tenant's act of vacating the premises was part of ordinary business activity where a business was being run down so the tenant was still in business occupation and entitled to statutory compensation.

In contrast, in *Sight and Sound Ltd v Books Etc*[160], where the tenant vacated five months before the section 25 notice expired and was held to have lost its right to compensation. So, tenants should wait to vacate or obtain the written agreement to avoid any risk.

10.3 How much compensation can be claimed?

The basic formula is:

$$A \times B \times C$$

where:

- A = Rateable value of the holding;
- B = 'The appropriate multiplier'; and
- C = 1 or 2 (i.e. single or double compensation)

Taking each part of the formula in turn:

- **A – Rateable value of the holding**
  The rateable value of commercial premises can be found in the local valuation office's list. The relevant list is the one that is in force at the date of service of the section 25 notice/26 request.
- **B – 'The appropriate multiplier'**
  As at 1 November 2005 this figure was 1. It can be changed by the Secretary of State making provision by statutory instrument (under section 37(8) LTA 1954) and has previously been as high as 3 (between 1985 and 1990).
- **C – Single or double compensation**
  Under section 37(3) of LTA 1954, if this figure is to be 2 (i.e. double compensation) then the tenant must show that:
  - the holding has been occupied for business purposes during the whole of the 14 years immediately preceding the termination/renewal date in the section 25 notice/26 request;
  - the business has been carried on by 'the occupier' (this does not have to be a tenant or even a predecessor in title). It is enough if the business is carried on by the occupier of the holding for the time being); and
  - if 'the occupier' changed in the 14 year period, the new occupier was the successor to the same business carried on by the immediately preceding occupier (it does not matter if the nature of the business changes during the 14 year period).

In all other cases this figure will be 1 (i.e. single compensation). Under section 37(3A) of LTA 1954, if one part of the holding has been occupied for 14 years and the other parts for less, then the one part qualifies for double compensation and the others for single. However, for compensation claims where the section 25 notice/26 request was served before 1 June 2004, the tenant is entitled to double compensation for the entire holding even if it has only occupied part of the holding for the requisite 14 years). The total compensation figure will then be the aggregate of the different amounts of compensation allotted to each part of the holding (section 37(3A) of LTA 1954).

In 1992 A bought the freehold of a two-storey office block and runs an employment agency business from there. In 2000 A vacated the first floor and granted a tenancy of it to B who runs another employment business there. Then in 2001 A sold his freehold of the building to C and took a five-year leaseback of the ground floor. A continued to run his employment agency business throughout and then in 2008 C decides to demolish the building and serves section 25 notices to both A and B relying on ground (f) specifying 31 January 2009 as the termination date.

A will be entitled to double compensation for his tenancy of the ground floor as at 31 December 2008 (i.e. immediately preceding the termination of his tenancy) A will have occupied that floor for the purposes of the employment business for a continuous period of 14 years. B will only be entitled to compensation equal to the rateable value for her tenancy of the first floor as even though B carries on the same type of business as A, it is not the same *business – B did not acquire any part of A's business when taking the tenancy.*

In 1992 A was granted a 15 year tenancy of premises which he used for an insurance business and then in 1995 A sold the business to B and lawfully assigned the tenancy of the premises. Then in 2002 B sold the insurance business and started a catering business from the same premises.

In 2004 B sold the catering business to and lawfully assigned the tenancy over to C who remains in business occupation until the tenancy expires in 2007, when the landlord serves a section 25 notice opposing renewal on ground (f) specifying a termination date of 31 January 2008.

C will be entitled to double compensation, because for the 14 years before the termination date either she or another occupier was occupying the holding for business purposes. The change of business in 2002 does not affect the double compensation entitlement because B changed the business during the period of occupation and C was the successor to that business in 2004.

However, if at the time of the 2004 assignment C had occupied the premises for a different business, then C would not have complied with part 'C' in the basic compensation formula and would only be entitled to single compensation.

I have been a business tenant of the same premises for 25 years. However, my business used to be that of an undertaker and then, seven years ago, I changed my business and became an accountant. My tenancy has now ended and my landlord has served me with a section 25 notice opposing the grant of a new tenancy on ground (f). Will my change of business affect my double compensation entitlement?'

No. Provided you are occupying your premises for business purposes when the section 25 notice expires, you will have been in continuous business occupation for the necessary 14 years and your business change is not important.

Split reversions

If the reversion to the tenancy is held separately by different legal owners (as opposed to joint owners), then under section 37(3B) of LTA 1954 compensation is determined and payable separately for each part held by the relevant landlord.

10.4 Contracting out of the compensation provisions

As discussed in chapter 2, it is possible to avoid compensation provisions (and security of tenure provisions) entirely by adopting the contracting-out procedure when granting the tenancy. Where a tenancy is not contracted out it is still possible to exclude or reduce the tentant's right to compensation.

In most modern tenancy agreements there are clauses that purport to exclude the right to statutory compensation. The clause in the tenancy agreement will be invalid, however, if:

- the holding has been occupied for business purposes during the whole of the five years immediately preceding the date on which the tenant has to quit the holding (i.e. the date in the section 25/26 notice or, if later, three months after the final disposal of any renewal/termination proceedings); and
- the business has been carried on by 'the occupier' (if 'the occupier' changed in the five year period, but the new occupier was the successor to the same business carried on by the immediately preceding occupier then the clause is still invalid).

However, an agreement made _after_ the right to compensation has accrued, is valid. Further, if the above conditions are not met (so that in essence the continuous business occupation at the premises has been for less than five years) then the clause limiting or excluding the right to statutory compensation will be valid.

So, if a tenant has only been in business occupation for three years and the tenancy agreement contains a clause excluding the right to compensation then that clause will not be void and the tenant will not be entitled to compensation if the landlord successfully opposes renewal of its tenancy on any of grounds (e)–(g).

Equally, if there is a break in the chain of business occupation so that only four years continuous occupation can be shown, then a clause excluding or reducing the compensation payable will be valid.

When does the right to compensation accrue?

The Act is not clear. Arguably, the right to compensation accrues as soon as the landlord serves a notice/counter-notice opposing renewal solely on any of grounds (e)–(g). However, some commentators[160] also argue that the right might accrue after the tenant has quit the holding. In the rare circumstance where a landlord and tenant might wish to agree to exclude or reduce the amount of compensation, the authors would suggest that they only do so after the tenant has quit the holding. To do otherwise would run the risk that the agreement was void.

10.5 Compensation for misrepresentation

It is important to note what happens if the landlord misrepresents or conceals material facts about his or her ability to rely on the compensation grounds of (e), (f) and/or (g) and as a result:

- induces the tenant not to apply for a new tenancy;
- induces the tenant to withdraw its application for a new tenancy;
- obtains a termination order; or
- successfully opposes the tenant's application for a new tenancy.

If the tenant quits its premises as a result of such a misrepresentation or concealment, the tenant will be entitled to damages under section 37A LTA 1954.

Section 37A states:

'(1) Where the court –

(a) makes an order for the termination of the current tenancy but does not make an order for the grant of a new tenancy, or

(b) refuses an order for the grant of a new tenancy,

and it is subsequently made to appear to the court that the order was obtained, or the court was induced to refuse the grant, by misrepresentation or the concealment of material facts, the court may order the landlord to pay the tenant such sum as appears sufficient as compensation for damage or loss sustained by the tenant as the result of the order or refusal.

(2) Where –

(a) the tenant has quit the holding –

(i) after making but withdrawing an application [for a renewal tenancy]; or

(ii) without making such an application; and

(b) it is made to appear to the court that the tenant did so by reason of misrepresentation or the concealment of material facts,

the court may order the landlord to pay to the tenant such sum as appears sufficient as compensation for damage or loss sustained by the tenant as a result of quitting the holding.'

Whether the tenant will actually obtain damages will depend on its ability to prove to the court that the landlord has misrepresented or concealed material facts. 'Material facts' is not defined by LTA 1954, but will include representations by the landlord about its intention or ability to rely on a statutory ground of opposition if these were made to induce the tenant to leave the premises in circumstances where the landlord has no real intention or ability to rely on those grounds, or to persuade the court to refuse to order the grant of a new tenancy.

The tenant must also show that the landlord's misrepresentation has caused it to suffer a loss.

Any damages awarded would take into account any statutory compensation that has already been paid to the tenant.

11

Alternative Dispute Resolution and LTA 1954

As discussed in previous chapters the standard legal process for resolving business tenancy renewal disputes is through litigation. However, there are other methods of dispute resolution available that might avoid the inflexibility, expense and delay of litigation.

This chapter provides an overview of the different ways of resolving issues that arise during the lease renewal/termination process. It explains the advantages and disadvantages of ADR compared with going to court and considers:

- Professional Arbitration on Court Terms (PACT) (section 11.1);
- Arbitration (section 11.2);
- Independent expert determination (section 11.3); and
- Mediation (section 11.4).

11.1 'PACT'

Professional Arbitration on Court Terms was devised by the Law Society and the Incorporated Society of Valuers and Auctioneers (which is now part of RICS) and was first introduced in 1997. It is designed to deal with unopposed renewal claims where there is a dispute about rent and/or other terms of the new tenancy.

Under the scheme the parties agree to refer one or more disputed issues to a specialist solicitor or surveyor, as appropriate. A dispute on rent levels would be referred to a surveyor whereas a dispute on tenancy terms might be referred to a solicitor. There is, though, nothing to stop the parties agreeing to appoint a surveyor/solicitor to deal with rent and tenancy terms.

The referral is achieved by the parties signing a consent order (samples of which are available in the *PACT – Professional*

Arbitration on Court Terms document available on the RICS website[162]) in which they agree to have the dispute decided by the surveyor/solicitor. If the judge agrees the order, the dispute is then referred to the third party expert.

PACT works by the parties agreeing to exclude the court's jurisdiction to decide the disputed issue(s) that the parties have specifically identified within the consent order. The parties also decide whether the third party expert will act as an arbitrator or an independent expert when dealing with the dispute (see below for the main differences between arbitration and independent expert determination). In addition, the third party expert is usually given the power to decide who should bear the costs of the PACT process.

Subject to any rights of appeal, the PACT decision will be binding on the parties. If necessary, the parties can then formally apply to the court for the new tenancy to be granted on the terms decided by the third party expert/arbitrator.

Advantages over litigation	Disadvantages over litigation
Flexibility: The parties are free to agree the procedure that the third party expert adopts to decide the disputed point(s).	A PACT decision will not produce a binding legal authority. If you are acting for a landlord or tenant with a large portfolio of properties, you might need a court decision to create case-law on a particular point.
Cost: As the parties are able to decide the procedure, they can save time and therefore often cut costs when compared to the litigation process.	A PACT referral might be used by one side to delay a decision on the disputed point (e.g. for valuation reasons in a rising market).
Speed: Compared to the generally lengthy and time-consuming court process, PACT referrals can be decided in a matter of weeks.	The difficulty in appealing a PACT decision. If the third party expert acted as an arbitrator then there is a limited right of appeal (if they acted as an independent expert there is no right of appeal).
Quality of decision: As a specialist decides the dispute, the decisions are likely to be more commercial than if decided by a non-specialist judge.	

Given the advantages, it is perhaps surprising that parties involved in business tenancy renewal disputes have not really taken up the PACT scheme. This may be the result of a lack of detailed knowledge of PACT amongst the legal and surveying professions. PACT referrals may increase as a result of the 1 June 2004 changes, which the authors believe has led to the courts starting to push renewal proceedings to early trials.

11.2 Arbitration

As with PACT, the parties have to agree to refer the disputed issues to an arbitrator. If court proceedings have already been issued, the parties would be best advised to adopt the PACT procedure.

PACT has been specifically established to deal with referrals to third party experts during business tenancy renewal proceedings. Where PACT cannot be used, the parties will usually need to enter into a written, binding agreement to refer a dispute to arbitration (unless the tenancy agreement contains one). Without that agreement, the arbitrator's decision will not be binding on the parties (specialist legal advice should be taken about the drafting of an agreement).

Arbitrators within England and Wales are governed by the *Arbitration Act* 1996, which sets out the arbitrator's powers. The arbitration process tends to be relatively formal and the usual steps following an arbitrator's appointment are:

1. The parties identify the issue in dispute and submit their case statements.
2. The arbitrator requires disclosure of all relevant documents and exchange of evidence.
3. The arbitrator invites written submissions and counter-submissions from each party on the other's statements of case.
4. The arbitrator may hold a hearing to allow for oral submissions and/or cross-examination of any witness.
5. The arbitrator is required to give a decision with reasons (unless the parties agree otherwise).
6. Unless agreed otherwise, the arbitrator decides who pays the costs. The court can formally determine fees if they are not agreed.

An arbitrator sits in a quasi-judicial capacity and cannot make a decision without having received evidence and submissions from the parties (subject to the limited right to make a decision where one party refuses to participate in the case). As a result (and due to the specific provisions of the *Arbitration Act* 1996) the arbitrator cannot be sued in negligence for any errors in the decision unless the arbitrator has shown bias.

Due to the relatively formal (and potentially expensive) nature of the arbitration process, it is generally considered more suited to higher value disputes. In disputes under LTA 1954, this type of ADR is particularly suited to valuation disputes where the new or interim rents cannot be agreed.

Advantages over litigation	Disadvantages over litigation
Confidentiality: An arbitrator's decision is confidential.	Speed: Unless the parties curtail the process, arbitration can be as lengthy as the litigation process.
Quality of decision: The arbitrator is usually a person chosen because of their specialism in the field that concerns the dispute. Judges are often not.	Binding authority: An arbitrator's decision is only binding on the parties on the particular point in dispute. It will not serve as a legal authority for any similar disputes between the parties or the world at large.
Certainty: There is only a limited right of appeal from an arbitrator's decision either for an obvious error on a point of law, a serious irregularity or bias. Accordingly, it is harder to appeal an arbitrator's decision than a court order.	Cost: The statutory procedural framework under the *Arbitration Act* 1996 is not that dissimilar from the court process. As a result, costs also tend to be relatively equal to those in the litigation process. Also, if an arbitrator needs help on a point of law that affects the arbitration, they will usually appoint counsel for advice – at extra cost to the parties. However, as the parties are free to agree the arbitration process there is some scope for reducing costs.
Flexibility: Subject to the arbitrator's power to actively manage the case, the parties can agree in advance the arbitration procedure and so can also control its speed.	

11.3 Independent expert determination

As with PACT, the parties have to agree to refer the disputed issues for independent expert determination. Again, if court proceedings have already been issued, the parties would be best advised to adopt the PACT procedure. Where PACT cannot be used, the parties will need to enter into a written, binding agreement to refer a dispute for independent expert determination. Without that agreement, the independent expert's decision will not be binding on the parties (specialist legal advice should be taken about the drafting of an agreement).

Unlike arbitrations, there is no statutory framework governing independent expert determinations. The independent expert's powers and duties should be contained within the document appointing him. In general terms and unless the contract appointing him or her provides otherwise, the independent expert:

- has a duty to investigate the facts for him- or herself, including details of comparables and all other information relevant to the question he or she has been asked to decide;

- bases the decision on his or her own knowledge and experience;
- has no power to award costs when making the decision;
- is not obliged to give any reasons for the decision;
- cannot require the parties to disclose evidence, provide written or oral submissions or attend a hearing;
- may be liable to the parties in negligence for any defects in the decision; and
- cannot have the decision appealed (the court does have very limited powers to set the decision aside, e.g. if an expert made a decision about something that was not actually referred to them).

As can be seen, the independent expert is almost entirely a creature of the parties' own making. Unless they set down detailed and specific guidelines for how the expert is to act, the independent expert has a free rein to decide how to reach the decision.

Advantages over litigation	Disadvantages over litigation
Quality of decision: The independent expert is usually a person chosen because of their specialism in the field that concerns the dispute. Judges are often not.	Their fees may be higher than an arbitrator as they are being asked to take liability for their decision.
Flexibility and speed: Because the parties can decide the procedure, they can also control the speed of the process. Depending on the procedure agreed by the parties, the independent expert determination can take place within days or weeks of the independent expert's appointment.	Lack of thoroughness: Unless given specific powers, the expert cannot compel the parties to provide evidence or attend hearings. As a result, the decision may be based on weak or scant evidence.
Certainty: Unless agreed otherwise, there is no right of appeal from an independent expert determination. There is a very limited right for the court to set a decision aside, e.g. if the expert decided on the wrong issue.	Certainty: Ironically, the advantage of certainty can also be a serious disadvantage. If an expert makes a negligent decision, then a party who suffers loss as a result can recover damages against him. However, if the expert made 'the wrong decision about the right point in dispute', there is nothing the wronged party can do to avoid the fact that it is bound by that wrong decision.
Cost: Unless the parties adopt a procedure that allows detailed submissions and counter-submissions, the costs will be limited to instructing and paying the independent expert.	

Confidentiality: An independent expert's decision is given in private and is not automatically a matter of public record. In addition, the parties could agree to the decision remaining confidential.	Lack of reasoned decision: The parties will not be able to understand why the independent expert reached the decision. Even if they wanted to set a decision aside, this lack of reasons means that they will probably not be able to.
Personal liability: The independent expert owes a legal duty of care to the parties for the decision. The expert can be sued in negligence for any errors in their decision. A judge cannot be sued, even if the decision is utterly wrong.	

Independent expert determination is normally only suited to lower value disputes where the inability to appeal an obviously wrong decision is not that important. Its main advantage is that it can be a very quick and relatively cheap method of dispute resolution when compared with arbitration or litigation. In disputes under LTA 1954, this type of ADR is particularly suited to minor new tenancy terms or where the amount in dispute is relatively small.

11.4 Mediation

Mediation is the most informal of the different types of ADR and is in essence a glorified (but often effective) negotiation. The mediator's role is not a judgmental one and they do not make any decisions about the disputed issue. Their task is to understand each parties' position in detail and see whether there is any common ground on which to build the basis of a settlement. A mediator is also always very careful to secure the confidence of both parties by not disclosing without agreement any aspect of their case to the other side.

Whilst a mediator does not decide who is right or wrong, they should challenge each party's standpoint on the dispute and should also encourage the parties to move from their entrenched positions so that a deal can eventually be reached. This is undertaken during 'without prejudice' discussions that take place between the parties and the mediator. Any eventual settlement is only ever binding once both parties have agreed it.

If the parties agree to enter into mediation, they must agree the appointment of a suitable mediator. They then have to agree what information the mediator should be provided with and where the mediation takes place, as well as agreeing who will bear the costs of the mediation process (normally each side bears their own costs of the meditation and pays half of the mediator's fee).

Advantages over litigation	Disadvantages over litigation
Flexibility: As mediation is a form of negotiation, the parties are free to enter or leave it at any point. They are not bound by any settlement until it is formally agreed. The 'without prejudice' nature of the process means information revealed in a mediation cannot normally be used against them in court.	Delay: If no settlement is reached in the mediation the parties will have to spend yet more time seeking a final resolution. Also, mediation might be used by one party as an attempt to waste time to improve their own position.
Speed: As there is no formal procedure, the mediation process can be set up quickly. Mediations themselves often take only a few hours and rarely more than a day.	No final decision: Mediation is entirely dependent on the parties agreeing to settle. If they cannot reach a settlement, then the dispute remains live.
Cost: As each party tends to bear their own costs of the mediation, it is only the mediator's fee that is an additional expense. However, parties might want their professional advisers to attend the mediation and these costs must be factored in.	Giving away secrets: Due to its informal nature, mediation can encourage parties to divulge information that normally they would not. Although given on a 'without prejudice' basis, this disclosure might strengthen the other party's hand in the litigation. Alternatively, it might lead them on a chain of enquiry so that the disclosed information is placed before the court via other means.
Confidentiality: A settlement achieved by mediation is not a matter of public record (unlike a court judgment). The parties can also agree that the settlement remains confidential to them.	
Courts like mediation: Where one party unreasonably refuses to attempt mediation it might be penalised by the court on costs, even if it later wins the dispute at court[163].	

Relationship: Settlements achieved by mediation tend to arise because both parties are 'happy' to reach a settlement. The settlement is one reached by agreement, rather than being forced on one side or the other by the court. In turn, this can help maintain a more harmonious landlord and tenant relationship.	
Possibilities: The court is constrained by sections 32–35 LTA 1954 in terms of what it can order. In a mediation the parties can be more creative about any settlement terms.	

Mediation is not always a suitable form of ADR. For example, a dispute as to whether a landlord can prove its intention to demolish under ground (f) is not likely to be suited to mediation. The tenant is unlikely to agree to give up possession and the landlord is equally unlikely to agree the grant of a new tenancy, so a judicial decision will still be needed.

However, mediation can be ideally suited to situations where all that is really in dispute is a sum of money. In disputes under LTA 1954, this type of ADR can be particularly suited to differences on the parties' valuation positions (no matter how large). Good mediators are adept at encouraging the parties to find common ground from which to reach a settlement. They also have the advantage that they are entirely independent of the dispute in a way that the parties and their representatives are not. This is useful where the parties have become entrenched and have lost sight of the strengths (as well as the weaknesses) of the other side's position.

Agreeing the appointment

If parties cannot agree who should be appointed as arbitrator or independent expert etc they are usually able to agree that the appointment should be made by an independent third party organisation. Both the Law Society and RICS offer this type of service for surveyors and solicitors. The Centre for Effective Dispute Resolution offers a similar service for the appointment of mediators. More information can be found on their respective websites[164].

Appendices

Appendix 1: *Landlord and Tenant Act* 1954

1954 CHAPTER 56

An Act to provide security of tenure for occupying tenants under certain leases of residential property at low rents and for occupying sub-tenants of tenants under such leases; to enable tenants occupying property for business, professional or certain other purposes to obtain new tenancies in certain cases; to amend and extend the Landlord and Tenant Act 1927, the Leasehold Property (Repairs) Act 1938; and section eighty-four of the Law of Property Act 1925; to confer jurisdiction on the County Court in certain disputes between landlords and tenants; to make provision for the termination of tenancies of derelict land; and for purposes connected with the matters aforesaid.

30th July 1954

Part II

Security of Tenure for Business, Professional and other Tenants

Tenancies to which Part II applies

23 Tenancies to which Part II applies

(1) Subject to the provisions of this Act, this Part of this Act applies to any tenancy where the property comprised in the tenancy is or includes premises which are occupied by the tenant and are so occupied for the purposes of a business carried on by him or for those and other purposes.

(1A) Occupation or the carrying on of a business –

    (a) by a company in which the tenant has a controlling interest; or

    (b) where the tenant is a company, by a person with a controlling interest in the company, shall be treated for the purposes of this section as equivalent to occupation or, as the case may be, the carrying on of a business by the tenant.

(1B) Accordingly references (however expressed) in this Part of this Act to the business of, or to use, occupation or enjoyment by, the tenant shall be construed as including references to the business of, or to use, occupation or enjoyment by, a company falling within subsection (1A)(a) above or a person falling within subsection (1A)(b) above.

(2) In this Part of this Act the expression 'business' includes a trade, profession or employment and includes any activity carried on by a body of persons, whether corporate or unincorporated.

(3) In the following provisions of this Part of this Act the expression 'the holding', in relation to a tenancy to which this Part of this Act applies, means the property comprised in the tenancy, there being excluded any part thereof which is occupied neither by the tenant nor by a person employed by the tenant and so employed for the purposes of a business by reason of which the tenancy is one to which this Part of this Act applies.

(4) Where the tenant is carrying on a business, in all or any part of the property comprised in a tenancy, in breach of a prohibition (however expressed) of use for business purposes which subsists under the terms of the tenancy and extends to the whole of that property, this Part of this Act shall not apply to the tenancy unless the immediate landlord or his predecessor in title has consented to the breach or the immediate landlord has acquiesced therein.

In this subsection the reference to a prohibition of use for business purposes does not include a prohibition of use for the purposes of a specified business, or of use for purposes of any but a specified business, but save as aforesaid includes a prohibition of use for the purposes of some one or more only of the classes of business specified in the definition of that expression in subsection (2) of this section.

Continuation and renewal of tenancies

24 Continuation of tenancies to which Part II applies and grant of new tenancies

(1) A tenancy to which this Part of this Act applies shall not come to an end unless terminated in accordance with the provisions of this Part of this Act; and, subject to the following provisions of this Act either the tenant or the landlord under such a tenancy may apply to the court for an order for the grant of a new tenancy –

(a) if the landlord has given notice under section 25 of this Act to terminate the tenancy, or
(b) if the tenant has made a request for a new tenancy in accordance with section twenty-six of this Act.

(2) The last foregoing subsection shall not prevent the coming to an end of a tenancy by notice to quit given by the tenant, by surrender or forfeiture, or by the forfeiture of a superior tenancy unless –

(a) in the case of a notice to quit, the notice was given before the tenant had been in occupation in right of the tenancy for one month; ...

(b) ... [repealed]

(2A) Neither the tenant nor the landlord may make an application under subsection (1) above if the other has made such an application and the application has been served.

(2B) Neither the tenant nor the landlord may make such an application if the landlord has made an application under section 29(2) of this Act and the application has been served.

(2C) The landlord may not withdraw an application under subsection (1) above unless the tenant consents to its withdrawal.

(3) Notwithstanding anything in subsection (1) of this section –

(a) where a tenancy to which this Part of this Act applies ceases to be such a tenancy, it shall not come to an end by reason only of the cesser, but if it was granted for a term of years certain and has been continued by subsection (1) of this section then (without prejudice to the termination thereof in accordance with any terms of the tenancy) it may be terminated by not less than three nor more than six months' notice in writing given by the landlord to the tenant;

(b) where, at a time when a tenancy is not one to which this Part of this Act applies, the landlord gives notice to quit, the operation of the notice shall not be affected by reason that the tenancy becomes one to which this Part of this Act applies after the giving of the notice.

24A Applications for determination of interim rent while tenancy continues

(1) Subject to subsection (2) below, if –

(a) the landlord of a tenancy to which this Part of this Act applies has given notice under section 25 of this Act to terminate the tenancy; or

(b) the tenant of such a tenancy has made a request for a new tenancy in accordance with section 26 of this Act,

either of them may make an application to the court to determine a rent (an 'interim rent') which the tenant is to pay while the tenancy ('the relevant tenancy') continues by virtue of section 24 of this Act and the court may order payment of an interim rent in accordance with section 24C or 24D of this Act.

(2) Neither the tenant nor the landlord may make an application under subsection (1) above if the other has made such an application and has not withdrawn it.

(3) No application shall be entertained under subsection (1) above if it is made more than six months after the termination of the relevant tenancy.

24B Date from which interim rent is payable

(1) The interim rent determined on an application under section 24A(1) of this Act shall be payable from the appropriate date.

(2) If an application under section 24A(1) of this Act is made in a case where the landlord has given a notice under section 25 of this Act, the appropriate date is the earliest date of termination that could have been specified in the landlord's notice.

(3) If an application under section 24A(1) of this Act is made in a case where the tenant has made a request for a new tenancy under section 26 of this Act, the appropriate date is the earliest date that could have been specified in the tenant's request as the date from which the new tenancy is to begin.

24C Amount of interim rent where new tenancy of whole premises granted and landlord not opposed

(1) This section applies where –

  (a) the landlord gave a notice under section 25 of this Act at a time when the tenant was in occupation of the whole of the property comprised in the relevant tenancy for purposes such as are mentioned in section 23(1) of this Act and stated in the notice that he was not opposed to the grant of a new tenancy; or
  (b) the tenant made a request for a new tenancy under section 26 of this Act at a time when he was in occupation of the whole of that property for such purposes and the landlord did not give notice under subsection (6) of that section,

and the landlord grants a new tenancy of the whole of the property comprised in the relevant tenancy to the tenant (whether as a result of an order for the grant of a new tenancy or otherwise).

(2) Subject to the following provisions of this section, the rent payable under and at the commencement of the new tenancy shall also be the interim rent.

(3) Subsection (2) above does not apply where –

  (a) the landlord or the tenant shows to the satisfaction of the court that the interim rent under that subsection differs substantially from the relevant rent; or

(b) the landlord or the tenant shows to the satisfaction of the court that the terms of the new tenancy differ from the terms of the relevant tenancy to such an extent that the interim rent under that subsection is substantially different from the rent which (in default of such agreement) the court would have determined under section 34 of this Act to be payable under a tenancy which commenced on the same day as the new tenancy and whose other terms were the same as the relevant tenancy.

(4) In this section 'the relevant rent' means the rent which (in default of agreement between the landlord and the tenant) the court would have determined under section 34 of this Act to be payable under the new tenancy if the new tenancy had commenced on the appropriate date (within the meaning of section 24B of this Act).

(5) The interim rent in a case where subsection (2) above does not apply by virtue only of subsection (3)(a) above is the relevant rent.

(6) The interim rent in a case where subsection (2) above does not apply by virtue only of subsection (3)(b) above, or by virtue of subsection (3)(a) and (b) above, is the rent which it is reasonable for the tenant to pay while the relevant tenancy continues by virtue of section 24 of this Act.

(7) In determining the interim rent under subsection (6) above the court shall have regard –

(a) to the rent payable under the terms of the relevant tenancy; and
(b) to the rent payable under any sub-tenancy of part of the property comprised in the relevant tenancy,

but otherwise subsections (1) and (2) of section 34 of this Act shall apply to the determination as they would apply to the determination of a rent under that section if a new tenancy of the whole of the property comprised in the relevant tenancy were granted to the tenant by order of the court and the duration of that new tenancy were the same as the duration of the new tenancy which is actually granted to the tenant.

(8) In this section and section 24D of this Act 'the relevant tenancy' has the same meaning as in section 24A of this Act.

24D Amount of interim rent in any other case

(1) The interim rent in a case where section 24C of this Act does not apply is the rent which it is reasonable for the tenant to pay while the relevant tenancy continues by virtue of section 24 of this Act.

(2) In determining the interim rent under subsection (1) above the court shall have regard –

(a) to the rent payable under the terms of the relevant tenancy; and
(b) to the rent payable under any sub-tenancy of part of the property comprised in the relevant tenancy,

but otherwise subsections (1) and (2) of section 34 of this Act shall apply to the determination as they would apply to the determination of a rent under that section if a new tenancy from year to year of the whole of the property comprised in the relevant tenancy were granted to the tenant by order of the court.

(3) If the court –

(a) has made an order for the grant of a new tenancy and has ordered payment of interim rent in accordance with section 24C of this Act, but
(b) either –

(i) it subsequently revokes under section 36(2) of this Act the order for the grant of a new tenancy; or
(ii) the landlord and tenant agree not to act on the order,

the court on the application of the landlord or the tenant shall determine a new interim rent in accordance with subsections (1) and (2) above without a further application under section 24A(1) of this Act.

25 Termination of tenancy by the landlord

(1) The landlord may terminate a tenancy to which this Part of this Act applies by a notice given to the tenant in the prescribed form specifying the date at which the tenancy is to come to an end (hereinafter referred to as 'the date of termination'):

Provided that this subsection has effect subject to the provisions of section 29B(4) of this Act and the provisions of Part IV of this Act as to the interim continuation of tenancies pending the disposal of applications to the court.

(2) Subject to the provisions of the next following subsection, a notice under this section shall not have effect unless it is given not more than twelve nor less than six months before the date of termination specified therein.

(3) In the case of a tenancy which apart from this Act could have been brought to an end by notice to quit given by the landlord –

(a) the date of termination specified in a notice under this section shall not be earlier than the earliest date on which apart from this Part of this Act the tenancy could have been brought to an end by notice to quit given by the landlord on the date of the giving of the notice under this section; and

(b) where apart from this Part of this Act more than six months' notice to quit would have been required to bring the tenancy to an end, the last foregoing subsection shall have effect with the substitution for twelve months of a period six months longer than the length of notice to quit which would have been required as aforesaid.

(4) In the case of any other tenancy, a notice under this section shall not specify a date of termination earlier than the date on which apart from this Part of this Act the tenancy would have come to an end by effluxion of time.

(5) ... [repealed]

(6) A notice under this section shall not have effect unless it states whether the landlord is opposed to the grant of a new tenancy to the tenant.

(7) A notice under this section which states that the landlord is opposed to the grant of a new tenancy to the tenant shall not have effect unless it also specifies one or more of the grounds specified in section 30(1) of this Act as the ground or grounds for his opposition.

(8) A notice under this section which states that the landlord is not opposed to the grant of a new tenancy to the tenant shall not have effect unless it sets out the landlord's proposals as to –

(a) the property to be comprised in the new tenancy (being either the whole or part of the property comprised in the current tenancy);
(b) the rent to be payable under the new tenancy; and
(c) the other terms of the new tenancy.

26 Tenant's request for a new tenancy

(1) A tenant's request for a new tenancy may be made where the current tenancy is a tenancy granted for a term of years certain exceeding one year, whether or not continued by section twenty-four of this Act, or granted for a term of years certain and thereafter from year to year.

(2) A tenant's request for a new tenancy shall be for a tenancy beginning with such date, not more than twelve nor less than six months after the making of the request, as may be specified therein:

Provided that the said date shall not be earlier than the date on which apart from this Act the current tenancy would come to an end by effluxion of time or could be brought to an end by notice to quit given by the tenant.

(3) A tenant's request for a new tenancy shall not have effect unless it is made by notice in the prescribed form given to the landlord and sets out the tenant's proposals as to the property to be comprised in the new tenancy (being either the whole or part of the property comprised in the current tenancy), as to the rent to be payable under the new tenancy and as to the other terms of the new tenancy.

(4) A tenant's request for a new tenancy shall not be made if the landlord has already given notice under the last foregoing section to terminate the current tenancy, or if the tenant has already given notice to quit or notice under the next following section; and no such notice shall be given by the landlord or the tenant after the making by the tenant of a request for a new tenancy.

(5) Where the tenant makes a request for a new tenancy in accordance with the foregoing provisions of this section, the current tenancy shall, subject to the provisions of sections 29B(4) and 36(2) of this Act and the provisions of Part IV of this Act as to the interim continuation of tenancies, terminate immediately before the date specified in the request for the beginning of the new tenancy.

(6) Within two months of the making of a tenant's request for a new tenancy the landlord may give notice to the tenant that he will oppose an application to the court for the grant of a new tenancy, and any such notice shall state on which of the grounds mentioned in section thirty of this Act the landlord will oppose the application.

27 Termination by tenant of tenancy for fixed term

(1) Where the tenant under a tenancy to which this Part of this Act applies, being a tenancy granted for a term of years certain, gives to the immediate landlord, not later than three months before the date on which apart from this Act the tenancy would come to an end by effluxion of time, a notice in writing that the tenant does not desire the tenancy to be continued, section twenty-four of this Act shall not have effect in relation to the tenancy unless the notice is given before the tenant has been in occupation in right of the tenancy for one month.

(1A) Section 24 of this Act shall not have effect in relation to a tenancy for a term of years certain where the tenant is not in occupation of the property comprised in the tenancy at the time when, apart from this Act, the tenancy would come to an end by effluxion of time.

(2) A tenancy granted for a term of years certain which is continuing by virtue of section twenty-four of this Act shall not come to an end by reason only of the tenant ceasing to occupy the property comprised in the tenancy but may be brought to an end on any ...

day by not less than three months' notice in writing given by the tenant to the immediate landlord, whether the notice is given ... after the date on which apart from this Act the tenancy would have come to an end or before that date, but not before the tenant has been in occupation in right of the tenancy for one month.

(3) Where a tenancy is terminated under subsection (2) above, any rent payable in respect of a period which begins before, and ends after, the tenancy is terminated shall be apportioned, and any rent paid by the tenant in excess of the amount apportioned to the period before termination shall be recoverable by him.

28 Renewal of tenancies by agreement

Where the landlord and tenant agree for the grant to the tenant of a future tenancy of the holding, or of the holding with other land, on terms and from a date specified in the agreement, the current tenancy shall continue until that date but no longer, and shall not be a tenancy to which this Part of this Act applies.

Applications to court

29 Order by court for grant of new tenancy or termination of current tenancy

(1) Subject to the provisions of this Act, on an application under section 24(1) of this Act, the court shall make an order for the grant of a new tenancy and accordingly for the termination of the current tenancy immediately before the commencement of the new tenancy.

(2) Subject to the following provisions of this Act, a landlord may apply to the court for an order for the termination of a tenancy to which this Part of this Act applies without the grant of a new tenancy –

    (a) if he has given notice under section 25 of this Act that he is opposed to the grant of a new tenancy to the tenant; or
    (b) if the tenant has made a request for a new tenancy in accordance with section 26 of this Act and the landlord has given notice under subsection (6) of that section.

(3) The landlord may not make an application under subsection (2) above if either the tenant or the landlord has made an application under section 24(1) of this Act.

(4) Subject to the provisions of this Act, where the landlord makes an application under subsection (2) above –

    (a) if he establishes, to the satisfaction of the court, any of the grounds on which he is entitled to make the application in accordance with section 30 of this Act, the court shall make an order for the termination of the current tenancy in accordance with section 64 of this Act without the grant of a new tenancy; and

(b) if not, it shall make an order for the grant of a new tenancy and accordingly for the termination of the current tenancy immediately before the commencement of the new tenancy.

(5) The court shall dismiss an application by the landlord under section 24(1) of this Act if the tenant informs the court that he does not want a new tenancy.

(6) The landlord may not withdraw an application under subsection (2) above unless the tenant consents to its withdrawal.

29A Time limits for applications to court

(1) Subject to section 29B of this Act, the court shall not entertain an application –

(a) by the tenant or the landlord under section 24(1) of this Act; or
(b) by the landlord under section 29(2) of this Act,

if it is made after the end of the statutory period.

(2) In this section and section 29B of this Act 'the statutory period' means a period ending –

(a) where the landlord gave a notice under section 25 of this Act, on the date specified in his notice; and
(b) where the tenant made a request for a new tenancy under section 26 of this Act, immediately before the date specified in his request.

(3) Where the tenant has made a request for a new tenancy under section 26 of this Act, the court shall not entertain an application under section 24(1) of this Act which is made before the end of the period of two months beginning with the date of the making of the request, unless the application is made after the landlord has given a notice under section 26(6) of this Act.

29B Agreements extending time limits

(1) After the landlord has given a notice under section 25 of this Act, or the tenant has made a request under section 26 of this Act, but before the end of the statutory period, the landlord and tenant may agree that an application such as is mentioned in section 29A(1) of this Act, may be made before the end of a period specified in the agreement which will expire after the end of the statutory period.

(2) The landlord and tenant may from time to time by agreement further extend the period for making such an application, but any such agreement must be made before the end of the period specified in the current agreement.

(3) Where an agreement is made under this section, the court may entertain an application such as is mentioned in section 29A(1) of this Act if it is made before the end of the period specified in the agreement.

(4) Where an agreement is made under this section, or two or more agreements are made under this section, the landlord's notice under section 25 of this Act or tenant's request under section 26 of this Act shall be treated as terminating the tenancy at the end of the period specified in the agreement or, as the case may be, at the end of the period specified in the last of those agreements.

30 Opposition by landlord to application for a new tenancy

(1) The grounds on which a landlord may oppose an application under section 24(1) of this Act, or make an application under section 29(2) of this Act, are such of the following grounds as may be stated in the landlord's notice under section twenty-five of this Act or, as the case may be, under subsection (6) of section twenty-six thereof, that is to say –

- (a) where under the current tenancy the tenant has any obligations as respects the repair and maintenance of the holding, that the tenant ought not to be granted a new tenancy in view of the state of repair of the holding, being a state resulting from the tenant's failure to comply with the said obligations;
- (b) that the tenant ought not to be granted a new tenancy in view of his persistent delay in paying rent which has become due;
- (c) that the tenant ought not to be granted a new tenancy in view of other substantial breaches by him of his obligations under the current tenancy, or for any other reason connected with the tenant's use or management of the holding;
- (d) that the landlord has offered and is willing to provide or secure the provision of alternative accommodation for the tenant, that the terms on which the alternative accommodation is available are reasonable having regard to the terms of the current tenancy and to all other relevant circumstances, and that the accommodation and the time at which it will be available are suitable for the tenant's requirements (including the requirement to preserve goodwill) having regard to the nature and class of his business and to the situation and extent of, and facilities afforded by, the holding;
- (e) where the current tenancy was created by the sub-letting of part only of the property comprised in a superior tenancy and

the landlord is the owner of an interest in reversion expectant on the termination of that superior tenancy, that the aggregate of the rents reasonably obtainable on separate lettings of the holding and the remainder of that property would be substantially less than the rent reasonably obtainable on a letting of that property as a whole, that on the termination of the current tenancy the landlord requires possession of the holding for the purpose of letting or otherwise disposing of the said property as a whole, and that in view thereof the tenant ought not to be granted a new tenancy;

(f) that on the termination of the current tenancy the landlord intends to demolish or reconstruct the premises comprised in the holding or a substantial part of those premises or to carry out substantial work of construction on the holding or part thereof and that he could not reasonably do so without obtaining possession of the holding;

(g) subject as hereinafter provided, that on the termination of the current tenancy the landlord intends to occupy the holding for the purposes, or partly for the purposes, of a business to be carried on by him therein, or as his residence.

(1A) Where the landlord has a controlling interest in a company, the reference in subsection (1)(g) above to the landlord shall be construed as a reference to the landlord or that company.

(1B) Subject to subsection (2A) below, where the landlord is a company and a person has a controlling interest in the company, the reference in subsection (1)(g) above to the landlord shall be construed as a reference to the landlord or that person.

(2) The landlord shall not be entitled to oppose an application under section 24(1) of this Act, or make an application under section 29(2) of this Act, on the ground specified in paragraph (g) of the last foregoing subsection if the interest of the landlord, or an interest which has merged in that interest and but for the merger would be the interest of the landlord, was purchased or created after the beginning of the period of five years which ends with the termination of the current tenancy, and at all times since the purchase or creation thereof the holding has been comprised in a tenancy or successive tenancies of the description specified in subsection (1) of section twenty-three of this Act.

(2A) Subsection (1B) above shall not apply if the controlling interest was acquired after the beginning of the period of five years which ends with the termination of the current tenancy, and at all times since the acquisition of the controlling interest the holding has been comprised in a tenancy or successive tenancies of the description specified in section 23(1) of this Act.

(3) ... [repealed]

31 Dismissal of application for new tenancy where landlord successfully opposes

(1) If the landlord opposes an application under subsection (1) of section twenty-four of this Act on grounds on which he is entitled to oppose it in accordance with the last foregoing section and establishes any of those grounds to the satisfaction of the court, the court shall not make an order for the grant of a new tenancy.

(2) Where the landlord opposes an application under section 24(1) of this Act, or makes an application under section 29(2) of this Act, on one or more of the grounds specified in section 30(1)(d) to (f) of this Act but establishes none of those grounds, and none of the other grounds specified in section 30(1) of this Act, to the satisfaction of the court, then if the court would have been satisfied on any of the grounds specified in section 30(1)(d) to (f) of this Act if the date of termination specified in the landlord's notice or, as the case may be, the date specified in the tenant's request for a new tenancy as the date from which the new tenancy is to begin, had been such later date as the court may determine, being a date not more than one year later than the date so specified –

(a) the court shall make a declaration to that effect, stating of which of the said grounds the court would have been satisfied as aforesaid and specifying the date determined by the court as aforesaid, but shall not make an order for the grant of a new tenancy;
(b) if, within fourteen days after the making of the declaration, the tenant so requires the court shall make an order substituting the said date for the date specified in the said landlord's notice or tenant's request, and thereupon that notice or request shall have effect accordingly.

31A Grant of new tenancy in some cases where section 30(1)(f) applies

(1) Where the landlord opposes an application under section 24(1) of this Act on the ground specified in paragraph (f) of section 30(1) of this Act, or makes an application under section 29(2) of this Act on that ground, the court shall not hold that the landlord could not reasonably carry out the demolition, reconstruction or work of construction intended without obtaining possession of the holding if –

(a) the tenant agrees to the inclusion in the terms of the new tenancy of terms giving the landlord access and other facilities for carrying out the work intended and, given that access and those facilities, the landlord could reasonably carry out the work without obtaining possession of the holding and without interfering to a substantial extent or for a substantial time with the use of the holding for the purposes of the business carried on by the tenant; or

(b) the tenant is willing to accept a tenancy of an economically separable part of the holding and either paragraph (a) of this section is satisfied with respect to that part or possession of the remainder of the holding would be reasonably sufficient to enable the landlord to carry out the intended work.

(2) For the purposes of subsection (1)(b) of this section a part of a holding shall be deemed to be an economically separable part if, and only if, the aggregate of the rents which, after the completion of the intended work, would be reasonably obtainable on separate lettings of that part and the remainder of the premises affected by or resulting from the work would not be substantially less than the rent which would then be reasonably obtainable on a letting of those premises as a whole.

32 Property to be comprised in new tenancy

(1) Subject to the following provisions of this section, an order under section twenty-nine of this Act for the grant of a new tenancy shall be an order for the grant of a new tenancy of the holding; and in the absence of agreement between the landlord and the tenant as to the property which constitutes the holding the court shall in the order designate that property by reference to the circumstances existing at the date of the order.

(1A) Where the court, by virtue of paragraph (b) of section 31A(1) of this Act, makes an order under section 29 of this Act for the grant of a new tenancy in a case where the tenant is willing to accept a tenancy of part of the holding, the order shall be an order for the grant of a new tenancy of that part only.

(2) The foregoing provisions of this section shall not apply in a case where the property comprised in the current tenancy includes other property besides the holding and the landlord requires any new tenancy ordered to be granted under section twenty-nine of this Act to be a tenancy of the whole of the property comprised in the current tenancy; but in any such case –

(a) any order under the said section twenty-nine for the grant of a new tenancy shall be an order for the grant of a new tenancy of the whole of the property comprised in the current tenancy; and
(b) references in the following provisions of this Part of this Act to the holding shall be construed as references to the whole of that property.

(3) Where the current tenancy includes rights enjoyed by the tenant in connection with the holding, those rights shall be included in a tenancy ordered to be granted under section twenty-nine of this Act except as otherwise agreed between the landlord and the tenant or, in default of such agreement, determined by the court.

33 Duration of new tenancy

Where on an application under this Part of this Act the court makes an order for the grant of a new tenancy, the new tenancy shall be such tenancy as may be agreed between the landlord and the tenant, or, in default of such an agreement, shall be such a tenancy as may be determined by the court to be reasonable in all the circumstances, being, if it is a tenancy for a term of years certain, a tenancy for a term not exceeding fifteen years, and shall begin on the coming to an end of the current tenancy.

34 Rent under new tenancy

(1) The rent payable under a tenancy granted by order of the court under this Part of this Act shall be such as may be agreed between the landlord and the tenant or as, in default of such agreement, may be determined by the court to be that at which, having regard to the terms of the tenancy (other than those relating to rent), the holding might reasonably be expected to be let in the open market by a willing lessor, there being disregarded –

- (a) any effect on rent of the fact that the tenant has or his predecessors in title have been in occupation of the holding,
- (b) any goodwill attached to the holding by reason of the carrying on thereat of the business of the tenant (whether by him or by a predecessor of his in that business),
- (c) any effect on rent of an improvement to which this paragraph applies,
- (d) in the case of a holding comprising licensed premises, any addition to its value attributable to the licence, if it appears to the court that having regard to the terms of the current tenancy and any other relevant circumstances the benefit of the licence belongs to the tenant.

(2) Paragraph (c) of the foregoing subsection applies to any improvement carried out by a person who at the time it was carried out was the tenant, but only if it was carried out otherwise than in pursuance of an obligation to his immediate landlord, and either it was carried out during the current tenancy or the following conditions are satisfied, that is to say –

- (a) that it was completed not more than twenty-one years before the application to the court was made; and
- (b) that the holding or any part of it affected by the improvement has at all times since the completion of the improvement been comprised in tenancies of the description specified in section 23(1) of this Act; and
- (c) that at the termination of each of those tenancies the tenant did not quit.

(2A) If this Part of this Act applies by virtue of section 23(1A) of this Act, the reference in subsection (1)(d) above to the tenant shall be construed as including –

    (a) a company in which the tenant has a controlling interest, or

    (b) where the tenant is a company, a person with a controlling interest in the company.

(3) Where the rent is determined by the court the court may, if it thinks fit, further determine that the terms of the tenancy shall include such provision for varying the rent as may be specified in the determination.

(4) It is hereby declared that the matters which are to be taken into account by the court in determining the rent include any effect on rent of the operation of the provisions of the *Landlord and Tenant (Covenants) Act* 1995.

35 Other terms of new tenancy

(1) The terms of a tenancy granted by order of the court under this Part of this Act (other than terms as to the duration thereof and as to the rent payable there under), including, where different persons own interests which fulfil the conditions specified in section 44(1) of this Act in different parts of it, terms as to the apportionment of the rent, shall be such as may be agreed between the landlord and the tenant or as, in default of such agreement, may be determined by the court; and in determining those terms the court shall have regard to the terms of the current tenancy and to all relevant circumstances.

(2) In subsection (1) of this section the reference to all relevant circumstances includes (without prejudice to the generality of that reference) a reference to the operation of the provisions of the *Landlord and Tenant (Covenants) Act* 1995.

36 Carrying out of order for new tenancy

(1) Where under this Part of this Act the court makes an order for the grant of a new tenancy, then, unless the order is revoked under the next following subsection or the landlord and the tenant agree not to act upon the order, the landlord shall be bound to execute or make in favour of the tenant, and the tenant shall be bound to accept, a lease or agreement for a tenancy of the holding embodying the terms agreed between the landlord and the tenant or determined by the court in accordance with the foregoing provisions of this Part of this Act; and where the landlord executes or makes such a lease or agreement the tenant shall be bound, if so required by the landlord, to execute a counterpart or duplicate thereof.

(2) If the tenant, within fourteen days after the making of an order under this Part of this Act for the grant of a new tenancy, applies to

the court for the revocation of the order the court shall revoke the order; and where the order is so revoked, then, if it is so agreed between the landlord and the tenant or determined by the court, the current tenancy shall continue, beyond the date at which it would have come to an end apart from this subsection, for such period as may be so agreed or determined to be necessary to afford to the landlord a reasonable opportunity for re-letting or otherwise disposing of the premises which would have been comprised in the new tenancy; and while the current tenancy continues by virtue of this subsection it shall not be a tenancy to which this Part of this Act applies.

(3) Where an order is revoked under the last foregoing subsection any provision thereof as to payment of costs shall not cease to have effect by reason only of the revocation; but the court may, if it thinks fit, revoke or vary any such provision or, where no costs have been awarded in the proceedings for the revoked order, award such costs.

(4) A lease executed or agreement made under this section, in a case where the interest of the lessor is subject to a mortgage, shall be deemed to be one authorised by section ninety-nine of the Law of Property Act 1925 (which confers certain powers of leasing on mortgagors in possession), and subsection (13) of that section (which allows those powers to be restricted or excluded by agreement) shall not have effect in relation to such a lease or agreement.

37 Compensation where order for new tenancy precluded on certain grounds

(1) Subject to the provisions of this Act, in a case specified in subsection (1A), (1B) or (1C) below (a 'compensation case') the tenant shall be entitled on quitting the holding to recover from the landlord by way of compensation an amount determined in accordance with this section.

(1A) The first compensation case is where on the making of an application by the tenant under section 24(1) of this Act the court is precluded (whether by subsection (1) or subsection (2) of section 31 of this Act) from making an order for the grant of a new tenancy by reason of any of the grounds specified in paragraphs (e), (f) and (g) of section 30(1) of this Act (the 'compensation grounds') and not of any grounds specified in any other paragraph of section 30(1).

(1B) The second compensation case is where on the making of an application under section 29(2) of this Act the court is precluded (whether by section 29(4)(a) or section 31(2) of this Act) from making an order for the grant of a new tenancy by reason of any of the compensation grounds and not of any other grounds specified in section 30(1) of this Act.

(1C) The third compensation case is where –

(a) the landlord's notice under section 25 of this Act or, as the case may be, under section 26(6) of this Act, states his opposition to the grant of a new tenancy on any of the compensation grounds and not on any other grounds specified in section 30(1) of this Act; and

(b) either –

(i) no application is made by the tenant under section 24(1) of this Act or by the landlord under section 29(2) of this Act; or

(ii) such an application is made but is subsequently withdrawn.

(2) Subject to the following provisions of this section, compensation under this section shall be as follows, that is to say –

(a) where the conditions specified in the next following subsection are satisfied in relation to the whole of the holding it shall be the product of the appropriate multiplier and twice the rateable value of the holding,

(b) in any other case it shall be the product of the appropriate multiplier and the rateable value of the holding.

(3) The said conditions are –

(a) that, during the whole of the fourteen years immediately preceding the termination of the current tenancy, premises being or comprised in the holding have been occupied for the purposes of a business carried on by the occupier or for those and other purposes;

(b) that, if during those fourteen years there was a change in the occupier of the premises, the person who was the occupier immediately after the change was the successor to the business carried on by the person who was the occupier immediately before the change.

(3A) If the conditions specified in subsection (3) above are satisfied in relation to part of the holding but not in relation to the other part, the amount of compensation shall be the aggregate of sums calculated separately as compensation in respect of each part, and accordingly, for the purpose of calculating compensation in respect of a part any reference in this section to the holding shall be construed as a reference to that part.

(3B) Where section 44(1A) of this Act applies, the compensation shall be determined separately for each part and compensation determined for any part shall be recoverable only from the person who is the owner of an interest in that part which fulfils the conditions specified in section 44(1) of this Act.

(4) Where the court is precluded from making an order for the grant of a new tenancy under this Part of this Act in a compensation case, the court shall on the application of the tenant certify that fact.

(5) For the purposes of subsection (2) of this section the rateable value of the holding shall be determined as follows –

    (a) where in the valuation list in force at the date on which the landlord's notice under section twenty-five or, as the case may be, subsection (6) of section twenty-six of this Act is given a value is then shown as the annual value (as hereinafter defined) of the holding, the rateable value of the holding shall be taken to be that value;

    (b) where no such value is so shown with respect to the holding but such a value or such values is or are so shown with respect to premises comprised in or comprising the holding or part of it, the rateable value of the holding shall be taken to be such value as is found by a proper apportionment or aggregation of the value or values so shown;

    (c) where the rateable value of the holding cannot be ascertained in accordance with the foregoing paragraphs of this subsection, it shall be taken to be the value which, apart from any exemption from assessment to rates, would on a proper assessment be the value to be entered in the said valuation list as the annual value of the holding;

and any dispute arising, whether in proceedings before the court or otherwise, as to the determination for those purposes of the rateable value of the holding shall be referred to the Commissioners of Inland Revenue for decision by a valuation officer.

An appeal shall lie to the Lands Tribunal from any decision of a valuation officer under this subsection, but subject thereto any such decision shall be final.

(5A) If part of the holding is domestic property, as defined in section 66 of the Local Government Finance Act 1988 –

    (a) the domestic property shall be disregarded in determining the rateable value of the holding under subsection (5) of this section; and

    (b) if, on the date specified in subsection (5)(a) of this section, the tenant occupied the whole or any part of the domestic property, the amount of compensation to which he is entitled under subsection (1) of this section shall be increased by the addition of a sum equal to his reasonable expenses in removing from the domestic property.

(5B) Any question as to the amount of the sum referred to in paragraph (b) of subsection (5A) of this section shall be determined by agreement between the landlord and the tenant or, in default of agreement, by the court.

(5C) If the whole of the holding is domestic property, as defined in section 66 of the Local Government Finance Act 1988, for the purposes of subsection (2) of this section the rateable value of the holding shall be taken to be an amount equal to the rent at which it is estimated the holding might reasonably be expected to let from year to year if the tenant undertook to pay all usual tenant's rates and taxes and to bear the cost of the repairs and insurance and the other expenses (if any) necessary to maintain the holding in a state to command that rent.

(5D) The following provisions shall have effect as regards a determination of an amount mentioned in subsection (5C) of this section –

(a) the date by reference to which such a determination is to be made is the date on which the landlord's notice under section 25 or, as the case may be, subsection (6) of section 26 of this Act is given;

(b) any dispute arising, whether in proceedings before the court or otherwise, as to such a determination shall be referred to the Commissioners of Inland Revenue for decision by a valuation officer;

(c) an appeal shall lie to the Lands Tribunal from such a decision but subject to that, such a decision shall be final.

(5E) Any deduction made under paragraph 2A of Schedule 6 to the Local Government Finance Act 1988 (deduction from valuation of hereditaments used for breeding horses etc) shall be disregarded, to the extent that it relates to the holding, in determining the rateable value of the holding under subsection (5) of this section.

(6) The Commissioners of Inland Revenue may by statutory instrument make rules prescribing the procedure in connection with references under this section.

(7) In this section –

the reference to the termination of the current tenancy is a reference to the date of termination specified in the landlord's notice under section twenty-five of this Act or, as the case may be, the date specified in the tenant's request for a new tenancy as the date from which the new tenancy is to begin;

the expression 'annual value' means rateable value except that where the rateable value differs from the net annual value the said expression means net annual value;

the expression 'valuation officer' means any officer of the Commissioners of Inland Revenue for the time being authorised by a certificate of the Commissioners to act in relation to a valuation list.

(8) In subsection (2) of this section 'the appropriate multiplier' means such multiplier as the Secretary of State may by order made by statutory instrument prescribe and different multipliers may be so prescribed in relation to different cases.

(9) A statutory instrument containing an order under subsection (8) of this section shall be subject to annulment in pursuance of a resolution of either House of Parliament.

37A Compensation for possession obtained by misrepresentation

(1) Where the court –

(a) makes an order for the termination of the current tenancy but does not make an order for the grant of a new tenancy; or
(b) refuses an order for the grant of a new tenancy,

and it subsequently made to appear to the court that the order was obtained, or the court was induced to refuse the grant, by misrepresentation or the concealment of material facts, the court may order the landlord to pay to the tenant such sum as appears sufficient as compensation for damage or loss sustained by the tenant as the result of the order or refusal.

(2) Where –

(a) the tenant has quit the holding –

(i) after making but withdrawing an application under section 24(1) of this Act; or
(ii) without making such an application; and

(b) it is made to appear to the court that he did so by reason of misrepresentation or the concealment of material facts,

the court may order the landlord to pay to the tenant such sum as appears sufficient as compensation for damage or loss sustained by the tenant as the result of quitting the holding.

38 Restriction on agreements excluding provisions of Part II

(1) Any agreement relating to a tenancy to which this Part of this Act applies (whether contained in the instrument creating the tenancy or not) shall be void (except as provided by section 38A of this Act) in

so far as it purports to preclude the tenant from making an application or request under this Part of this Act or provides for the termination or the surrender of the tenancy in the event of his making such an application or request or for the imposition of any penalty or disability on the tenant in that event.

(2) Where –

  (a) during the whole of the five years immediately preceding the date on which the tenant under a tenancy to which this Part of this Act applies is to quit the holding, premises being or comprised in the holding have been occupied for the purposes of a business carried on by the occupier or for those and other purposes; and

  (b) if during those five years there was a change in the occupier of the premises, the person who was the occupier immediately after the change was the successor to the business carried on by the person who was the occupier immediately before the change,

any agreement (whether contained in the instrument creating the tenancy or not and whether made before or after the termination of that tenancy) which purports to exclude or reduce compensation under section 37 of this Act shall to that extent be void, so however that this subsection shall not affect any agreement as to the amount of any such compensation which is made after the right to compensation has accrued.

(3) In a case not falling within the last foregoing subsection the right to compensation conferred by section 37 of this Act may be excluded or modified by agreement.

(4) … [repealed]

38A Agreements to exclude provisions of Part 2

(1) The persons who will be the landlord and the tenant in relation to a tenancy to be granted for a term of years certain which will be a tenancy to which this Part of this Act applies may agree that the provisions of sections 24 to 28 of this Act shall be excluded in relation to that tenancy.

(2) The persons who are the landlord and the tenant in relation to a tenancy to which this Part of this Act applies may agree that the tenancy shall be surrendered on such date or in such circumstances as may be specified in the agreement and on such terms (if any) as may be so specified.

(3) An agreement under subsection (1) above shall be void unless –

(a) the landlord has served on the tenant a notice in the form, or substantially in the form, set out in Schedule 1 to the Regulatory Reform (Business Tenancies) (England and Wales) Order 2003 ('the 2003 Order'); and

(b) the requirements specified in Schedule 2 to that Order are met.

(4) An agreement under subsection (2) above shall be void unless –

(a) the landlord has served on the tenant a notice in the form, or substantially in the form, set out in Schedule 3 to the 2003 Order; and

(b) the requirements specified in Schedule 4 to that Order are met.

General and supplementary provisions

39 Saving for compulsory acquisitions

(1) ... [repealed]

(2) If the amount of the compensation which would have been payable under section thirty-seven of this Act if the tenancy had come to an end in circumstances giving rise to compensation under that section and the date at which the acquiring authority obtained possession had been the termination of the current tenancy exceeds the amount of the compensation payable under section 121 of the Lands Clauses Consolidation Act 1845 or section 20 of the Compulsory Purchase Act 1965 in the case of a tenancy to which this Part of this Act applies, that compensation shall be increased by the amount of the excess.

(3) Nothing in section twenty-four of this Act shall affect the operation of the said section one hundred and twenty-one.

40 Duties of tenants and landlords of business premises to give information to each other

(1) Where a person who is an owner of an interest in reversion expectant (whether immediately or not) on a tenancy of any business premises has served on the tenant a notice in the prescribed form requiring him to do so, it shall be the duty of the tenant to give the appropriate person in writing the information specified in subsection (2) below.

(2) That information is –

(a) whether the tenant occupies the premises or any part of them wholly or partly for the purposes of a business carried on by him;
(b) whether his tenancy has effect subject to any sub-tenancy on which his tenancy is immediately expectant and, if so –

    (i) what premises are comprised in the sub-tenancy;

    (ii) for what term it has effect (or, if it is terminable by notice, by what notice it can be terminated);

    (iii) what is the rent payable under it;

    (iv) who is the sub-tenant;

    (v) (to the best of his knowledge and belief) whether the sub-tenant is in occupation of the premises or of part of the premises comprised in the sub-tenancy and, if not, what is the sub-tenant's address;

    (vi) whether an agreement is in force excluding in relation to the sub-tenancy the provisions of sections 24 to 28 of this Act; and

    (vii) whether a notice has been given under section 25 or 26(6) of this Act, or a request has been made under section 26 of this Act, in relation to the sub-tenancy and, if so, details of the notice or request; and

(c) (to the best of his knowledge and belief) the name and address of any other person who owns an interest in reversion in any part of the premises.

(3) Where the tenant of any business premises who is a tenant under such a tenancy as is mentioned in section 26(1) of this Act has served on a reversioner or a reversioner's mortgagee in possession a notice in the prescribed form requiring him to do so, it shall be the duty of the person on whom the notice is served to give the appropriate person in writing the information specified in subsection (4) below.

(4) That information is –

(a) whether he is the owner of the fee simple in respect of the premises or any part of them or the mortgagee in possession of such an owner,

(b) if he is not, then (to the best of his knowledge and belief) –

    (i) the name and address of the person who is his or, as the case may be, his mortgagor's immediate landlord in respect of those premises or of the part in respect of which he or his mortgagor is not the owner in fee simple;

    (ii) for what term his or his mortgagor's tenancy has effect and what is the earliest date (if any) at which that tenancy is terminable by notice to quit given by the landlord; and

    (iii) whether a notice has been given under section 25 or 26(6) of this Act, or a request has been made under section 26 of this Act, in relation to the tenancy and, if so, details of the notice or request;

(c) (to the best of his knowledge and belief) the name and address of any other person who owns an interest in reversion in any part of the premises; and

(d) if he is a reversioner, whether there is a mortgagee in possession of his interest in the premises and, if so, (to the best of his knowledge and belief) what is the name and address of the mortgagee.

(5) A duty imposed on a person by this section is a duty –

(a) to give the information concerned within the period of one month beginning with the date of service of the notice; and
(b) if within the period of six months beginning with the date of service of the notice that person becomes aware that any information which has been given in pursuance of the notice is not, or is no longer, correct, to give the appropriate person correct information within the period of one month beginning with the date on which he becomes aware.

(6) This section shall not apply to a notice served by or on the tenant more than two years before the date on which apart from this Act his tenancy would come to an end by effluxion of time or could be brought to an end by notice to quit given by the landlord.

(7) Except as provided by section 40A of this Act, the appropriate person for the purposes of this section and section 40A(1) of this Act is the person who served the notice under subsection (1) or (3) above.

(8) In this section –

'business premises' means premises used wholly or partly for the purposes of a business;

'mortgagee in possession' includes a receiver appointed by the mortgagee or by the court who is in receipt of the rents and profits, and 'his mortgagor' shall be construed accordingly;

'reversioner' means any person having an interest in the premises, being an interest in reversion expectant (whether immediately or not) on the tenancy;

'reversioner's mortgagee in possession' means any person being a mortgagee in possession in respect of such an interest; and

'sub-tenant' includes a person retaining possession of any premises by virtue of the Rent (Agriculture) Act 1976 or the Rent Act 1977 after the coming to an end of a sub-tenancy, and 'sub-tenancy' includes a right so to retain possession.

40A Duties in transfer cases

(1) If a person on whom a notice under section 40(1) or (3) of this Act has been served has transferred his interest in the premises or

any part of them to some other person and gives the appropriate person notice in writing –

> (a) of the transfer of his interest; and
> (b) of the name and address of the person to whom he transferred it,

on giving the notice he ceases in relation to the premises or (as the case may be) to that part to be under any duty imposed by section 40 of this Act.

(2) If –

> (a) the person who served the notice under section 40(1) or (3) of this Act ('the transferor') has transferred his interest in the premises to some other person ('the transferee'); and
> (b) the transferor or the transferee has given the person required to give the information notice in writing –
>
> > (i) of the transfer; and
> > (ii) of the transferee's name and address,

the appropriate person for the purposes of section 40 of this Act and subsection (1) above is the transferee.

(3) If –

> (a) a transfer such as is mentioned in paragraph (a) of subsection (2) above has taken place; but
> (b) neither the transferor nor the transferee has given a notice such as is mentioned in paragraph (b) of that subsection,

any duty imposed by section 40 of this Act may be performed by giving the information either to the transferor or to the transferee.

40B Proceedings for breach of duties to give information

A claim that a person has broken any duty imposed by section 40 of this Act may be made the subject of civil proceedings for breach of statutory duty; and in any such proceedings a court may order that person to comply with that duty and may make an award of damages.

41 Trusts

(1) Where a tenancy is held on trust, occupation by all or any of the beneficiaries under the trust, and the carrying on of a business by all or any of the beneficiaries, shall be treated for the purposes of section twenty-three of this Act as equivalent to occupation or the carrying on of a business by the tenant; and in relation to a tenancy to which this Part of this Act applies by virtue of the foregoing provisions of this subsection –

(a) references (however expressed) in this Part of this Act and in the Ninth Schedule to this Act to the business of, or to carrying on of business, use, occupation or enjoyment by, the tenant shall be construed as including references to the business of, or to carrying on of business, use, occupation or enjoyment by, the beneficiaries or beneficiary;

(b) the reference in paragraph (d) of subsection (1) of section thirty-four of this Act to the tenant shall be construed as including the beneficiaries or beneficiary; and

(c) a change in the persons of the trustees shall not be treated as a change in the person of the tenant.

(2) Where the landlord's interest is held on trust the references in paragraph (g) of subsection (1) of section thirty of this Act to the landlord shall be construed as including references to the beneficiaries under the trust or any of them; but, except in the case of a trust arising under a will or on the intestacy of any person, the reference in subsection (2) of that section to the creation of the interest therein mentioned shall be construed as including the creation of the trust.

41A Partnerships

(1) The following provisions of this section shall apply where –

(a) a tenancy is held jointly by two or more persons (in this section referred to as the joint tenants); and

(b) the property comprised in the tenancy is or includes premises occupied for the purposes of a business; and

(c) the business (or some other business) was at some time during the existence of the tenancy carried on in partnership by all the persons who were then the joint tenants or by those and other persons and the joint tenants' interest in the premises was then partnership property; and

(d) the business is carried on (whether alone or in partnership with other persons) by one or some only of the joint tenants and no part of the property comprised in the tenancy is occupied, in right of the tenancy, for the purposes of a business carried on (whether alone or in partnership with other persons) by the other or others.

(2) In the following provisions of this section those of the joint tenants who for the time being carry on the business are referred to as the business tenants and the others as the other joint tenants.

(3) Any notice given by the business tenants which, had it been given by all the joint tenants, would have been –

(a) a tenant's request for a new tenancy made in accordance with section 26 of this Act; or

(b) a notice under subsection (1) or subsection (2) of section 27 of this Act;

shall be treated as such if it states that it is given by virtue of this section and sets out the facts by virtue of which the persons giving it are the business tenants; and references in those sections and in section 24A of this Act to the tenant shall be construed accordingly.

(4) A notice given by the landlord to the business tenants which, had it been given to all the joint tenants, would have been a notice under section 25 of this Act shall be treated as such a notice, and references in that section to the tenant shall be construed accordingly.

(5) An application under section 24(1) of this Act for a new tenancy may, instead of being made by all the joint tenants, be made by the business tenants alone; and where it is so made –

(a) this Part of this Act shall have effect, in relation to it, as if the references therein to the tenant included references to the business tenants alone; and
(b) the business tenants shall be liable, to the exclusion of the other joint tenants, for the payment of rent and the discharge of any other obligation under the current tenancy for any rental period beginning after the date specified in the landlord's notice under section 25 of this Act or, as the case may be, beginning on or after the date specified in their request for a new tenancy.

(6) Where the court makes an order under section 29 of this Act for the grant of a new tenancy it may order the grant to be made to the business tenants or to them jointly with the persons carrying on the business in partnership with them, and may order the grant to be made subject to the satisfaction, within a time specified by the order, of such conditions as to guarantors, sureties or otherwise as appear to the court equitable, having regard to the omission of the other joint tenants from the persons who will be the tenant under the new tenancy.

(7) The business tenants shall be entitled to recover any amount payable by way of compensation under section 37 or section 59 of this Act.

42 Groups of companies

(1) For the purposes of this section two bodies corporate shall be taken to be members of a group if and only if one is a subsidiary of the other or both are subsidiaries of a third body corporate or the same person has a controlling interest in both.

(2) Where a tenancy is held by a member of a group, occupation by another member of the group, and the carrying on of a business by another member of the group, shall be treated for the purposes of section twenty-three of this Act as equivalent to occupation or the carrying on of a business by the member of the group holding the tenancy; and in relation to a tenancy to which this Part of this Act applies by virtue of the foregoing provisions of this subsection–

    (a) references (however expressed) in this Part of this Act and in the Ninth Schedule to this Act to the business of or to use occupation or enjoyment by the tenant shall be construed as including references to the business of or to use occupation or enjoyment by the said other member;

    (b) the reference in paragraph (d) of subsection (1) of section thirty-four of this Act to the tenant shall be construed as including the said other member; and

    (c) an assignment of the tenancy from one member of the group to another shall not be treated as a change in the person of the tenant.

(3) Where the landlord's interest is held by a member of a group –

    (a) the reference in paragraph (g) of subsection (1) of section 30 of this Act to intended occupation by the landlord for the purposes of a business to be carried on by him shall be construed as including intended occupation by any member of the group for the purposes of a business to be carried on by that member; and

    (b) the reference in subsection (2) of that section to the purchase or creation of any interest shall be construed as a reference to a purchase from or creation by a person other than a member of the group.

43 Tenancies excluded from Part II

(1) This Part of this Act does not apply –

    (a) to a tenancy of an agricultural holding which is a tenancy in relation to which the Agricultural Holdings Act 1986 applies or a tenancy which would be a tenancy of an agricultural holding in relation to which that Act applied if subsection (3) of section 2 of that Act did not have effect or, in a case where approval was given under subsection (1) of that section, if that approval had not been given;

    (aa) to a farm business tenancy;

    (b) to a tenancy created by a mining lease;

    (c), (d) … [repealed]

(2) This Part of this Act does not apply to a tenancy granted by reason that the tenant was the holder of an office, appointment or employment from the grantor thereof and continuing only so long as the tenant holds the office, appointment or employment, or terminable by the grantor on the tenant's ceasing to hold it, or coming to an end at a time fixed by reference to the time at which the tenant ceases to hold it:

> Provided that this subsection shall not have effect in relation to a tenancy granted after the commencement of this Act unless the tenancy was granted by an instrument in writing which expressed the purpose for which the tenancy was granted.

(3) This Part of this Act does not apply to a tenancy granted for a term certain not exceeding six months unless –

(a) the tenancy contains provision for renewing the term or for extending it beyond six months from its beginning; or
(b) the tenant has been in occupation for a period which, together with any period during which any predecessor in the carrying on of the business carried on by the tenant was in occupation, exceeds twelve months.

43A Jurisdiction of county court to make declaration

Where the rateable value of the holding is such that the jurisdiction conferred on the court by any other provision of this Part of this Act is, by virtue of section 63 of this Act, exercisable by the county court, the county court shall have jurisdiction (but without prejudice to the jurisdiction of the High Court) to make any declaration as to any matter arising under this Part of this Act, whether or not any other relief is sought in the proceedings.

44 Meaning of 'the landlord' in Part II, and provisions as to mesne landlords, etc.

(1) Subject to subsections (1A) and (2) below, in this Part of this Act the expression 'the landlord', in relation to a tenancy (in this section referred to as 'the relevant tenancy'), means the person (whether or not he is the immediate landlord) who is the owner of that interest in the property comprised in the relevant tenancy which for the time being fulfils the following conditions, that is to say –

(a) that it is an interest in reversion expectant (whether immediately or not) on the termination of the relevant tenancy; and
(b) that it is either the fee simple or a tenancy which will not come to an end within fourteen months by effluxion of time and, if it is such a tenancy, that no notice has been given by virtue of which it will come to an end within fourteen months

or any further time by which it may be continued under
section 36(2) or section 64 of this Act,

and is not itself in reversion expectant (whether immediately or not)
on an interest which fulfils those conditions.

(1A) The reference in subsection (1) above to a person who is the
owner of an interest such as is mentioned in that subsection is to be
construed, where different persons own such interests in different
parts of the property, as a reference to all those persons collectively.

(2) References in this Part of this Act to a notice to quit given by the
landlord are references to a notice to quit given by the immediate
landlord.

(3) The provisions of the Sixth Schedule to this Act shall have effect
for the application of this Part of this Act to cases where the
immediate landlord of the tenant is not the owner of the fee simple in
respect of the holding.

45 ... [repealed]

46 Interpretation of Part II

(1) In this Part of this Act: –

'business' has the meaning assigned to it by subsection (2) of
section twenty-three of this Act;

'current tenancy' means the tenancy under which the tenant
holds for the time being;

'date of termination' has the meaning assigned to it by subsection
(1) of section twenty-five of this Act; subject to the provisions of
section thirty-two of this Act, 'the holding' has the meaning
assigned to it by subsection (3) of section twenty-three of this Act;

'interim rent' has the meaning given by section 24A(1) of this Act;

'mining lease' has the same meaning as in the Landlord and
Tenant Act 1927.

(2) For the purposes of this Part of this Act, a person has a
controlling interest in a company, if, had he been a company, the
other company would have been its subsidiary; and in this Part –

'company' has the meaning given by section 735 of the
Companies Act 1985; and

'subsidiary' has the meaning given by section 736 of that Act.

Part IV
Miscellaneous and Supplementary

56 Application to Crown

(1) Subject to the provisions of this and the four next following sections, Part II of this Act shall apply where there is an interest belonging to Her Majesty in right of the Crown or the Duchy of Lancaster or belonging to the Duchy of Cornwall, or belonging to a Government department or held on behalf of Her Majesty for the purposes of a Government department, in like manner as if that interest were an interest not so belonging or held.

(2) The provisions of the Eighth Schedule to this Act shall have effect as respects the application of Part II of this Act to cases where the interest of the landlord belongs to Her Majesty in right of the Crown or the Duchy of Lancaster or to the Duchy of Cornwall.

(3) Where a tenancy is held by or on behalf of a Government department and the property comprised therein is or includes premises occupied for any purposes of a Government department, the tenancy shall be one to which Part II of this Act applies; and for the purposes of any provision of the said Part II or the Ninth Schedule to this Act which is applicable only if either or both of the following conditions are satisfied, that is to say –

(a) that any premises have during any period been occupied for the purposes of the tenant's business;

(b) that on any change of occupier of any premises the new occupier succeeded to the business of the former occupier,

the said conditions shall be deemed to be satisfied respectively, in relation to such a tenancy, if during that period or, as the case may be, immediately before and immediately after the change, the premises were occupied for the purposes of a Government department.

(4) The last foregoing subsection shall apply in relation to any premises provided by a Government department without any rent being payable to the department therefor as if the premises were occupied for the purposes of a Government department.

(5) The provisions of Parts III and IV of this Act amending any other enactment which binds the Crown or applies to land belonging to Her Majesty in right of the Crown or the Duchy of Lancaster, or land belonging to the Duchy of Cornwall, or to land belonging to any Government department, shall bind the Crown or apply to such land.

(6) Sections fifty-three and fifty-four of this Act shall apply where the interest of the landlord, or any other interest in the land in question,

belongs to Her Majesty in right of the Crown or the Duchy of Lancaster or to the Duchy of Cornwall, or belongs to a Government department or is held on behalf of Her Majesty for the purposes of a Government department, in like manner as if that interest were an interest not so belonging or held.

(7) Part I of this Act shall apply where –

(a) there is an interest belonging to Her Majesty in right of the Crown and that interest is under the management of the Crown Estate Commissioners; or
(b) there is an interest belonging to Her Majesty in right of the Duchy of Lancaster or belonging to the Duchy of Cornwall;

as if it were an interest not so belonging.

57 Modification on grounds of public interest of rights under Part II

(1) Where the interest of the landlord or any superior landlord in the property comprised in any tenancy belongs to or is held for the purposes of a Government department or is held by a local authority, statutory undertakers or a development corporation, the Minister or Board in charge of any Government department may certify that it is requisite for the purposes of the first-mentioned department, or, as the case may be, of the authority, undertakers or corporation, that the use or occupation of the property or a part thereof shall be changed by a specified date.

(2) A certificate under the last foregoing subsection shall not be given unless the owner of the interest belonging or held as mentioned in the last foregoing subsection has given to the tenant a notice stating –

(a) that the question of the giving of such a certificate is under consideration by the Minister or Board specified in the notice, and
(b) that if within twenty-one days of the giving of the notice the tenant makes to that Minister or Board representations in writing with respect to that question, they will be considered before the question is determined,

and if the tenant makes any such representations within the said twenty-one days the Minister or Board shall consider them before determining whether to give the certificate.

(3) Where a certificate has been given under subsection (1) of this section in relation to any tenancy, then –

(a) if a notice given under subsection (1) of section twenty-five of this Act specifies as the date of termination a date not earlier than the date specified in the certificate and contains a copy of the certificate subsection (6) of that section shall not apply to the notice and no application for a new tenancy shall be made by the tenant under subsection (1) of section twenty-four of this Act;

(b) if such a notice specifies an earlier date as the date of termination and contains a copy of the certificate, then if the court makes an order under Part II of this Act for the grant of a new tenancy the new tenancy shall be for a term expiring not later than the date specified in the certificate and shall not be a tenancy to which Part II of this Act applies.

(4) Where a tenant makes a request for a new tenancy under section twenty-six of this Act, and the interest of the landlord or any superior landlord in the property comprised in the current tenancy belongs or is held as mentioned in subsection (1) of this section, the following provisions shall have effect: −

(a) if a certificate has been given under the said subsection (1) in relation to the current tenancy, and within two months after the making of the request the landlord gives notice to the tenant that the certificate has been given and the notice contains a copy of the certificate, then −

(i) if the date specified in the certificate is not later than that specified in the tenant's request for a new tenancy, the tenant shall not make an application under section twenty-four of this Act for the grant of a new tenancy;

(ii) if, in any other case, the court makes an order under Part II of this Act for the grant of a new tenancy the new tenancy shall be for a term expiring not later than the date specified in the certificate and shall not be a tenancy to which Part II of this Act applies;

(b) if no such certificate has been given but notice under subsection (2) of this section has been given before the making of the request or within two months thereafter, the request shall not have effect, without prejudice however to the making of a new request when the Minister or Board has determined whether to give a certificate.

(5) Where application is made to the court under Part II of this Act for the grant of a new tenancy and the landlord's interest in the property comprised in the tenancy belongs or is held as mentioned in subsection (1) of this section, the Minister or Board in charge of any Government department may certify that it is necessary in the public interest that if the landlord makes an application in that behalf

the court shall determine as a term of the new tenancy that it shall be terminable by six months' notice to quit given by the landlord.

Subsection (2) of this section shall apply in relation to a certificate under this subsection, and if notice under the said subsection (2) has been given to the tenant –

(a) the court shall not determine the application for the grant of a new tenancy until the Minister or Board has determined whether to give a certificate;

(b) if a certificate is given, the court shall on the application of the landlord determine as a term of the new tenancy that it shall be terminable as aforesaid, and section twenty-five of this Act shall apply accordingly.

(6) The foregoing provisions of this section shall apply to an interest held by a Health Authority or Special Health Authority, as they apply to an interest held by a local authority but with the substitution, for the reference to the purposes of the authority, of a reference to the purposes of the National Health Service Act 1977.

(7) Where the interest of the landlord or any superior landlord in the property comprised in any tenancy belongs to the National Trust the Minister of Works may certify that it is requisite for the purpose of securing that the property will as from a specified date be used or occupied in a manner better suited to the nature thereof that the use or occupation of the property should be changed; and subsections (2) to (4) of this section shall apply in relation to certificates under this subsection, and to cases where the interest of the landlord or any superior landlord belongs to the National Trust, as those subsections apply in relation to certificates under subsection (1) of this section and to cases where the interest of the landlord or any superior landlord belongs or is held as mentioned in that subsection.

(8) In this and the next following section the expression 'Government department' does not include the Commissioners of Crown Lands and the expression 'landlord' has the same meaning as in Part II of this Act; and in the last foregoing subsection the expression 'National Trust' means the National Trust for Places of Historic Interest or Natural Beauty.

58 Termination on special grounds of tenancies to which Part II applies

(1) Where the landlord's interest in the property comprised in any tenancy belongs to or is held for the purposes of a Government department, and the Minister or Board in charge of any Government department certifies that for reasons of national security it is necessary that the use or occupation of the property should be discontinued or changed, then –

(a) if the landlord gives a notice under subsection (1) of section twenty-five of this Act containing a copy of the certificate, subsection (6) of that section shall not apply to the notice and no application for a new tenancy shall be made by the tenant under subsection (1) of section twenty-four of this Act;

(b) if (whether before or after the giving of the certificate) the tenant makes a request for a new tenancy under section twenty-six of this Act, and within two months after the making of the request the landlord gives notice to the tenant that the certificate has been given and the notice contains a copy of the certificate –

(i) the tenant shall not make an application under section twenty-four of this Act for the grant of a new tenancy, and

(ii) if the notice specifies as the date on which the tenancy is to terminate a date earlier than that specified in the tenant's request as the date on which the new tenancy is to begin but neither earlier than six months from the giving of the notice nor earlier than the earliest date at which apart from this Act the tenancy would come to an end or could be brought to an end, the tenancy shall terminate on the date specified in the notice instead of that specified in the request.

(2) Where the landlord's interest in the property comprised in any tenancy belongs to or is held for the purposes of a Government department, nothing in this Act shall invalidate an agreement to the effect –

(a) that on the giving of such a certificate as is mentioned in the last foregoing subsection the tenancy may be terminated by notice to quit given by the landlord of such length as may be specified in the agreement, if the notice contains a copy of the certificate; and

(b) that after the giving of such a notice containing such a copy the tenancy shall not be one to which Part II of this Act applies.

(3) Where the landlord's interest in the property comprised in any tenancy is held by statutory undertakers, nothing in this Act shall invalidate an agreement to the effect –

(a) that where the Minister or Board in charge of a Government department certifies that possession of the property comprised in the tenancy or a part thereof is urgently required for carrying out repairs (whether on that property or elsewhere) which are needed for the proper operation of the landlord's undertaking, the tenancy may be terminated by notice to quit given by the landlord of such length as may be specified in the agreement, if the notice contains a copy of the certificate; and

(b) that after the giving of such a notice containing such a copy, the tenancy shall not be one to which Part II of this Act applies.

(4) Where the court makes an order under Part II of this Act for the grant of a new tenancy and the Minister or Board in charge of any Government department certifies that the public interest requires the tenancy to be subject to such a term as is mentioned in paragraph (a) or (b) of this subsection, as the case may be, then –

(a) if the landlord's interest in the property comprised in the tenancy belongs to or is held for the purposes of a Government department, the court shall on the application of the landlord determine as a term of the new tenancy that such an agreement as is mentioned in subsection (2) of this section and specifying such length of notice as is mentioned in the certificate shall be embodied in the new tenancy;

(b) if the landlord's interest in that property is held by statutory undertakers, the court shall on the application of the landlord determine as a term of the new tenancy that such an agreement as is mentioned in subsection (3) of this section and specifying such length of notice as is mentioned in the certificate shall be embodied in the new tenancy.

59 Compensation for exercise of powers under sections 57 and 58

(1) Where by virtue of any certificate given for the purposes of either of the two last foregoing sections or, subject to subsection (1A) below, section 60A below the tenant is precluded from obtaining an order for the grant of a new tenancy, or of a new tenancy for a term expiring later than a specified date, the tenant shall be entitled on quitting the premises to recover from the owner of the interest by virtue of which the certificate was given an amount by way of compensation, and subsections (2), (3) to (3B) and (5) to (7) of section thirty-seven of this Act shall with the necessary modifications apply for the purposes of ascertaining the amount.

(1A) No compensation shall be recoverable under subsection (1) above where the certificate was given under section 60A below and either –

(a) the premises vested in the Welsh Development Agency under section 7 (property of Welsh Industrial Estates Corporation) or 8 (land held under Local Employment Act 1972) of the Welsh Development Agency Act 1975; or

(b) the tenant was not tenant of the premises when the said Agency acquired the interest by virtue of which the certificate was given.

(1B) ....

(2) Subsections (2) and (3) of section thirty-eight of this Act shall apply to compensation under this section as they apply to compensation under section thirty-seven of this Act.

60 Special provisions as to premises provided under Distribution of Industry Acts 1945 and 1950, etc

(1) Where the property comprised in a tenancy consists of premises of which the Minister of Technology or the English Industrial Estates Corporation the Urban Regeneration Agency is the landlord, being premises situated in a locality which is either –

(a) a development area ... or
(b) an intermediate area ...

and the Minister of Technology certifies that it is necessary or expedient for achieving the purpose mentioned in section 2(1) of the said Act of 1972 that the use or occupation of the property should be changed, paragraphs (a) and (b) of subsection (1) of section fifty-eight of this Act shall apply as they apply where such a certificate is given as is mentioned in that subsection.

(2) Where the court makes an order under Part II of this Act for the grant of a new tenancy of any such premises as aforesaid, and the Secretary of State certifies that it is necessary or expedient as aforesaid that the tenancy should be subject to a term, specified in the certificate, prohibiting or restricting the tenant from assigning the tenancy or sub-letting, charging or parting with possession of the premises or any part thereof or changing the use of premises or any part thereof, the court shall determine that the terms of the tenancy shall include the terms specified in the certificate.

(3) In this section 'development area' and 'intermediate area' mean an area for the time being specified as a development area or, as the case may be, as an intermediate area by an order made, or having effect as if made, under section 1 of the Industrial Development Act 1982.

60A Welsh Development Agency premises

(1) Where the property comprised in a tenancy consists of premises of which the Welsh Development Agency is the landlord, and the Secretary of State certifies that it is necessary or expedient, for the purpose of providing employment appropriate to the needs of the

area in which the premises are situated, that the use or occupation of the property should be changed, paragraphs (a) and (b) of section 58(1) above shall apply as they apply where such a certificate is given as is mentioned in that subsection.

(2) Where the court makes an order under Part II of this Act for the grant of a new tenancy of any such premises as aforesaid, and the Secretary of State certifies that it is necessary or expedient as aforesaid that the tenancy should be subject to a term, specified in the certificate, prohibiting or restricting the tenant from assigning the tenancy or sub-letting, charging or parting with possession of the premises or any part of the premises or changing the use of the premises or any part of the premises, the court shall determine that the terms of the tenancy shall include the terms specified in the certificate.

...

63 Jurisdiction of court for purposes of Parts I and II and of Part I of Landlord and Tenant Act 1927

(1) Any jurisdiction conferred on the court by any provision of Part I of this Act shall be exercised by the county court.

(2) Any jurisdiction conferred on the court by any provision of Part II of this Act or conferred on the tribunal by Part I of the Landlord and Tenant Act 1927, shall, subject to the provisions of this section, be exercised by the High Court or a County Court.

(3) ... [repealed]

(4) The following provisions shall have effect as respects transfer of proceedings from or to the High Court or the county court, that is to say –

    (a) where an application is made to the one but by virtue of an Order under section 1 of the Courts and Legal Services Act 1990 cannot be entertained except by the other, the application shall not be treated as improperly made but any proceedings thereon shall be transferred to the other court;

    (b) any proceedings under the provisions of Part II of this Act or of Part I of the Landlord and Tenant Act 1927, which are pending before one of those courts may by order of that court made on the application of any person interested be transferred to the other court, if it appears to the court making the order that it is desirable that the proceedings and any proceedings before the other court should both be entertained by the other court.

(5) In any proceedings where in accordance with the foregoing provisions of this section the county court exercises jurisdiction the powers of the judge of summoning one or more assessors under subsection (1) of section eighty-eight of the County Courts Act 1934, may be exercised notwithstanding that no application is made in that behalf by any party to the proceedings.

(6) Where in any such proceedings an assessor is summoned by a judge under the said subsection

(1) –

> (a) he may, if so directed by the judge, inspect the land to which the proceedings relate without the judge and report to the judge in writing thereon;
> (b) the judge may on consideration of the report and any observations of the parties thereon give such judgment or make such order in the proceedings as may be just;
> (c) the remuneration of the assessor shall be at such rate as may be determined by the Lord Chancellor with the approval of the Treasury and shall be defrayed out of moneys provided by Parliament.

(7) In this section the expression 'the holding' –

> (a) in relation to proceedings under Part II of this Act, has the meaning assigned to it by subsection (3) of section twenty-three of this Act,
> (b) in relation to proceedings under Part I of the Landlord and Tenant Act 1927, has the same meaning as in the said Part I.

(8) ... [repealed]

(9) Nothing in this section shall prejudice the operation of section 41 of the County Courts Act 1984 (which relates to the removal into the High Court of proceedings commenced in a county court).

(10) ... [repealed]

64 Interim continuation of tenancies pending determination by court

(1) In any case where –

> (a) a notice to terminate a tenancy has been given under Part I or Part II of this Act or a request for a new tenancy has been made under Part II thereof, and
> (b) an application to the court has been made under the said Part I or under section 24(1) or 29(2) of this Act, as the case may be, and

(c) apart from this section the effect of the notice or request would be to terminate the tenancy before the expiration of the period of three months beginning with the date on which the application is finally disposed of,

the effect of the notice or request shall be to terminate the tenancy at the expiration of the said period of three months and not at any other time.

(2) The reference in paragraph (c) of subsection (1) of this section to the date on which an application is finally disposed of shall be construed as a reference to the earliest date by which the proceedings on the application (including any proceedings on or in consequence of an appeal) have been determined and any time for appealing or further appealing has expired, except that if the application is withdrawn or any appeal is abandoned the reference shall be construed as a reference to the date of the withdrawal or abandonment.

65 Provisions as to reversions

(1) Where by virtue of any provision of this Act a tenancy (in this subsection referred to as 'the inferior tenancy') is continued for a period such as to extend to or beyond the end of the term of a superior tenancy, the superior tenancy shall, for the purposes of this Act and of any other enactment and of any rule of law, be deemed so long as it subsists to be an interest in reversion expectant upon the termination of the inferior tenancy and, if there is no intermediate tenancy, to be the interest in reversion immediately expectant upon the termination thereof.

(2) In the case of a tenancy continuing by virtue of any provision of this Act after the coming to an end of the interest in reversion immediately expectant upon the termination thereof, subsection (1) of section one hundred and thirty-nine of the Law of Property Act 1925 (which relates to the effect of the extinguishment of a reversion) shall apply as if references in the said subsection (1) to the surrender or merger of the reversion included references to the coming to an end of the reversion for any reason other than surrender or merger.

(3) Where by virtue of any provision of this Act a tenancy (in this subsection referred to as 'the continuing tenancy') is continued beyond the beginning of a reversionary tenancy which was granted (whether before or after the commencement of this Act) so as to begin on or after the date on which apart from this Act the continuing tenancy would have come to an end, the reversionary tenancy shall have effect as if it had been granted subject to the continuing tenancy.

(4) Where by virtue of any provision of this Act a tenancy (in this subsection referred to as 'the new tenancy') is granted for a period beginning on the same date as a reversionary tenancy or for a period such as to extend beyond the beginning of the term of a reversionary tenancy, whether the reversionary tenancy in question was granted before or after the commencement of this Act, the reversionary tenancy shall have effect as if it had been granted subject to the new tenancy.

66 Provisions as to notices

(1) Any form of notice required by this Act to be prescribed shall be prescribed by regulations made by the Lord Chancellor by statutory instrument.

(2) Where the form of a notice to be served on persons of any description is to be prescribed for any of the purposes of this Act, the form to be prescribed shall include such an explanation of the relevant provisions of this Act as appears to the Lord Chancellor requisite for informing persons of that description of their rights and obligations under those provisions.

(3) Different forms of notice may be prescribed for the purposes of the operation of any provision of this Act in relation to different cases.

(4) Section twenty-three of the Landlord and Tenant Act 1927 (which relates to the service of notices) shall apply for the purposes of this Act.

(5) Any statutory instrument under this section shall be subject to annulment in pursuance of a resolution of either House of Parliament.

67 Provisions as to mortgagees in possession

Anything authorised or required by the provisions of this Act, other than subsection ... (3) of section forty, to be done at any time by, to or with the landlord, or a landlord of a specified description, shall, if at that time the interest of the landlord in question is subject to a mortgage and the mortgagee is in possession or a receiver appointed by the mortgagee or by the court is in receipt of the rents and profits, be deemed to be authorised or required to be done by, to or with the mortgagee instead of that landlord.

68 Repeal of enactments and transitional provisions

(1) ... [repealed]

(2) The transitional provisions set out in the Ninth Schedule to this Act shall have effect.

69 Interpretation

(1) In this Act the following expressions have the meanings hereby assigned to them respectively, that is to say: –

'agricultural holding' has the same meaning as in the Agricultural Holdings Act 1986;

'development corporation' has the same meaning as in the New Towns Act 1946;

'farm business tenancy' has the same meaning as in the Agricultural Tenancies Act 1995;

'local authority' means any local authority within the meaning of the Town and Country Planning Act 1990, any National Park authority, the Broads Authority, the London Fire and Emergency Planning Authority or ... a joint authority established by Part IV of the Local Government Act 1985;

'mortgage' includes a charge or lien and 'mortgagor' and 'mortgagee' shall be construed accordingly;

'notice to quit' means a notice to terminate a tenancy (whether a periodical tenancy or a tenancy for a term of years certain) given in accordance with the provisions (whether express or implied) of that tenancy;

'repairs' includes any work of maintenance, decoration or restoration, and references to repairing, to keeping or yielding up in repair and to state of repair shall be construed accordingly;

'statutory undertakers' has the same meaning as in the Town and Country Planning Act 1947 ... ;

'tenancy' means a tenancy created either immediately or derivatively out of the freehold, whether by a lease or underlease, by an agreement for a lease or underlease or by a tenancy agreement or in pursuance of any enactment (including this Act), but does not include a mortgage term or any interest arising in favour of a mortgagor by his attorning tenant to his mortgagee, and references to the granting of a tenancy and to demised property shall be construed accordingly;

'terms', in relation to a tenancy, includes conditions.

(2) References in this Act to an agreement between the landlord and the tenant (except in section seventeen and subsections (1) and (2) of section thirty-eight thereof) shall be construed as references to an agreement in writing between them.

(3) References in this Act to an action for any relief shall be construed as including references to a claim for that relief by way of counter-claim in any proceedings.

70 Short title and citation, commencement and extent

(1) This Act may be cited as the Landlord and Tenant Act 1954, and the Landlord and Tenant Act 1927, and this Act may be cited together as the Landlord and Tenant Acts 1927 and 1954.

(2) This Act shall come into operation on the first day of October, nineteen hundred and fifty-four.

(3) This Act shall not extend to Scotland or to Northern Ireland.

SCHEDULE 6

Provisions for purposes of Part II where immediate landlord is not the freeholder

Section 44

Definitions

1

In this Schedule the following expressions have the meanings hereby assigned to them in relation to a tenancy (in this Schedule referred to as 'the relevant tenancy'), that is to say –

'the competent landlord' means the person who in relation to the tenancy is for the time being the landlord (as defined by section forty-four of this Act) for the purposes of Part II of this Act;

'mesne landlord' means a tenant whose interest is intermediate between the relevant tenancy and the interest of the competent landlord; and

'superior landlord' means a person (whether the owner of the fee simple or a tenant) whose interest is superior to the interest of the competent landlord.

Power of court to order reversionary tenancies

2

Where the period for which in accordance with the provisions of Part II of this Act it is agreed or determined by the court that a new tenancy should be granted there under will extend beyond the date on which the interest of the immediate landlord will come to an end, the power of the court under Part II of this Act to order such a grant shall include power to order the grant of a new tenancy until the expiration of that interest and also to order the grant of such a reversionary tenancy or reversionary tenancies as may be required to secure that the combined effects of those grants will be equivalent to the grant of a tenancy for that period; and the provisions of Part II of this Act shall, subject to the necessary modifications, apply in relation to the grant of a tenancy together with one or more reversionary tenancies as they apply in relation to the grant of one new tenancy.

Acts of competent landlord binding on other landlords

3

(1) Any notice given by the competent landlord under Part II of this Act to terminate the relevant tenancy, and any agreement made between that landlord and the tenant as to the granting, duration, or terms of a future tenancy, being an agreement made for the purposes of the said Part II, shall bind the interest of any mesne landlord notwithstanding that he has not consented to the giving of the notice or was not a party to the agreement.

(2) The competent landlord shall have power for the purposes of Part II of this Act to give effect to any agreement with the tenant for the grant of a new tenancy beginning with the coming to an end of the relevant tenancy notwithstanding that the competent landlord will not be the immediate landlord at the commencement of the new tenancy, and any instrument made in the exercise of the power conferred by this sub-paragraph shall have effect as if the mesne landlord had been a party thereto.

(3) Nothing in the foregoing provisions of this paragraph shall prejudice the provisions of the next following paragraph.

Provisions as to consent of mesne landlord to acts of competent landlord

4

(1) If the competent landlord, not being the immediate landlord, gives any such notice or makes any such agreement as is mentioned in sub-paragraph (1) of the last foregoing paragraph without the consent of every mesne landlord, any mesne landlord whose consent has not been given thereto shall be entitled to compensation from the competent landlord for any loss arising in consequence of the giving of the notice or the making of the agreement.

(2) If the competent landlord applies to any mesne landlord for his consent to such a notice or agreement, that consent shall not be unreasonably withheld, but may be given subject to any conditions which may be reasonable (including conditions as to the modification

of the proposed notice or agreement or as to the payment of compensation by the competent landlord).

(3) Any question arising under this paragraph whether consent has been unreasonably withheld or whether any conditions imposed on the giving of consent are unreasonable shall be determined by the court.

Consent of superior landlord required for agreements affecting his interest

5

An agreement between the competent landlord and the tenant made for the purposes of Part II of this Act in a case where –

(a) the competent landlord is himself a tenant, and
(b) the agreement would apart from this paragraph operate as respects any period after the coming to an end of the interest of the competent landlord,

shall not have effect unless every superior landlord who will be the immediate landlord of the tenant during any part of that period is a party to the agreement.

Withdrawal by competent landlord of notice given by mesne landlord

6

Where the competent landlord has given a notice under section 25 of this Act to terminate the relevant tenancy and, within two months after the giving of the notice, a superior landlord –

(a) becomes the competent landlord; and
(b) gives to the tenant notice in the prescribed form that he withdraws the notice previously given,

the notice under section 25 of this Act shall cease to have effect, but without prejudice to the giving of a further notice under that section by the competent landlord.

Duty to inform superior landlords

7

If the competent landlord's interest in the property comprised in the relevant tenancy is a tenancy which will come or can be brought to an end within sixteen months (or any further time by which it may be continued under section 36(2) or section 64 of this Act) and he gives to the tenant under the relevant tenancy a notice under section

25 of this Act to terminate the tenancy or is given by him a notice under section 26(3) of this Act: –

(a) the competent landlord shall forthwith send a copy of the notice to his immediate landlord; and
(b) any superior landlord whose interest in the property is a tenancy shall forthwith send to his immediate landlord any copy which has been sent to him in pursuance of the preceding sub-paragraph or this sub-paragraph.

SCHEDULE 8

Application of Part II to land belonging to Crown and Duchies of Lancaster and Cornwall

Section 56

1

Where an interest in any property comprised in a tenancy belongs to Her Majesty in right of the Duchy of Lancaster, then for the purposes of Part II of this Act the Chancellor of the Duchy shall represent Her Majesty and shall be deemed to be the owner of the interest.

2

Where an interest in any property comprised in a tenancy belongs to the Duchy of Cornwall, then for the purposes of Part II of this Act such person as the Duke of Cornwall, or other the possessor for the time being of the Duchy of Cornwall, appoints shall represent the Duke of Cornwall or other the possessor aforesaid, and shall be deemed to be the owner of the interest and may do any act or thing under the said Part II which the owner of that interest is authorised or required to do there under.

3

...

4

The amount of any compensation payable under section thirty-seven of this Act by the Chancellor of the Duchy of Lancaster shall be raised and paid as an expense incurred in improvement of land belonging to Her Majesty in right of the Duchy within section twenty-five of the Act of the fifty-seventh year of King George the Third, Chapter ninety-seven.

5

Any compensation payable under section thirty-seven of this Act by the person representing the Duke of Cornwall or other the possessor for the time being of the Duchy of Cornwall shall be paid, and advances therefore made, in the manner and subject to the provisions of section eight of the Duchy of Cornwall Management Act 1863 with respect to improvements of land mentioned in that section.

SCHEDULE 9

Transitional provisions

Sections 41, 42, 56, 68

1, 2

...

3

Where immediately before the commencement of this Act a person was protected by section seven of the Leasehold Property (Temporary Provisions) Act 1951, against the making of an order or giving of a judgment for possession or ejectment, the Rent Acts shall apply in relation to the dwelling-house to which that person's protection extended immediately before the commencement of this Act as if section fifteen of this Act had always had effect.

4

For the purposes of section twenty-six and subsection (2) of section forty of this Act a tenancy which is not such a tenancy as is mentioned in subsection (1) of the said section twenty-six but is a tenancy to which Part II of this Act applies and in respect of which the following conditions are satisfied, that is to say –

(a) that it took effect before the commencement of this Act at the coming to an end by effluxion of time or notice to quit of a tenancy which is such a tenancy as is mentioned in subsection (1) of the said section twenty-six or is by virtue of this paragraph deemed to be such a tenancy; and

(b) that if this Act had then been in force the tenancy at the coming to an end of which it took effect would have been one to which Part II of this Act applies; and

(c) that the tenant is either the tenant under the tenancy at the coming to an end of which it took effect or a successor to his business,

shall be deemed to be such a tenancy as is mentioned in subsection (1) of the said section twenty-six.

5

(1) A tenant under a tenancy which was current at the commencement of this Act shall not in any case be entitled to compensation under section thirty-seven or fifty-nine of this Act

unless at the date on which he is to quit the holding the holding or part thereof has continuously been occupied for the purposes of the carrying on of the tenant's business (whether by him or by any other person) for at least five years.

(2) Where a tenant under a tenancy which was current at the commencement of this Act would but for this sub-paragraph be entitled both to –

(a) compensation under section thirty-seven or section fifty-nine of this Act; and
(b) compensation payable, under the provisions creating the tenancy, on the termination of the tenancy,

he shall be entitled, at his option, to the one or the other, but not to both.

6

(1) Where the landlord's interest in the property comprised in a tenancy which, immediately before the commencement of this Act, was terminable by less than six months' notice to quit given by the landlord belongs to or is held for the purposes of a Government Department or is held by statutory undertakers, the tenancy shall have effect as if that shorter length of notice were specified in such an agreement as is mentioned in subsection (2) or (3) of section fifty-eight of this Act, as the case may be, and the agreement were embodied in the tenancy.

(2) The last foregoing sub-paragraph shall apply in relation to a tenancy where the landlord's interest belongs or is held as aforesaid and which, immediately before the commencement of this Act, was terminable by the landlord without notice as if the tenancy had then been terminable by one month's notice to quit given by the landlord.

7

... [repealed]

8

Where at the commencement of this Act any proceedings are pending on an application made before the commencement of this Act to the tribunal under section five of the Landlord and Tenant Act 1927, no further step shall be taken in the proceedings except for the purposes of an order as to costs; and where the tribunal has made an interim order in the proceedings under subsection (13) of section five of that Act authorising the tenant to remain in possession of the property comprised in his tenancy for any period, the tenancy shall be deemed not to have come to an end before the expiration of that period, and section twenty-four of this Act shall have effect in relation to it accordingly.

9, 10

... [repealed]

11

Notwithstanding the repeal of Part II of the Leasehold Property (Temporary Provisions) Act 1951, where immediately before the commencement of this Act a tenancy was being continued by subsection (3) of section eleven of that Act it shall not come to an end at the commencement of this Act, and section twenty-four of this Act shall have effect in relation to it accordingly.

Appendix 2 – *Landlord and Tenant Act* 1927

1927 Chapter 36

An Act to provide for the payment of compensation for improvements and goodwill to tenants of premises used for business purposes, or the grant of a new lease in lieu thereof; and to amend the law of landlord and tenant

[22 December 1927]

23 Service of notices

(1) Any notice, request, demand or other instrument under this Act shall be in writing and may be served on the person on whom it is to be served either personally, or by leaving it for him at his last known place of abode in England or Wales, or by sending it through the post in a registered letter addressed to him there, or, in the case of a local or public authority or a statutory or a public utility company, to the secretary or other proper officer at the principal office of such authority or company, and in the case of a notice to a landlord, the person on whom it is to be served shall include any agent of the landlord duly authorised in that behalf.

(2) Unless or until a tenant of a holding shall have received notice that the person theretofore entitled to the rents and profits of the holding (hereinafter referred to as 'the original landlord') has ceased to be so entitled, and also notice of the name and address of the person who has become entitled to such rents and profits, any claim, notice, request, demand, or other instrument, which the tenant shall serve upon or deliver to the original landlord shall be deemed to have been served upon or delivered to the landlord of such holding.

25 Interpretation

(1) For the purposes of this Act, unless the context otherwise requires –

The expression 'tenant' means any person entitled in possession to the holding under any contract of tenancy, whether the interest of such tenant was acquired by original contract, assignment, operation of law or otherwise;

The expression 'landlord' means any person who under a lease is, as between himself and the tenant or other lessee, for the time being entitled to the rents and profits of the demised premises payable under the lease;

The expression 'predecessor in title' in relation to a tenant or landlord means any person through whom the tenant or landlord has derived title, whether by assignment, by will, by intestacy, or by operation of law;

The expression 'lease' means a lease, under-lease or other tenancy, assignment operating as a lease or under-lease, or an agreement for such lease, under-lease tenancy, or assignment;

The expression 'mining lease' means a lease for any mining purpose or purposes connected therewith, and 'mining purposes' include the sinking and searching for, winning, working, getting, making merchantable, smelting or otherwise converting or working for the purposes of any manufacture, carrying away, and disposing of mines and minerals, in or under land, and the erection of buildings, and the execution of engineering and other works suitable for those purposes;

The expression 'term of years absolute' has the same meaning as in the Law of Property Act 1925;

The expression 'statutory company' means any company constituted by or under an Act of Parliament to construct, work or carry on any … , tramway, hydraulic power, dock, canal or railway undertaking; and the expression 'public utility company' means any company within the meaning of the *Companies (Consolidation) Act* 1908, or a society registered under the *Industrial and Provident Societies Acts* 1893 to 1913, carrying on any such undertaking;

The expression 'prescribed' means prescribed by rules of court or by a practice direction.

(2) The designation of landlord and tenant shall continue to apply to the parties until the conclusion of any proceedings taken under or in pursuance of this Act in respect of compensation.

Appendix 3: Hostile section 25 notice

**Landlord's notice ending a business tenancy
and reasons for refusing a new one
Section 25 of the Landlord and Tenant Act 1954**

IMPORTANT NOTE FOR THE LANDLORD: If you wish to oppose the grant of a new tenancy on any of the grounds in section 30(1) of the *Landlord and Tenant Act* 1954, complete this form and send it to the tenant. If the tenant may be entitled to acquire the freehold or an extended lease, use form 7 in Schedule 2 to the Landlord and Tenant Act 1954, Part 2 (Notices) Regulations 2004 instead of this form.

To: *(insert name and address of tenant)*

From: *(insert name and address of landlord)*

1. This notice relates to the following property: (insert address or description of property).

2. I am giving you notice under section 25 of the Landlord and Tenant Act 1954 to end your tenancy on (insert date).

3. I am opposed to the grant of a new tenancy.

4. You may ask the court to order the grant of a new tenancy. If you do, I will oppose your application on the ground(s) mentioned in paragraph(s)* of section 30(1) of that Act. I draw your attention to the Table in the Notes below, which sets out all the grounds of opposition.
(insert letter(s) of the paragraph(s) relied on)

5. If you wish to ask the court for a new tenancy you must do so before the date in paragraph 2 unless, before that date, we agree in writing to a later date.

6. I can ask the court to order the ending of your tenancy without granting you a new tenancy. I may have to pay you compensation if I have relied only on one or more of the grounds mentioned in paragraphs (e), (f) and (g) of section 30(1). If I ask the court to end your tenancy, you can challenge my application.

7. Please send all correspondence about this notice to:

Name:
Address:

Signed:
Date:
*[Landlord] *[On behalf of the landlord] *[Mortgagee] *[On behalf of the mortgagee]
(*delete if inapplicable)

IMPORTANT NOTE FOR THE TENANT:

This notice is intended to bring your tenancy to an end on the date specified in paragraph 2.

Your landlord is not prepared to offer you a new tenancy. You will not get a new tenancy unless you successfully challenge in court the grounds on which your landlord opposes the grant of a new tenancy.

If you want to continue to occupy your property you must act quickly. The notes below should help you to decide what action you now need to take. If you want to challenge your landlord's refusal to renew your tenancy, get advice immediately from a solicitor or a surveyor.

NOTES

The sections mentioned below are sections of the *Landlord and Tenant Act* 1954, as amended, (most recently by the Regulatory Reform (Business Tenancies) (England and Wales) Order 2003).

Ending of your tenancy

This notice is intended to bring your tenancy to an end on the date given in paragraph 2. Section 25 contains rules about the date that the landlord can put in that paragraph.

Your landlord is not prepared to offer you a new tenancy. If you want a new tenancy you will need to apply to the court for a new tenancy and successfully challenge the landlord's grounds for opposition (see the section below headed 'Landlord's opposition to new tenancy'). If you wish to apply to the court you must do so before the date given in paragraph 2 of this notice, unless you and your landlord have agreed in writing, before that date, to extend the deadline (sections 29A and 29B).

If you apply to the court your tenancy will continue after the date given in paragraph 2 of this notice while your application is being considered (section 24). You may not apply to the court if your landlord has already done so (section 24(2A) and (2B)).

You may only stay in the property after the date given in paragraph 2 (or such later date as you and the landlord may have agreed in writing) if before that date you have asked the court to order the grant of a new tenancy or the landlord has asked the court to order the ending of your tenancy without granting you a new one.

If you are in any doubt about what action you should take, get advice immediately from a solicitor or a surveyor.

Landlord's opposition to new tenancy

If you apply to the court for a new tenancy, the landlord can only oppose your application on one or more of the grounds set out in section 30(1). If you match the letter(s) specified in paragraph 4 of this notice with those in the first column in the Table below, you can see from the second column the ground(s) on which the landlord relies.

Paragraph of section 30(1)	Grounds
(a)	Where under the current tenancy the tenant has any obligations as respects the repair and maintenance of the holding, that the tenant ought not to be granted a new tenancy in view of the state of repair of the holding, being a state resulting from the tenant's failure to comply with the said obligations.
(b)	That the tenant ought not to be granted a new tenancy in view of his persistent delay in paying rent which has become due.
(c)	That the tenant ought not to be granted a new tenancy in view of other substantial breaches by him of his obligations under the current tenancy, or for any other reason connected with the tenant's use or management of the holding.
(d)	That the landlord has offered and is willing to provide or secure the provision of alternative accommodation for the tenant, that the terms on which the alternative accommodation is available are reasonable having regard to the terms of the current tenancy and to all other relevant circumstances, and that the accommodation and the time at which it will be available are suitable for the tenant's requirements (including the requirement to preserve goodwill) having regard to the nature and class of his business and to the situation and extent of, and facilities afforded by, the holding.

(e)	Where the current tenancy was created by the sub-letting of part only of the property comprised in a superior tenancy and the landlord is the owner of an interest in reversion expectant on the termination of that superior tenancy, that the aggregate of the rents reasonably obtainable on separate lettings of the holding and the remainder of that property would be substantially less than the rent reasonably obtainable on a letting of that property as a whole, that on the termination of the current tenancy the landlord requires possession of the holding for the purposes of letting or otherwise disposing of the said property as a whole, and that in view thereof the tenant ought not to be granted a new tenancy.
(f)	That on the termination of the current tenancy the landlord intends to demolish or reconstruct the premises comprised in the holding or a substantial part of those premises or to carry out substantial work of construction on the holding or part thereof and that he could not reasonably do so without obtaining possession of the holding.
(g)	On the termination of the current tenancy the landlord intends to occupy the holding for the purposes, or partly for the purposes, of a business to be carried on by him therein, or as his residence.

In this Table 'the holding' means the property that is the subject of the tenancy.

In ground (e), 'the landlord is the owner of an interest in reversion expectant on the termination of that superior tenancy' means that the landlord has an interest in the property that will entitle him or her, when your immediate landlord's tenancy comes to an end, to exercise certain rights and obligations in relation to the property that are currently exercisable by your immediate landlord.

If the landlord relies on ground (f), the court can sometimes still grant a new tenancy if certain conditions set out in section 31A are met.

If the landlord relies on ground (g), please note that 'the landlord' may have an extended meaning. Where a landlord has a controlling interest in a company then either the landlord or the company can rely on ground (g). Where the landlord is a company and a person has a controlling interest in that company then either of them can rely on ground (g) (section 30(1A) and (1B)). A person has a 'controlling interest' in a company if, had he been a company, the other company would have been its subsidiary (section 46(2)).

The landlord must normally have been the landlord for at least five years before he or she can rely on ground (g).

Compensation

If you cannot get a new tenancy solely because one or more of grounds (e), (f) and (g) applies, you may be entitled to compensation under section 37. If your landlord has opposed your application on any of the other grounds as well as (e), (f) or (g) you can only get compensation if the court's refusal to grant a new tenancy is based solely on one or more of grounds (e), (f) and (g). In other words, you cannot get compensation under section 37 if the court has refused your tenancy on other grounds, even if one or more of grounds (e), (f) and (g) also applies.

If your landlord is an authority possessing compulsory purchase powers (such as a local authority) you may be entitled to a disturbance payment under Part 3 of the Land Compensation Act 1973.

Validity of this notice

The landlord who has given you this notice may not be the landlord to whom you pay your rent (sections 44 and 67). This does not necessarily mean that the notice is invalid.

If you have any doubts about whether this notice is valid, get advice immediately from a solicitor or a surveyor.

Further information

An explanation of the main points to consider when renewing or ending a business tenancy, *'Renewing and Ending Business Leases: a Guide for Tenants and Landlords'*, can be found at *www.odpm.gov.uk*. Printed copies of the explanation, but not of this form, are available from 1st June 2004 from Free Literature, PO Box 236, Wetherby, West Yorkshire, LS23 7NB (0870 1226 236).

Appendix 4: Non-hostile section 25 notice

**Landlord's notice ending a business tenancy
with proposals for a new one**

Section 25 of the Landlord and Tenant Act 1954

IMPORTANT NOTE FOR THE LANDLORD: If you are willing to grant a new tenancy, complete this form and send it to the tenant. If you wish to oppose the grant of a new tenancy, use form 2 in Schedule 2 to the Landlord and Tenant Act 1954, Part 2 (Notices) Regulations 2004 or, where the tenant may be entitled to acquire the freehold or an extended lease, form 7 in that Schedule, instead of this form.

To: *(insert name and address of tenant)*

From: *(insert name and address of landlord)*

1. This notice applies to the following property: (insert address or description of property).

2. I am giving you notice under section 25 of the Landlord and Tenant Act 1954 to end your tenancy on *(insert date)*.

3. I am not opposed to granting you a new tenancy. You will find my proposals for the new tenancy, which we can discuss, in the Schedule to this notice.

4. If we cannot agree on all the terms of a new tenancy, either you or I may ask the court to order the grant of a new tenancy and settle the terms on which we cannot agree.

5. If you wish to ask the court for a new tenancy you must do so by the date in paragraph 2, unless we agree in writing to a later date and do so before the date in paragraph 2.

6. Please send all correspondence about this notice to:

Name:
Address:

Signed:
Date:
*[Landlord] *[On behalf of the landlord] *[Mortgagee] *[On behalf of the mortgagee]
*(delete if inapplicable)

Schedule
Landlord's proposals for a new tenancy
(attach or insert proposed terms of the new tenancy)

IMPORTANT NOTE FOR THE TENANT:

This Notice is intended to bring your tenancy to an end. If you want to continue to occupy your property after the date specified in paragraph 2 you must act quickly. If you are in any doubt about the action that you should take, get advice immediately from a solicitor or a surveyor.

The landlord is prepared to offer you a new tenancy and has set out proposed terms in the Schedule to this notice. You are not bound to accept these terms. They are merely suggestions as a basis for negotiation. In the event of disagreement, ultimately the court would settle the terms of the new tenancy.

It would be wise to seek professional advice before agreeing to accept the landlord's terms or putting forward your own proposals.

NOTES:

The sections mentioned below are sections of the Landlord and Tenant Act 1954, as amended, (most recently by the Regulatory Reform (Business Tenancies) (England and Wales) Order 2003).

Ending of tenancy and grant of new tenancy

This notice is intended to bring your tenancy to an end on the date given in paragraph 2. Section 25 contains rules about the date that the landlord can put in that paragraph.

However, your landlord is prepared to offer you a new tenancy and has set out proposals for it in the Schedule to this notice (section 25(8)). You are not obliged to accept these proposals and may put forward your own.

If you and your landlord are unable to agree terms either one of you may apply to the court. You may not apply to the court if your landlord has already done so (section 24(2A)). If you wish to apply to the court you must do so by the date given in paragraph 2 of this notice, unless you and your landlord have agreed in writing to extend the deadline (sections 29A and 29B).

The court will settle the rent and other terms of the new tenancy or those on which you and your landlord cannot agree (sections 34 and 35). If you apply to the court your tenancy will continue after the date shown in paragraph 2 of this notice while your application is being considered (section 24).

If you are in any doubt about what action you should take, get advice immediately from a solicitor or a surveyor.

Negotiating a new tenancy

Most tenancies are renewed by negotiation. You and your landlord may agree in writing to extend the deadline for making an application to the court while negotiations continue. Either you or your landlord can ask the court to fix the rent that you will have to pay while the tenancy continues (sections 24A to 24D).

You may only stay in the property after the date in paragraph 2 (or if we have agreed in writing to a later date, that date), if by then you or the landlord has asked the court to order the grant of a new tenancy.

If you do try to agree a new tenancy with your landlord remember:

that your present tenancy will not continue after the date in paragraph 2 of this notice without the agreement in writing mentioned above, unless you have applied to the court or your landlord has done so, and

that you will lose your right to apply to the court once the deadline in paragraph 2 of this notice has passed, unless there is a written agreement extending the deadline.

Validity of this notice

The landlord who has given you this notice may not be the landlord to whom you pay your rent (sections 44 and 67). This does not necessarily mean that the notice is invalid.

If you have any doubts about whether this notice is valid, get advice immediately from a solicitor or a surveyor.

Further information

An explanation of the main points to consider when renewing or ending a business tenancy, *'Renewing and Ending Business Leases: a Guide for Tenants and Landlords'*, can be found at *www.odpm.gov.uk*. Printed copies of the explanation, but not of this form, are available from 1st June 2004 from Free Literature, PO Box 236, Wetherby, West Yorkshire, LS23 7NB (0870 1226 236).

Appendix 5: Section 26 request

Tenant's request for a new business tenancy

Section 26 of the Landlord and Tenant Act 1954

To *(insert name and address of landlord):*

From *(insert name and address of tenant)*:

1. This notice relates to the following property: (insert address or description of property).

2. I am giving you notice under section 26 of the Landlord and Tenant Act 1954 that I request a new tenancy beginning on *(insert date)*.

3. You will find my proposals for the new tenancy, which we can discuss, in the Schedule to this notice.

4. If we cannot agree on all the terms of a new tenancy, either you or I may ask the court to order the grant of a new tenancy and settle the terms on which we cannot agree.

5. If you wish to ask the court to order the grant of a new tenancy you must do so by the date in paragraph 2, unless we agree in writing to a later date and do so before the date in paragraph 2.

6. You may oppose my request for a new tenancy only on one or more of the grounds set out in section 30(1) of the Landlord and Tenant Act 1954. You must tell me what your grounds are within two months of receiving this notice. If you miss this deadline you will not be able to oppose renewal of my tenancy and you will have to grant me a new tenancy.

7. Please send all correspondence about this notice to:

Name:

Address:

Signed:
Date:
*[Tenant] *[On behalf of the tenant]
(*delete whichever is inapplicable)

Schedule
Tenant's proposals for a new tenancy
(attach or insert proposed terms of the new tenancy)

IMPORTANT NOTE FOR THE LANDLORD

This notice requests a new tenancy of your property or part of it. If you want to oppose this request you must act quickly.

Read the notice and all the Notes carefully. It would be wise to seek professional advice.

NOTES

The sections mentioned below are sections of the Landlord and Tenant Act 1954, as amended, (most recently by the Regulatory Reform (Business Tenancies) (England and Wales) Order 2003)

Tenant's request for a new tenancy

This request by your tenant for a new tenancy brings his or her current tenancy to an end on the day before the date mentioned in paragraph 2 of this notice. Section 26 contains rules about the date that the tenant can put in paragraph 2 of this notice.

Your tenant can apply to the court under section 24 for a new tenancy. You may apply for a new tenancy yourself, under the same section, but not if your tenant has already served an application. Once an application has been made to the court, your tenant's current tenancy will continue after the date mentioned in paragraph 2 while the application is being considered by the court. Either you or your tenant can ask the court to fix the rent which your tenant will have to pay whilst the tenancy continues (sections 24A to 24D). The court will settle any terms of a new tenancy on which you and your tenant disagree (sections 34 and 35).

Time limit for opposing your tenant's request

If you do not want to grant a new tenancy, you have two months from the making of your tenant's request in which to notify him or her that you will oppose any application made to the court for a new tenancy. You do not need a special form to do this, but the notice must be in writing and it must state on which of the grounds set out in section 30(1) you will oppose the application. If you do not use the same wording of the ground (or grounds), as set out below, your notice may be ineffective.

If there has been any delay in your seeing this notice, you may need to act very quickly. If you are in any doubt about what action you should take, get advice immediately from a solicitor or a surveyor.

Grounds for opposing tenant's application

If you wish to oppose the renewal of the tenancy, you can do so by opposing your tenant's application to the court, or by making your own application to the court for termination without renewal. However, you can only oppose your tenant's application, or apply for termination without renewal, on one or more of the grounds set out in section 30(1). These grounds are set out below. You will only be able to rely on the ground(s) of opposition that you have mentioned in your written notice to your tenant.

Paragraph of section 30(1)	Grounds
(a)	Where under the current tenancy the tenant has any obligations as respects the repair and maintenance of the holding, that the tenant ought not to be granted a new tenancy in view of the state of repair of the holding, being a state resulting from the tenant's failure to comply with the said obligations.
(b)	That the tenant ought not to be granted a new tenancy in view of his persistent delay in paying rent which has become due.
(c)	That the tenant ought not to be granted a new tenancy in view of other substantial breaches by him of his obligations under the current tenancy, or for any other reason connected with the tenant's use or management of the holding.
(d)	That the landlord has offered and is willing to provide or secure the provision of alternative accommodation for the tenant, that the terms on which the alternative accommodation is available are reasonable having regard to the terms of the current tenancy and to all other relevant circumstances, and that the accommodation and the time at which it will be available are suitable for the tenant's requirements (including the requirement to preserve goodwill) having regard to the nature and class of his business and to the situation and extent of, and facilities afforded by, the holding.
(e)	Where the current tenancy was created by the sub-letting of part only of the property comprised in a superior tenancy and the landlord is the owner of an interest in reversion expectant on the termination of that superior tenancy, that the aggregate of the rents reasonably obtainable on separate lettings of the holding and the remainder of that property would be substantially less than the rent reasonably obtainable on a letting of that property as a whole, that on the termination of the current tenancy the landlord requires possession of the holding for the purposes of letting or otherwise disposing of the said property as a whole, and that in view thereof the tenant ought not to be granted a new tenancy.

(f)	That on the termination of the current tenancy the landlord intends to demolish or reconstruct the premises comprised in the holding or a substantial part of those premises or to carry out substantial work of construction on the holding or part thereof and that he could not reasonably do so without obtaining possession of the holding.
(g)	On the termination of the current tenancy the landlord intends to occupy the holding for the purposes, or partly for the purposes, of a business to be carried on by him therein, or as his residence.

In this Table 'the holding' means the property that is the subject of the tenancy.

Compensation

If your tenant cannot get a new tenancy solely because one or more of grounds (e), (f) and (g) applies, he or she is entitled to compensation under section 37. If you have opposed your tenant's application on any of the other grounds mentioned in section 30(1), as well as on one or more of grounds (e), (f) and (g), your tenant can only get compensation if the court's refusal to grant a new tenancy is based solely on ground (e), (f) or (g). In other words, your tenant cannot get compensation under section 37 if the court has refused the tenancy on other grounds, even if one or more of grounds (e), (f) and (g) also applies.

If you are an authority possessing compulsory purchase powers (such as a local authority), your tenant may be entitled to a disturbance payment under Part 3 of the Land Compensation Act 1973.

Negotiating a new tenancy

Most tenancies are renewed by negotiation and your tenant has set out proposals for the new tenancy in paragraph 3 of this notice. You are not obliged to accept these proposals and may put forward your own. You and your tenant may agree in writing to extend the deadline for making an application to the court while negotiations continue. Your tenant may not apply to the court for a new tenancy until two months have passed from the date of the making of the request contained in this notice, unless you have already given notice opposing your tenant's request as mentioned in paragraph 6 of this notice (section 29A(3)).

If you try to agree a new tenancy with your tenant, remember:

that one of you will need to apply to the court before the date in paragraph 2 of this notice, unless you both agree to extend the period for making an application.

that any such agreement must be in writing and must be made before the date in paragraph 2 (sections 29A and 29B).

Validity of this notice

The tenant who has given you this notice may not be the person from whom you receive rent (sections 44 and 67). This does not necessarily mean that the notice is invalid.

If you have any doubts about whether this notice is valid, get advice immediately from a solicitor or a surveyor.

Further information

An explanation of the main points to consider when renewing or ending a business tenancy, 'Renewing and Ending Business Leases: a Guide for Tenants and Landlords', can be found at www.odpm.gov.uk. Printed copies of the explanation, but not of this form, are available from 1st June 2004 from Free Literature, PO Box 236, Wetherby, West Yorkshire, LS23 7NB (0870 1226 236).

Appendix 6: Specimen counter-notice to section 26 request

Landlord's counter-notice following the service by the tenant of a notice under the Landlord and Tenant Act 1954 Section 26(6)

Landlord and Tenant Act 1954 Section 26

Counter-notice

To: *(name of tenant)*

of: *[(address) (or as appropriate) whose registered office is at (address)]*

From: *(name of landlord)*

of: *[(address) (or as appropriate) whose registered office is at) (address)]*
(briefly describe the premises)

I have received your request for a new tenancy of the above premises dated *(date of tenant's request)* given under the Landlord and Tenant Act 1954 Section 26 and now give you notice that I will oppose an application to the court for the grant of a new tenancy on the ground[s] set out in paragraph[s] *(insert relevant paragraph letter or letters)* of Section 30(1) of that Act.

Dated: *(date)*

Signed: *(signature of, or on behalf of, the landlord)*
(on duplicate)
*[Landlord] *[On behalf of landlord] *[Mortgagee] *[On behalf of mortgagee]
(delete if inapplicable)

Received a notice of which the above is a true copy.

Dated: *(date)*

Signed: *(signature of, or on behalf of, the tenant)*

Appendix 7: Specimen section 27(1) notice

**Tenant's notice to terminate under
the Landlord and Tenant Act 1954 Section 27(1)**

Landlord and Tenant Act 1954 Section 27(1)

Notice to terminate

To: *(name of landlord)*

[of (address) (or as appropriate) whose registered office is at (address)]

From: (name of tenant)
[of (address) (or as appropriate) whose registered office is at (address)]
(briefly describe the premises)

I am the tenant of the above premises by virtue of a [sub]lease dated *(date of lease)* and made between (1) *(name of landlord)* and (2) *(name of tenant)* which will expire on *(termination date)* and now give you notice under the Landlord and Tenant Act 1954 Section 27(1) that I do not desire the tenancy to be continued under the provisions of Part II of that Act.

Dated: *(date)*

Signed: *(signature of, or on behalf of, the tenant)*
(on duplicate)
*[Tenant] *[On behalf of tenant]
(delete if inapplicable)

Received a notice of which the above is a true copy.

Dated: *(date)*

Signed: *(signature of, or on behalf of, the landlord)*

Appendix 8: Specimen section 27(2) notice

Tenant's notice to terminate under the Landlord and Tenant Act 1954 Section 27(2)

Landlord and Tenant Act 1954 Section 27(2)

Notice to terminate

To: *(name of landlord)*

[of (address) (or as appropriate) whose registered office is at (address)]

From: *(name of tenant)*

[of (address) (or as appropriate) whose registered office is at (address)]
(briefly describe the premises)

I am the tenant of the above premises by virtue of a [sub]lease dated *(date of lease)* and made between (1) *(name of landlord)* and (2) *(name of tenant)* which [will expire *(or as appropriate)* expired] on *(termination date)* and which [will continue *(or as appropriate)* continues] after that date under the *Landlord and Tenant Act* 1954 Section 24, and now give you notice under Section 27(2) of that Act that the tenancy will be brought to an end on *(date tenancy to end)* by virtue of this notice.

Dated: *(date)*

Signed: *(signature of, or on behalf of, the tenant)*
(on duplicate)
*[Tenant] *[On behalf of tenant]

(delete if inapplicable)

Received a notice of which the above is a true copy.

Dated: *(date)*

Signed: *(signature of, or on behalf of, the landlord)*

Appendix 9A: Landlord's warning notice

**Landlord's warning notice that sections 24 to 28
of the *Landlord and Tenant Act* 1954
are not to apply to a business tenancy**

To: (*Name and address of tenant*)

From: (*Name and address of landlord*)

IMPORTANT NOTICE

**You are being offered a lease without security of tenure.
Do not commit yourself to the lease unless you have read
this message carefully and have discussed it with a
professional adviser.**

Business tenants normally have security of tenure – the right to
stay in their business premises when the lease ends.

**If you commit yourself to the lease you will be giving up
these important legal rights.**

- You will have no right to stay in the premises when the lease
  ends.
- Unless the landlord chooses to offer you another lease, you
  will need to leave the premises.
- You will be unable to claim compensation for the loss of your
  business premises, unless the lease specifically gives you this
  right.
- If the landlord offers you another lease, you will have no right
  to ask the court to fix the rent.

It is therefore important to get professional advice – from a
qualified surveyor, lawyer or accountant -before agreeing to give
up these rights.

If you want to ensure that you can stay in the same business
premises when the lease ends, you should consult your adviser
about another form of lease that does not exclude the protection
of the *Landlord and Tenant Act* 1954.

If you receive this notice at least 14 days before committing yourself to the lease, you will need to sign a simple declaration that you have received this notice and have accepted its consequences, before signing the lease.

But if you do not receive at least 14 days notice, you will need to sign a 'statutory' declaration. To do so, you will need to visit an independent solicitor (or someone else empowered to administer oaths).

Unless there is a special reason for committing yourself to the lease sooner, you may want to ask the landlord to let you have at least 14 days to consider whether you wish to give up your statutory rights. If you then decided to go ahead with the agreement to exclude the protection of the *Landlord and Tenant Act* 1954, you would only need to make a simple declaration, and so you would not need to make a separate visit to an independent solicitor.

(The form of lease is annexed.)

Date: *(insert date)*
(On duplicate)

I *(Name of tenant)* have received notice of which the above is a copy.

Signed _____

Full name _____

Date   _____

Appendix 9B: Tenant's ordinary declaration

Tenant's ordinary declaration that sections 24 to 28 of the Landlord and Tenant Act 1954 are not to apply to a business tenancy

I *(Name of tenant)*

of
(Address)

declare that:

1. I propose to enter into a tenancy of premises at *(address of premises)* for a term commencing on *(commencement date)*.

2. [I][The tenant] propose[s] to enter into an agreement with [*name of landlord*] that the provisions of sections 24 to 28 of the *Landlord and Tenant Act* 1954 (security of tenure) shall be excluded in relation to the tenancy.

3. The landlord has, not less than 14 days before [I] [the tenant] enter[s] into the tenancy, or (if earlier) become[s] contractually bound to do so served on [me][the tenant] a notice in the form, or substantially in the form, set out in Schedule 1 to *Regulatory Reform (Business Tenancies) (England and Wales) Order 2003*. The form of notice set out in that Schedule is reproduced below.

4. [I have][The tenant has] read the notice referred to in paragraph 3 above and accept[s] the consequences of entering into the agreement referred to in paragraph 2 above.

5. [I am duly authorised by the tenant to make this declaration.] – *(form can be modified for tenant's representative)*

DECLARED this   day of   .

To:

_____

_____

(Name and address of tenant)

From:

_____

_____

_____

(*Name and address of landlord*)

Appendix 9C: Tenant's statutory declaration

**Tenant's statutory declaration that sections 24 to 28
of the Landlord and Tenant Act 1954
are not to apply to a business tenancy**

I (*Name of tenant*)

of
(*Address*)
do solemnly and sincerely declare that:

1. I propose to enter into a tenancy of premises at (*address of premises*) for a term commencing on (*commencement date*).

2. I propose to enter into an agreement with (*name of landlord*) that the provisions of sections 24 to 28 of the *Landlord and Tenant Act 1954* (security of tenure) shall be excluded in relation to the tenancy.

3. The landlord has served on me a notice in the form, or substantially in the form, set out in Schedule 1 to *Regulatory Reform (Business Tenancies) (England and Wales) Order 2003*. The form of notice set out in that Schedule is reproduced below.

4. I have read the notice referred to in paragraph 3 above and accept the consequences of entering into the agreement referred to in paragraph 2 above.

5. [I am duly authorised by the tenant to make this declaration.] – *(form can be modified for tenant's representative)*

To:

_____
_____
_____

(Name and address of tenant)

From:

_____
_____
_____

(Name and address of landlord)

IMPORTANT NOTICE

You are being offered a lease without security of tenure. Do not commit yourself to the lease unless you have read this message carefully and have discussed it with a professional adviser.

Business tenants normally have security of tenure – the right to stay in their business premises when the lease ends.

If you commit yourself to the lease you will be giving up these important legal rights.

- You will have no right to stay in the premises when the lease ends.
- Unless the landlord chooses to offer you another lease, you will need to leave the premises.
- You will be unable to claim compensation for the loss of your business premises, unless the lease specifically gives you this right.
- If the landlord offers you another lease, you will have no right to ask the court to fix the rent.

It is therefore important to get professional advice – from a qualified surveyor, lawyer or accountant -before agreeing to give up these rights.

If you want to ensure that you can stay in the same business premises when the lease ends, you should consult your adviser about another form of lease that does not exclude the protection of the *Landlord and Tenant Act* 1954.

If you receive this notice at least 14 days before committing yourself to the lease, you will need to sign a simple declaration that you have received this notice and have accepted its consequences, before signing the lease.

But if you do not receive at least 14 days notice, you will need to sign a 'statutory' declaration. To do so, you will need to visit an independent solicitor (or someone else empowered to administer oaths).

Unless there is a special reason for committing yourself to the lease sooner, you may want to ask the landlord to let you have at least 14 days to consider whether you wish to give up your statutory rights. If you then decided to go ahead with the agreement to exclude the protection of the *Landlord and Tenant Act* 1954, you would only need to make a simple declaration, and so you would not need to make a separate visit to an independent solicitor.

AND I make this solemn declaration conscientiously believing the same to be true and by virtue of the *Statutory Declarations Act* 1835.

DECLARED at
this   day of

Before me
(signature of person before whom declaration is made)
A commissioner for oaths or a solicitor empowered to administer oaths *(or as appropriate)*

Appendix 9D: Landlord's warning notice

**Landlord's warning notice that an agreement
to surrender a business tenancy is to be made**

To: (*Name and address of tenant*)

From: (*Name and address of landlord*)

IMPORTANT NOTICE FOR TENANT

**<u>Do not commit yourself to any agreement to surrender
your lease unless you have read this message carefully
and discussed it with a professional advisor.</u>**

Normally, you have the right to renew your lease when it expires.
By committing yourself to an agreement to surrender, **you will be
giving up this important statutory right.**

- You will not be able to continue occupying the premises
  beyond the date provided for under the agreement for
  surrender, unless the landlord chooses to offer you a further
  term (in which case you would lose the right to ask the
  court to determine the new rent). You will need to leave the
  premises.
- You will be unable to claim compensation for the loss of your
  premises, unless the lease or agreement for surrender gives
  you this right.

A qualified surveyor, lawyer or accountant would be able to offer
you professional advice on your options.

**<u>You do not have to commit yourself to the agreement to
surrender your lease unless you want to.</u>**

If you receive this notice at least 14 days before committing
yourself to the agreement to surrender, you will need to sign a
simple declaration that you have received this notice and have
accepted its consequences, before signing the agreement to
surrender.

> **But if you do not receive at least 14 days notice, you will need to sign a 'statutory' declaration. To do so, you will need to visit an independent solicitor (or someone else empowered to administer oaths).**
>
> Unless there is a special reason for committing yourself to the agreement to surrender sooner, you may want to ask the landlord to let you have at least 14 days to consider whether you wish to give up your statutory rights. If you then decided to go ahead with the agreement to end your lease, you would only need to make a simple declaration, and so you would not need to make a separate visit to an independent solicitor.

(The form of agreement to surrender is annexed.)

Date: *(insert date)*
(On duplicate)

I have received notice of which the above is a copy

Signed_____

Full name_____

Date_____

Appendix 9E: Tenant's ordinary declaration

**Tenant's ordinary declaration that an agreement
to surrender a business tenancy is to be made**

[I] [*Name of tenant or person authorised by tenant*]

of[*Address*]

declare that:

1   [I have] [(*name of tenant*) has] a tenancy of premises at [*address of premises*] for a term commencing on [*commencement date*].

2   [I][The tenant] propose[s] to enter into an agreement with [*name of landlord*] to surrender the tenancy on a date or in circumstances specified in the agreement.

3   The landlord has not less than 14 days before I/the tenant enter(s) into the agreement referred to in paragraph 2 above, or (if earlier) become(s) contractually bound to do so served on [me][the tenant] a notice in the form, or substantially in the form, set out in Schedule 3 to Regulatory Reform (Business Tenancies) (England and Wales) Order 2003. The form of notice set out in that Schedule is reproduced below.

4   [I have][The tenant has] read the notice referred to in paragraph 3 above and accept[s] the consequences of entering into the agreement referred to in paragraph 2 above.

5   [*I am duly authorised by the tenant to make this declaration.*]

DECLARED this   . day of   .

To:

_____

_____

[*Name and address of tenant*]

From:

_____

_____

[*Name and address of landlord*]

IMPORTANT NOTICE FOR TENANT

Do not commit yourself to any agreement to surrender your lease unless you have read this message carefully and discussed it with a professional advisor.

Normally, you have the right to renew your lease when it expires. By committing yourself to an agreement to surrender, **you will be giving up this important statutory right.**

- You will not be able to continue occupying the premises beyond the date provided for under the agreement for surrender, unless the landlord chooses to offer you a further term (in which case you would lose the right to ask the court to determine the new rent). You will need to leave the premises.
- You will be unable to claim compensation for the loss of your premises, unless the lease or agreement for surrender gives you this right.

A qualified surveyor, lawyer or accountant would be able to offer you professional advice on your options.

You do not have to commit yourself to the agreement to surrender your lease unless you want to.

If you receive this notice at least 14 days before committing yourself to the agreement to surrender, you will need to sign a simple declaration that you have received this notice and have accepted its consequences, before signing the agreement to surrender.

But if you do not receive at least 14 days notice, you will need to sign a "statutory" declaration. To do so, you will need to visit an independent solicitor (or someone else empowered to administer oaths).

Unless there is a special reason for committing yourself to the agreement to surrender sooner, you may want to ask the landlord to let you have at least 14 days to consider whether you wish to give up your statutory rights. If you then decided to go ahead with the agreement to end your lease, you would only need to make a simple declaration, and so you would not need to make a separate visit to an independent solicitor.

Appendix 9F: Tenant's statutory declaration

Tenant's statutory declaration that an agreement to surrender a business tenancy is to be made

I *(Name of tenant)*

of
(Address)

do solemnly and sincerely declare that:

1   I have a tenancy of premises at *(address of premises)* for a term commencing on *(commencement date)*.

2   I propose to enter into an agreement with *(name of landlord*]) to surrender the tenancy on a date or in circumstances specified in the agreement.

3   The landlord has served on me a notice in the form, or substantially in the form, set out in Schedule 3 to *Regulatory Reform (Business Tenancies) (England and Wales) Order 2003*. The form of notice set out in that Schedule is reproduced below.

4   I have read the notice referred to in paragraph 3 above and accept the consequences of entering into the agreement referred to in paragraph 2 above.

5   [I am duly authorised by the tenant to make this declaration.] – *(form can be modified for tenant's representative)*

To:

_____

_____

_____

(Name and address of tenant)

From:

_____

_____

(Name and address of landlord)

IMPORTANT NOTICE FOR TENANT

<u>Do not commit yourself to any agreement to surrender your lease unless you have read this message carefully and discussed it with a professional advisor.</u>

Normally, you have the right to renew your lease when it expires. By committing yourself to an agreement to surrender, **you will be giving up this important statutory right.**

- You will not be able to continue occupying the premises beyond the date provided for under the agreement for surrender, unless the landlord chooses to offer you a further term (in which case you would lose the right to ask the court to determine the new rent). You will need to leave the premises.
- You will be unable to claim compensation for the loss of your premises, unless the lease or agreement for surrender gives you this right.

A qualified surveyor, lawyer or accountant would be able to offer you professional advice on your options.

You do not have to commit yourself to the agreement to surrender your lease unless you want to.

If you receive this notice at least 14 days before committing yourself to the agreement to surrender, you will need to sign a simple declaration that you have received this notice and have accepted its consequences, before signing the agreement to surrender.

But if you do not receive at least 14 days notice, you will need to sign a 'statutory' declaration. To do so, you will need to visit an independent solicitor (or someone else empowered to administer oaths).

Unless there is a special reason for committing yourself to the agreement to surrender sooner, you may want to ask the landlord to let you have at least 14 days to consider whether you wish to give up your statutory rights. If you then decided to go ahead with the agreement to end your lease, you would only need to make a simple declaration, and so you would not need to make a separate visit to an independent solicitor.

AND I make this solemn declaration conscientiously believing the same to be true and by virtue of the *Statutory Declarations Act 1835*.

DECLARED at
this   day of

Before me
(signature of person before whom declaration is made)

Appendix 10: Landlord's section 40(1) request

**Landlord's request for information about occupation
and subtenancies Section 40(1) of the
Landlord and Tenant Act 1954**

To: *(insert name and address of tenant)*

From: *(insert name and address of landlord)*

1. This notice relates to the following premises: *(insert address or description of premises)*.

2. I give you notice under section 40(1) of the *Landlord and Tenant Act* 1954 that I require you to provide information –

   (a) by answering questions (1) to (3) in the Table below;
   (b) if you answer 'yes' to question (2), by giving me the name and address of the person or persons concerned;
   (c) if you answer 'yes' to question (3), by also answering questions (4) to (10) in the Table below;
   (d) if you answer 'no' to question (8) by giving me the name and address of the sub-tenant; and
   (e) if you answer 'yes' to question (10), by giving me details of the notice or request.

TABLE

(1) Do you occupy the premises or any part of them wholly or partly for the purposes of a business that is carried on by you?
(2) To the best of your knowledge and belief, does any other person own an interest in reversion in any part of the premises?
(3) Does your tenancy have effect subject to any sub-tenancy on which your tenancy is immediately expectant?
(4) What premises are comprised in the sub-tenancy?
(5) For what term does it have effect or, if it is terminable by notice, by what notice can it be terminated'?
(6) What is the rent payable under it?
(7) Who is the sub-tenant?
(8) To the best of your knowledge and belief, is the sub-tenant in occupation of the premises or of part of the premises comprised in the sub-tenancy?
(9) Is an agreement in force excluding, in relation to the sub-tenancy, the provisions of sections 24 to 28 of the *Landlord and Tenant Act* 1954?

(10) Has a notice been given under section 25 or 26(6) of that Act, or has a request been made under section 26 of that Act, in relation to the sub-tenancy?

3. You must give the information concerned in writing and within the period of one month beginning with the date of service of this notice.

4. Please send all correspondence about this notice to:

Name:
Address:

Signed:
Date:
*[Landlord] *[on behalf of the landlord] *delete whichever is inapplicable

IMPORTANT NOTE FOR THE TENANT

This notice contains some words and phrases that you may not understand. The Notes below should help you, but it would be wise to seek professional advice, for example, from a solicitor or surveyor, before responding to this notice.

Once you have provided the information required by this notice, you must correct it if you realise that it is not, or is no longer, correct. This obligation lasts for six months from the date of service of this notice, but an exception is explained in the next paragraph. If you need to correct information already given, you must do so within one month of becoming aware that the information is incorrect.

The obligation will cease if, after transferring your tenancy, you notify the landlord of the transfer and of the name and address of the person to whom your tenancy has been transferred.

If you fail to comply with the requirements of this notice, or the obligation mentioned above, you may face civil proceedings for breach of the statutory duty that arises under section 40 of the Landlord and Tenant Act 1954. In any such proceedings a court may order you to comply with that duty and may make an award of damages.

NOTES

The sections mentioned below are sections of the Landlord and Tenant Act 1954, as amended, (most recently by the Regulatory Reform (Business Tenancies) (England and Wales) Order 2003)

Purpose of this notice

Your landlord (or, if he or she is a tenant, possibly your landlord's landlord) has sent you this notice in order to obtain information about your occupation and that of any sub-tenants. This information may be relevant to the taking of steps to end or renew your business tenancy.

Time limit for replying

You must provide the relevant information within one month of the date of service of this notice (section 40(1), (2) and (5)).

Information required

You do not have to give your answers on this form; you may use a separate sheet for this purpose. The notice requires you to provide, in writing, information in the form of answers to questions (1) to (3) in the Table above and, if you answer 'yes' to question (3), also to provide information in the form of answers to questions (4) to (10) in that Table. Depending on your answer to question (2) and, if applicable in your case, questions (8) and (10), you must also provide the information referred to in paragraph 2(b), (d) and (e) of this notice. Question (2) refers to a person who owns an interest in reversion. You should answer 'yes' to this question if you know or believe that there is a person who receives, or is entitled to receive, rent in respect of any part of the premises (other than the landlord who served this notice).

When you answer questions about sub-tenants, please bear in mind that, for these purposes, a sub-tenant includes a person retaining possession of premises by virtue of the *Rent (Agriculture) Act* 1976 or the Rent Act 1977 after the coming to an end of a sub-tenancy, and 'sub-tenancy' includes a right so to retain possession (section 40(8)).

You should keep a copy of your answers and of any other information provided in response to questions (2), (8) or (10) above.

If, once you have given this information, you realise that it is not, or is no longer, correct, you must give the correct information within one month of becoming aware that the previous information is incorrect.

Subject to the next paragraph, your duty to correct any information that you have already given continues for six months after you receive this notice (section 40(5)). You should give the correct information to the landlord who gave you this notice unless you receive notice of the transfer of his or her interest, and of the name and address of the person to whom that interest has been transferred. In that case, the correct information must be given to that person.

If you transfer your tenancy within the period of six months referred to above, your duty to correct information already given will cease if you notify the landlord of the transfer and of the name and address of the person to whom your tenancy has been transferred.

If you do not provide the information requested, or fail to correct information that you have provided earlier, after realising that it is not, or is no longer, correct, proceedings may be taken against you and you may have to pay damages (section 40B).

If you are in any doubt about the information that you should give, get immediate advice from a solicitor or a surveyor.

Validity of this notice

The landlord who has given you this notice may not be the landlord to whom you pay your rent (sections 44 and 67). This does not necessarily mean that the notice is invalid.

If you have any doubts about whether this notice is valid, get advice immediately from a solicitor or a surveyor.

Further information

An explanation of the main points to consider when renewing or ending a business tenancy, *'Renewing and Ending Business Leases: a Guide for Tenants and Landlords'*, can be found at www.odpm.gov.uk. Printed copies of the explanation, but not of this form, are available from 1st June 2004 from Free Literature, PO Box 236, Wetherby, West Yorkshire, LS23 7NB (0870 1226 236).

Appendix 11: Tenant's section 40(3) request

Tenant's request for information from landlord or landlord's mortgagee about landlord's interest

Section 40(3) of the Landlord and Tenant Act 1954

To: *(insert name and address of reversioner or reversioner's mortgagee in possession [see the first note below])*

From: *(insert name and address of tenant)*

1. This notice relates to the following premises: *(insert address or description of premises)*

2. In accordance with section 40(3) of the Landlord and Tenant Act 1954 I require you:

    (a) to state in writing whether you are the owner of the fee simple in respect of the premises or any part of them or the mortgagee in possession of such an owner,

    (b) if you answer 'no' to (a), to state in writing, to the best of your knowledge and belief:

    (i) the name and address of the person who is your or, as the case may be, your mortgagor's immediate landlord in respect of the premises or of the part in respect of which you are not, or your mortgagor is not, the owner in fee simple;

    (ii) for what term your or your mortgagor's tenancy has effect and what is the earliest date (if any) at which that tenancy is terminable by notice to quit given by the landlord; and

    (iii) whether a notice has been given under section 25 or 26(6) of the *Landlord and Tenant Act* 1954, or a request has been made under section 26 of that Act, in relation to the tenancy and, if so, details of the notice or request;

    (c) to state in writing, to the best of your knowledge and belief, the name and address of any other person who owns an interest in reversion in any part of the premises;

    (d) if you are a reversioner, to state in writing whether there is a mortgagee in possession of your interest in the premises; and

    (e) if you answer 'yes' to (d), to state in writing, to the best of your knowledge and belief, the name and address of the mortgagee in possession.

3. You must give the information concerned within the period of one month beginning with the date of service of this notice.

4. Please send all correspondence about this notice to:

Name:
Address:

Signed:
Date:
*[Tenant] *[on behalf of the tenant] (*delete whichever is inapplicable)

IMPORTANT NOTE FOR LANDLORD OR LANDLORD'S MORTGAGEE

This notice contains some words and phrases that you may not understand. The Notes below should help you, but it would be wise to seek professional advice, for example, from a solicitor or surveyor, before responding to this notice.

Once you have provided the information required by this notice, you must correct it if you realise that it is not, or is no longer, correct. This obligation lasts for six months from the date of service of this notice, but an exception is explained in the next paragraph. If you need to correct information already given, you must do so within one month of becoming aware that the information is incorrect.

The obligation will cease if, after transferring your interest, you notify the tenant of the transfer and of the name and address of the person to whom your interest has been transferred.

If you fail to comply with the requirements of this notice, or the obligation mentioned above, you may face civil proceedings for breach of the statutory duty that arises under section 40 of the *Landlord and Tenant Act* 1954. In any such proceedings a court may order you to comply with that duty and may make an award of damages.

NOTES

The sections mentioned below are sections of the *Landlord and Tenant Act* 1954, as amended, (most recently by the *Regulatory Reform (Business Tenancies) (England and Wales) Order 2003*).

Terms used in this notice
The following terms, which are used in paragraph 2 of this notice, are defined in section 40(8):

'mortgagee in possession' includes a receiver appointed by the mortgagee or by the court who is in receipt of the rents and profits;

'reversioner' means any person having an interest in the premises, being an interest in reversion expectant (whether immediately or not) on the tenancy; and

'reversioner's mortgagee in possession' means any person being a mortgagee in possession in respect of such an interest.

section 40(8) requires the reference in paragraph 2(b) of this notice to your mortgagor to be read in the light of the definition of 'mortgagee in possession'.

a mortgagee (mortgage lender) will be 'in possession' if the mortgagor (the person who owes money to the mortgage lender) has failed to comply with the terms of the mortgage. The mortgagee may then be entitled to receive rent that would normally have been paid to the mortgagor.

the term 'the owner of the fee simple' means the freehold owner.

the term 'reversioner' includes the freehold owner and any intermediate landlord as well as the immediate landlord of the tenant who served this notice.

Purpose of this notice and information required

This notice requires you to provide, in writing, the information requested in paragraph 2(a) and (c) of the notice and, if applicable in your case, in paragraph 2(b), (d) and (e). You do not need to use a special form for this purpose.

If, once you have given this information, you realise that it is not, or is no longer, correct, you must give the correct information within one month of becoming aware that the previous information is incorrect. Subject to the last paragraph in this section of these Notes, your duty to correct any information that you have already given continues for six months after you receive this notice (section 40(5)).

You should give the correct information to the tenant who gave you this notice unless you receive notice of the transfer of his or her interest, and of the name and address of the person to whom that interest has been transferred. In that case, the correct information must be given to that person.

If you do not provide the information requested, or fail to correct information that you have provided earlier, after realising that it is not, or is no longer, correct, proceedings may be taken against you and you may have to pay damages (section 40B).

If you are in any doubt as to the information that you should give, get advice immediately from a solicitor or a surveyor.

If you transfer your interest within the period of six months referred to above, your duty to correct information already given will cease if you notify the tenant of that transfer and of the name and address of the person to whom your interest has been transferred.

Time limit for replying

You must provide the relevant information within one month of the date of service of this notice (section 40(3), (4) and (5)).

Validity of this notice

The tenant who has given you this notice may not be the person from whom you receive rent (sections 44 and 67). This does not necessarily mean that the notice is invalid.

If you have any doubts about the validity of the notice, get advice immediately from a solicitor or a surveyor.

Further information

An explanation of the main points to consider when renewing or ending a business tenancy, 'Renewing and Ending Business Leases: a Guide for Tenants and Landlords', can be found at *www.odpm.gov.uk*. Printed copies of the explanation, but not of this form, are available from 1st June 2004 from Free Literature, PO Box 236, Wetherby, West Yorkshire, LS23 7NB (0870 1226 236).

Appendix 12: Specimen draft directions for an unopposed claim

[1. **Transfer to the Chancery List**

This case be transferred to this Court's Chancery List]

2. **Draft Lease**

The claimant shall serve on the defendant [either by email or on a computer disc, an electronic copy of] a draft lease by no later than 4.00pm on [insert date].

The defendant shall serve on the claimant its proposed amendments/counter-proposals to the lease [,either by email or on computer disc, marked in italics or underlined (if the draft lease was submitted electronically) or marked in red or by schedule (if the draft lease was submitted in paper form)], by no later than 4.00pm on [insert date].

The claimant shall by no later than 4.00pm on [insert date] notify the defendant which amendments, if any, are disputed and specify the claimant's additional amendments, [either by email or on computer disc, marked in italics or underlined (if the draft lease was submitted electronically) or marked in green (if the defendant's amendments were marked in red) or by counter-schedule (if the defendant's amendments were by schedule)].

3. **Disclosure** [optional]

Each party [the claimant/the defendant] shall give standard disclosure of documents to every other party [to the defendant/the claimant] by list by 4.00pm on [insert date].

The last date for service of any request to inspect or for a copy of any document is 4.00pm on [insert date].

4. **Witness Statements of Fact** [optional]

Each party shall serve on the other party the witness statements of all witnesses of fact on whom it intends to rely.

There shall be simultaneous exchange of such statements by no later than 4.00pm on [insert date].

5. Expert evidence

(1) each party has permission to adduce [oral] expert evidence in the field of:

[(a) conveyancing; and]
(b) valuation

limited to 1 expert per party [in each field].

(2) the experts' reports shall be exchanged by no later than 4.00pm on [insert date].

(3) the experts shall hold a discussion for the purpose of:

(a) identifying the issues, if any, between them; and
(b) where possible, reaching agreement on those issues.

(4) the experts shall by 4.00pm on [insert date] prepare and file a statement for the court showing:

(a) those issues on which they did agree; and
(b) those issues on which they disagree and a summary of their reasons for disagreeing.

(5) The time for service on another party of any question addressed to an expert instructed by that party is no later than [insert number] days after service of that expert's report. Any such question is to be answered within [insert number] days of service of the question(s).

6. Dates for filing Listing Questionnaires and Trial

Each party must file a completed Listing Questionnaire by no later than 4.00pm on [insert date].

This case [including the claim for interim rent] is to be tried as a fixture before a Circuit Judge in the period commencing on [insert date] and ending on [insert date] with a provisional time estimate of [insert].

The trial date is to be fixed by [a Listing Officer] [the Specialist Jurisdiction manager] at a listing appointment at [insert time] on [insert date] at [insert place] at which the parties are to attend and to have all available dates to avoid. The parties are to inform each other forthwith of the details of the listing appointment to ensure attendance at that appointment, so that it shall be effective.

If a party does not attend the listing appointment or does not then provide dates to avoid, the trial date will be fixed for such date as the Listing Officer/Specialist Jurisdiction Manager may decide, and any date so fixed shall only be varied upon an application to a Judge.

7. **Miscellaneous**

The parties shall seek to agree the contents of the trial bundle not less than 28 days before the start of the trial. The claimant shall provide to the defendant a copy of the said bundle not less than 21 days before the start of the trial.

The Claimant shall lodge at the court an indexed bundle of documents contained in a ring binder and with each page clearly numbered no more than 7 days and not less than 3 days before the start of trial.

Skeleton arguments on behalf of both parties shall be lodged not later than 3 days before the start of the trial.

Each party must inform the court immediately if the claim is settled, whether or not it is then possible to file a draft consent order to give effect to their agreement.

Costs in case.

Appendix 13: Specimen draft directions for an opposed claim

1. Allocation
The case is allocated to the multi-track.

[2. Transfer to the Chancery List
This case be transferred to this Court's Chancery List]

3. Preliminary issue
The trial of the issue(s) as to whether the [landlord] satisfies the grounds of opposition contained in section 30(1)[a-b-c-d-e-f-g] be tried as [a] preliminary issue(s).

[The trial of the issue of whether the court has jurisdiction to make an order granting the [tenant] a new lease of the premises be tried as a preliminary issue.]

The directions referred to below shall apply to the preliminary issue(s) only, and all further proceedings herein (save in relation to the preliminary issue(s)) shall be stayed until the determination of the preliminary issue(s) or further order in the meantime.

4. Disclosure [optional]
Each party [the claimant/the defendant] shall give standard disclosure of documents relating to the preliminary issue(s) to every other party [to the defendant/the claimant] by list by 4.00pm on [insert date].

The last date for service of any request to inspect or for a copy of any document is 4.00pm on [insert date].

5. Witness Statements of Fact [optional]
Each party shall serve on the other party the witness statements of all witnesses of fact on whom it intends to rely.

There shall be consecutive service of such statements. The [Landlord] shall serve its statements by 4.00pm on [insert date] and the [Tenant] by 4.00pm on [insert date].

6. **Expert evidence** [optional]

(1) each party has permission to adduce [oral] expert evidence in the field of:

[Insert field]

limited to 1 expert per party [in each field].

(2) the experts reports shall be exchanged consecutively. The [Landlord] shall serve its report by no later than 4.00pm on [insert date] and the [Tenant] by 4.00pm on [insert date].

(3) the experts shall hold a discussion for the purpose of:

    (a) identifying the issues, if any, between them; and
    (b) where possible, reaching agreement on those issues.

(4) the experts shall by 4.00pm on [insert date] prepare and file a statement for the court showing:

    (a) those issues on which they did agree; and
    (b) those issues on which they disagree and a summary of their reasons for disagreeing.

(5) The time for service on another party of any question addressed to an expert instructed by that party is no later than [insert number] days after service of that expert's report.

Any such question is to be answered within [insert number] days of service of the question(s).

7. **Dates for filing Listing Questionnaires and Trial**

Each party must file a completed Listing Questionnaire by no later than 4.00pm on [insert date].

The preliminary issue is to be tried as a fixture before a Circuit Judge in the period commencing on [insert date] and ending on [insert date] with a provisional time estimate of [insert].

The trial date is to be fixed by [a Listing Officer] [the Specialist Jurisdiction manager] at a listing appointment at [insert time] on [insert date] at [insert place] at which the parties are to attend and to have all available dates to avoid. The parties are to inform each other forthwith of the details of the listing appointment to ensure attendance at that appointment, so that it shall be effective.

If a party does not attend the listing appointment or does not then provide dates to avoid, the trial date will be fixed for such date as the Listing Officer/Specialist Jurisdiction Manager may decide, and any date so fixed shall only be varied upon an application to a Judge.

8. **Miscellaneous**

The parties shall seek to agree the contents of the trial bundle not less than 28 days before the start of the trial. The claimant shall provide to the defendant a copy of the said bundle not less than 21 days before the start of the trial.

The claimant shall lodge at the court an indexed bundle of documents contained in a ring binder and with each page clearly numbered no more than seven days and not less than three days before the start of trial.

Skeleton arguments on behalf of both parties shall be lodged not later than three days before the start of the trial.

Each party must inform the court immediately if the claim is settled, whether or not it is then possible to file a draft consent order to give effect to their agreement.

Costs in case.

Appendix 14: Specimen skeleton expert report

**Expert report for use in an unopposed claim
where only rent is in dispute**

1. Introduction

a) Expert's name and business address
b) Summary of the expert's qualifications and relevant experience (a more detailed CV should be appended)
c) Summary of the purpose of the report
d) Summary of material instructions received (consider appending the letter of instruction, but oral instructions must also be summarised).
e) List of the documents considered by the expert in the preparation of his report (this may be more conveniently included in a bibliography to be appended).

2. Background

a) Description of the demised premises
b) Summary of the terms of the current tenancy
c) Procedural background to the claim

3. The new tenancy

a) Consider appending any draft lease that has passed between the parties.
b) Summary of the terms agreed.
c) Summary of the terms disputed and detailed reasons why the expert disagrees with any terms which the other side contends for.
d) Identify the terms which are particularly relevant to the valuation of rent under section 34 of the Act and explain why.
e) Identify the form of lease which the valuation assumes.

4. Valuation

a) Identify the valuation date and any assumptions adopted or disregards made
b) Describe the valuation method (e.g. zoning)
c) Identify any particular valuation considerations affecting the demised premises

5. **Comparable transactions**

(for each comparable)

a) Details of the transaction (location, layout and floor area and other physical characteristics of the property; terms upon which the property was let or assumed to have been let)

b) Analysis of the comparable transaction

c) Identify which of the comparable transactions is/are most relevant, and explain why

6. **Conclusion**

a) Valuation of the rent payable under the new tenancy. This may be on alternative bases if the parties contend for significantly different terms.

7. **Expert's declaration and statement of truth**

Appendix 15: Specimen details of claim in an unopposed claim

IN THE CENTRAL LONDON COUNTY COURT   Claim No.

CHANCERY LIST

IN THE MATTER OF The Landlord and Tenant Act 1954

AND IN THE MATTER OF 3–4 High Street, London W2

BETWEEN:

ALEXA MARIA LIMITED

Claimant

-and-

PHILIP MATTHEW PLC

Defendant

DETAILS OF CLAIM

Remedies sought

The claimant claims:

(1) An order for the grant of a new tenancy of 3–4 High Street, London W2 pursuant to section 24(1) of the Landlord and Tenant Act 1954 ('the Act') for the period and on the terms referred to herein; and

(2) Costs

Information required by paragraphs 3.4 and 3.7 PD56

1. The claim relates to 3–4 High Street, London W2 ('the Property');

2. By deed dated 5 March 1981 one PreviousOwner Limited let the Property to the defendant for a term of 25 years commencing 25 December 1980 at a rent of £178,500 per annum ('the Lease'). The current rent is £245,000 per annum. The Lease expires by effluxion of time on 25 December 2005.

3. The claimant is the successor in title to PreviousOwner Limited.

4. On 10 January 2005, the claimant served notice on the defendant under section 25 of the Act.

5. The statutory period under section 29A(2) of the Act expires on 1 January 2006.

6. The claimant's proposed terms of the new tenancy are as follows:
   (a) Term: 10 years
   (b) Rent: £285,000 per annum
   (c) Other terms: in the same terms as the lease

7. So far as the claimant is aware, the defendant occupies the whole of the Property demised by the Lease and section 32(2) of the Act does not apply.

8. MortgageLender Express Limited has an interest in the reversion in the Property on the termination of the current tenancy and is likely to be affected by the grant of a new tenancy.

9. There is no person who has a freehold interest in the Property, other than the claimant.

Dated 31 January 2005

Statement of truth
The claimant believes that the facts stated in this statement of case are true. I am duly authorised to sign this statement on behalf of the claimant.

Full name:

Signed:

Position or office held:

Appendix 16: Specimen acknowledgement of service

**Acknowledgement of service in
an unopposed claim**

IN THE CENTRAL LONDON COUNTY COURT   Claim No.

CHANCERY LIST

IN THE MATTER OF The Landlord and Tenant Act 1954

AND IN THE MATTER OF 3–4 High Street, London W2

BETWEEN:

ALEXA MARIA LIMITED

Claimant

-and-

PHILIP MATTHEW PLC

Defendant

ACKNOWLEDGMENT OF SERVICE

Information required by paragraph 3.11 PD56

1. The business of menswear retailer is carried on at the property.

2. The defendant relies on section 23(1A) of the Act.

Particulars

The property is occupied by Mr Joe Brownhill (trading as 'High Fashions'), who holds a majority of the voting rights and therefore has a controlling interest in the defendant company.

3. The defendant does not rely on section 41 or 42 of the Act.

4. The whole of the Property let under the Lease is occupied by Mr Brownhill and, by virtue of section 23(1A) of the Act, the defendant.

5. The defendant does not know of any person:

    (a) who has an interest in the reversion of the Property on the termination of the current tenancy and who is likely to be affected by the grant of a new tenancy; or
    (b) who has a freehold interest in the Property, other than the claimant.

6. If a new tenancy is granted, the defendant objects to the following terms proposed by the claimant:

    (a) Term: 10 years
    (b) Rent: £285,000 per annum
    (c) Other terms: in the same terms as the Lease

    and proposes the following different terms:

    (a) Term: 5 years
    (b) Rent: £245,000 per annum
    (c) Other terms: in the same terms as the Lease save for the addition of the words '... except with the Landlord's consent, such consent not to be unreasonably withheld or delayed' to the existing clause 3.14 (prohibition on structural alterations).

    Dated 14 February 2005

Statement of truth

The defendant believes that the facts stated in this acknowledgment of service are true. I am duly authorised to sign this statement on behalf of the defendant.

Full name:

Signed:

Position or office held:

Appendix 17: Specimen particulars of claim

IN THE CENTRAL LONDON COUNTY COURT   **Claim No.**

CHANCERY LIST

IN THE MATTER OF The Landlord and Tenant Act 1954

AND IN THE MATTER OF 3–4 High Street, London W2

BETWEEN:

S.J.R. PLC

Claimant

-and-

OLIVERS LIMITED

Defendant

PARTICULARS OF CLAIM

---

1. The claim relates to 3–4 High Street, London W2 ('the Property').

2. By deed dated 5 March 1981 one PreviousOwner Limited let the Property to the defendant for a term of 25 years commencing 25 December 1980 at a rent of £178,500 per annum ('the Lease'). The current rent is £245,000 per annum. The Lease expires by effluxion of time on 25 December 2005.

3. The claimant is the successor in title to PreviousOwner Limited.

4. On 10 January 2005, the claimant served notice on the defendant under section 25 of the Landlord and Tenant Act 1954 ('the Act').

5. The statutory period under section 29A(2) of the Act expires on 1 January 2006.

6. The claimant opposes the grant of a new tenancy to the defendant and relies on section 30(1)(f) of the Act.

Particulars

As soon as practicable after 1 January 2006, the claimant intends to demolish a substantial part of the Property and replace it with a new four-storey office building. The claimant has obtained planning permission for its intended works and appointed contractors to carry them out. The claimant has sufficient financial resources to carry out the works, which have been approved through the claimant's own internal procedures. The claimant cannot carry out the works unless it obtains vacant possession of the Property from the defendant.

Copies of relevant documents are attached to this statement of case.

7. On termination of the current tenancy, the claimant will have an immediate right to possession of the Property and be entitled to obtain vacant possession thereof from the defendant.

8. In the event that the claim for an order pursuant to section 29(2) of the Act fails, the claimant's proposed terms of the new tenancy are as follows:

   (a) Term: 10 years
   (b) Rent: £285,000 per annum
   (c) Other terms: in the same terms as the Lease

AND the claimant claims:

(1) An order pursuant to section 29(2) of the Act for the termination of the Lease without the grant of a new tenancy; and

(2) An order that the defendant shall give possession of the property to the claimant on such date as the court shall determine;

(3) Further or other relief;

(4) Costs.

Dated 30 November 2005

Statement of truth

The claimant believes that the facts stated in this statement of case are true. I am duly authorised to sign this statement on behalf of the claimant.

Full name:

Signed:

Position or office held:

Appendix 18: Specimen defence in an opposed claim

IN THE CENTRAL LONDON COUNTY COURT   Claim No.

CHANCERY LIST

IN THE MATTER OF The Landlord and Tenant Act 1954

AND IN THE MATTER OF 3–4 High Street, London W2

BETWEEN:

S.J.R. PLC

Claimant

-and-

OLIVERS LIMITED

Defendant

DEFENCE

---

1. Paragraphs 1–5 of the Particulars of Claim are admitted.

2. Paragraph 6 of the Particulars of Claim is denied. It is denied that the claimant is entitled to rely on section 30(1)(f) of the Act, as alleged or at all.

Particulars

(a) The property is Grade II listed and is situated in the London Conservation Area. The claimant has not obtained listed buildings and conservation area consents, as it must before the works can begin. The claimant will not obtain listed buildings consent without a specialist archeological survey of the area underneath the basement of the property being carried out by English Heritage, and such survey cannot be completed before March 2007. In the circumstances, the claimant does not have the intention to carry out its works, alternatively does not have the intention to do so on termination of the current tenancy.

    (b) The claimant does not require vacant possession of all of the Property in order to complete its works, and the defendant further relies on the matters set out at paragraph 5 of this defence.

    (c) The claimant intends to demolish block 'A' of the Property, which comprises only 45% of the entire area of the property, and is not a substantial part thereof.

3. As to paragraph 7 of the Particulars of Claim:

    (a) It is admitted that on termination of the current tenancy (without the grant of a new tenancy) the claimant will have an immediate right to possession of the Property and be entitled to obtain vacant possession thereof from the defendant; but

    (b) it is denied that the claimant has any immediate right of possession or one arising out of its reliance on section 30(1)(f) for the reasons set out in paragraph 2 of this defence.

4. The defendant does not rely on section 23(1A), 41 or 42 of the Act.

5. The defendant relies on section 31A of the Act.

Particulars

The Property comprises two buildings (described in the Lease as block 'A' and block 'B'), linked together at ground level by a covered walkway. The claimant's planning permission only relates to demolition of block A. The defendant is willing to accept a tenancy of the block B, being an economically separable part of the holding, and possession of the remainder of the holding would be reasonably sufficient to enable the claimant to carry out its works.

6. Paragraph 8 of the Particulars of Claim is noted. The defendant proposes the following terms in the event that the claimant's claim to terminate the current tenancy fails:

    (a) Term: 5 years

    (b) Rent: £245,000 per annum

    (c) Other terms: in the same terms as the Lease save for the addition of the words ' ... except with the Landlord's consent, such consent not to be unreasonably withheld or delayed' to the existing clause 3.14 (prohibition on structural alterations).

7. In the circumstances, it is denied that the claimant is entitled to the relief claimed.

Dated 28 December 2005

Statement of truth

The defendant believes that the facts stated in this statement of case are true. I am duly authorised to sign this statement on behalf of the defendant.

Full name:

Signed:

Position or office held:

Glossary

Agreement to Surrender: An agreement by the landlord and the tenant that the lease will come to an end on the date provided for in the agreement.

Alienation The transfer of the ownership of property rights

Competent Landlord: The person (whether or not he is the immediate landlord) who from time to time is the relevant landlord for the purpose of the business tenancy renewal process. See Chapter 4 for information about how to identify the competent landlord.

'Contracted out': A lease or agreement to surrender that excludes the statutory protection of the LTA 1954. The tenant therefore has no right to his tenancy continuing beyond the end of the term or to statutory compensation. See Chapter 2 for more information.

CPR: Civil Procedure Rules 1998 are the rules of court which set out how the court and the parties are to deal with the different stages of litigation.

Holding: That part of the premises demised to the tenant under its tenancy agreement which the tenant occupies for business purposes. See Chapter 6 for more information.

Interim rent: Broadly speaking, the rent payable during the period between expiry of the current tenancy and execution of the renewal tenancy. See Chapter 6 for more information.

Lease: An agreement by which a landlord gives the right of exclusive possession to a tenant for a term and usually for a specified rent.

Licence: A right to enter or occupy property which takes effect as a personal right and not a property right. A licence is not an estate in land and cannot be sold or transferred in its own right.

LTA 1954: Landlord and Tenant Act 1954 – the code of conduct for dealing with contractual agreements between landlords and tenants.

Opposed Claim: A claim by a tenant for a new tenancy where the landlord relies on one or more of the 7 statutory grounds to oppose the new tenancy or applies for a termination order. See Chapter 8 for more information.

PACT: Professional Arbitration on Court Terms which is an alternative to litigating over lease renewals as set out in LTA 1954. Typically used when a landlord wishes to renew a lease, but some of the terms cannot be agreed upon.

PD: Practice Direction (form part of the CPR).

Periodic tenancy: A tenancy running periodically (e.g. from month to month or year to year).

Scott Schedule: A schedule that sets out information in a clear way allowing the court to more easily understand the parties' positions. For example, the court often orders that disputed lease terms should be listed in the first column, with the parties' comments in the second and third columns and a final column (left empty) for the judge's comments.

Surrender: The giving up of a lease by the tenant to the landlord with the agreement of both parties.

Tenancy agreement: A lease

Term: Usually the reference in a lease to the specified period of time the lease is granted for (e.g. a term of five years). Also it can mean the individual covenant within a lease (e.g. it was a term of the lease that the tenant). pay the rent on time."

Unopposed claim: A claim by a tenant or landlord for a new tenancy where the landlord does not use one of the statutory grounds for opposition. Also claims where the landlord does not oppose the grant of a new lease but terms are not agreed between the parties.

Endnotes

Chapter 1

1 Lord Hoffman in *Bruton v London and Quadrant Housing* [2000] 1 AC 406, referring to *Street v Mountford* [1985] AC 809
2 *R v Trinity Development Co (Banbury) Ltd, ex p National Car Parks Ltd* [2001] EWCA Civ 1686
3 *Clear Channel UK Ltd* v *Manchester City Council*, EWCA Civ 1304
4 *avad* v *Aqil* [1991] 1 WLR 1007
5 *Walji* v *Mount Cook Land Ltd* [2002] 1 P&CR 13
6 *Parc (Battersea) Ltd* v *Hutchinson* [1999] 2 EGLR 33
7 *Milmo* v *Carreras* [1946] KB 306
8 *Hemingway Securities Ltd* v *Dunraven Ltd* [1995] 1 EGLR 61
9 Lord Nicholls in *Graysim Holdings Ltd v P&O Property Holdings Ltd* [1996] AC 329
10 *Wandsworth London Borough Council v Singh* (1991) 62 P & CR 219
11 *Bacchiocchi v Academic Agency Ltd* [1998] 1 WLR 1313
12 Ward LJ in *Bacchiocchi v Academic Agency Ltd* [1998] 1 WLR 1313
13 *Jacobs v Chaudhuri* [1968] 2 QB 470
14 *Graysim Holdings Ltd v P&O Property Holdings Ltd* [1996] AC 329
15 *Lee-Velhurst (Investments) Ltd v Harwood Trust* [1973] QB 204; and *Smith v Titanate Ltd* [2005] 20 EG 262, Central London County Court, HHJ Cooke
16 *Hillil Property and Investment Company Ltd v Naraine Pharmacy Ltd* [1979] 2 EGLR 65
17 *Hawesbrook Leisure Ltd v The Reccc-Jones Partnership* [2003] EWHC 3333
18 *Addiscombe Garden Estates Ltd v Crabbe* [1958] 1 QB 513
19 Reynolds, K., and Clark, W., *Renewal of Business Tenancies* (2nd edition), Sweet and Maxwell, 2004 (ISBN 0 42182 960 5) paragraph 1.6.1.1
20 *Hansard,* 27 July 1954, columns: 409–410
21 *Groveside Properties Ltd v Westminster Medical School* [1983] 2 EGLR 68
22 *Cheryl Investments Ltd v Saldanha* [1978] 1 WLR 1329
23 *Bell v Alfred Franks and Bartlett Co. Ltd* [1980] 1 WLR 340
24 *Cheryl Investments v Saldanha* [1978] 1 WLR 1329
25 *Teasdale v Walker* [1958] 1 WLR 1076
26 Pearce LJ in *Teasdale v Walker* [1958] 1 WLR 1076
27 *I&H Caplan Ltd v Caplan (No.2)* [1963] 1 WLR 1247

Chapter 2

28 *Metropolitan Police District v Palacegate Properties Ltd*
[2001] Ch 131

29 *Metropolitan Police District v Palacegate Properties Ltd*
[2001] Ch 131

Chapter 3

30 *Meadows v Clerical Medical and General Life Assurance
Society* [1981] Ch 70

31 *Pennell v Payne* [1995] QB 192

32 *Cadogan v Dimovic* [1984] 1 WLR 609

33 *D'Silva v Lister House* [1971] Ch 17

34 *Crestfort Limited v Tesco Stores Ltd* [2005] EWHC 805

35 *Garston v Scottish Widows' Fund and Life Assurance Society*
[1996] 1 WLR 834; confirmed by Court of Appeal [1998] 1
WLR 1583

36 *Street v Mountford* [1985] AC 809

37 *Blunden v Frogmore Investments Ltd* [2002] EWCA Civ 573

Chapter 4

38 *Pearson v Alyo* [1990] 1 EGLR 114

39 *Shelley v United Artists Corporation Ltd* [1990] 60 P&CR 241

40 *Harris v Black* (1983) P&CR 366

41 *Booth v Reynolds* (1974) New LJ 119

42 *M&P Enterprises (London) Ltd v Norfolk Square Hotels Ltd*
[1994] 1 EGLR 129; and *Mannai Investment Co. Ltd v Eagle
Star Life Assurance Co. Ltd* [1997] AC 749

43 Companies House *www.companieshouse.gov.uk/info*

44 *M&P Enterprises (London) Ltd v Norfolk Square Hotels Ltd*
[1994] 1 EGLR 129

45 *Re Crowhurst Park* [1974] 1 WLR 583

46 *Code of Practice for Commercial Leases in England and Wales*
(2nd edition) www.commercialleasecodeew.co.uk/docs.html

47 *London County Council v Farren* [1956] 1 WLR 1297

48 *Stidolph v American School in London Educational Trust*
(1969) 20 P & CR 802

49 *Stradbrooke v Mitchell* [1991] 1 EGLR 1

50 *Sun Life Assurance plc v Thales Tracs Limited* [2001] 34 EG
100, CA

51 *Garston v Scottish Widows Fund and Life Assurance Society*
[1996] 1 WLR 834

52 *Stile Hall Properties Limited v Gooch* (1968) 207 EG 715

53 Reynolds, K., and Clark, W., *Renewal of Business Tenancies*
(2nd edition), Sweet and Maxwell, 2004 (ISBN 0 42182 960
5)

54 *C.A. Webber (Transport) Ltd v Railtrack Plc* [2003] EWCA Civ
1167, CA

55 *Stylo Shoes Ltd v Prices Tailors Ltd* [1960] Ch 396

56 *Price v West London Investment Building Society* [1964] 1 WLR 616
57 *Railtrack plc v Gojra* [1998] 1 EGLR 63
58 *Stylo Shoes Ltd v Prices Tailors Ltd* [1960] Ch 396
59 *Mannai Investment Co Ltd v Eagle Star Life Assurance Co Ltd* [1997] AC 749
60 *Keith Bailey Rogers & Co (A Firm) v Cubes Ltd* (1975) 31 P & CR 412
61 *Barclays Bank plc v Bee* [2001] EWCA Civ 1126
62 *Re 14 Grafton Street London W1, De Havilland (Antiques) Ltd v Centrovincial Estates (Mayfair) Ltd* [1971] Ch 935, approved in *Pennycook v Shaws (EAL) Ltd* [2004] EWCA Civ 100
63 *Pennycook v Shaws (EAL) Ltd* [2004] EWCA Civ 100

Chapter 5

64 *Code of Practice for Commercial Leases in England and Wales (2nd edition), www.commercialleasecodeew.co.uk*
65 *Waugh v British Railways Board* [1980] AC 521
66 *Code of Practice for Commercial Leases in England and Wales (2nd edition), www.commercialleasecodeew.co.uk*
67 *Code of Practice for Commercial Leases in England and Wales (2nd edition), www.commercialleasecodeew.co.uk"*
68 James LJ in *Behar, Ellis & Parnell v Territorial Investments Ltd* (unreported) CAT 237
69 *LB of Hackney v Hackney African Organisation* [1999] L&TR 117
70 *Shelley v United Artists Corporation Ltd* [1990] 1 EGLR 103
71 *Parsons v George* [2004] EWCA Civ 912
72 *Court Service www.hmcourts-service.gov.uk*
73 *Phillips & Sons Ltd v Milne* (1962) 106 S.J. 731, County Court

Chapter 6

74 *Chipperfield v Shell (UK) Ltd* [1981] 1 EGLR 51
75 *CBS United Kingdom Ltd v London Scottish Properties Limited* [1985] 2 EGLR 125
76 *National Car Parks Ltd v Paternoster Consortium Limited* [1990] 15 EG 53; and *Adams v Green* [1978] 2 EGLR 46
77 *Davy's of London (Wine Merchants) Ltd v The City of London Corporation* [2004] EWHC 2224
78 *Wallis Fashion Group Ltd v CGU Life Assurance Ltd* [2000] 2 EGLR 49
79 *Cairnplace Limited v CBL (Property Investment) Company Ltd* [1984] 1 WLR 696
80 *O'May v City of London Real Property Co Ltd* [1983] 2 AC 726
81 *O'May v City of London Real Property Co Ltd* [1983] 2 AC 726
82 *Cardshops v Davies* [1971] 1 WLR 591

83 *J Murphy and Sons Ltd v Railtrack plc* [2002] EWCA Civ 679 at para. 13
84 *GREA Real Property Investments Ltd v Williams* [1979] 1 EGLR 121
85 *Zubaida (Elley's Enterprises) v Hargreaves* [1995] 1 EGLR 127
86 *Lovely and Orchard Services Ltd v Daejan Investments (Grove Hall) Ltd* [1978] 1 EGLR 44
87 *Stride & Son v Chichester Corporation* [1960] EGD 117
88 *J Murphy and Sons Ltd v Railtrack plc* [2002] EWCA Civ 679
89 *Code of Practice for Commercial Leases in England and Wales (2nd edition), www.commercialleasecodeew.co.uk*
90 *Cairnplace Ltd v CBL (Property Investment) Company Ltd* [1984] 1 WLR 696
91 Joyce, J., *Business Tenancies The New Law*, Legalease, July 2004, ISBN 1 90392 742 0, pp. 127–128
92 Reynolds, K., and Clark, W., *Renewal of Business Tenancies* (2nd edition), Sweet and Maxwell, 2004 (ISBN 0 42182 960 5) p. 46
93 Joyce, J., *Business Tenancies The New Law*, Legalease, July 2004 (ISBN 1 90392 742 0)
94 Court Service *www.hmcourts-service.gov.uk*
95 HMCS website *www.hmcourts-service.gov.uk*
96 *Cranfield v Bridgegrove Ltd* [2003] EWCA Civ 656
97 Land Registry website www.landregistry.gov.uk
98 *Prudential Assurance Company Ltd v Genco (Stores) Ltd* (unreported, Central London County Court, District Judge Lightman 24/11/04)
99 *Calderbank v Calderbank* [1976] Fam 93
100 Trustees of Stokes Pension Fund v Western Power Distribution (South West) Plc [2005] EWCA Civ 854
101 *Neave v Neave (No. 2)* [2003] EWCA Civ 325
102 *Scammell v Dicker* [2001] 1 WLR 631
103 *Capital Bank plc v Stickland* [2004] EWCA Civ 1677

Chapter 7

104 *Escalus Properties Ltd v Robinson* [1996] QB 231
105 *City Centre Restaurants Ltd v Starburst Holdings Ltd* (unreported, Central London County Court, HHJ Cooke, 2/2/04)
106 *Hazel v Hassan Akhtar* [2001] EWCA Civ 1883
107 *Betty's Cafes Ltd v Phillips Furnishing Stores Ltd* [1959] AC 20
108 *Beard v Williams* [1986] 1 EGLR 148
109 *Chaplin (M.) Limited v Regent Capital Holdings Limited* [1994] 1 EGLR 249
110 Reynolds, K., and Clark, W., *Renewal of Business Tenancies* (2nd edition), Sweet and Maxwell, 2004 (ISBN 0 42182 960 5)
111 *Betty's Cafes Limited v Phillips Furnishing Stores Limited* [1959] AC 20
112 *Wessex Reserve Forces and Cadets Association v White* [2005] All ER (D) 310

113 *Zarvos v Pradhan* [2003] EWCA Civ 208

114 Lord Evershed MR in *Fleet Electrics Ltd v Jacey Investments Ltd* [1956] 1 WLR 1027 at 1032

115 *Westminster City Council v British Waterways Board* [1985] AC 676

116 *XL Fisheries Ltd v Leeds Corporation* [1955] QB 636

117 *Fisher v Taylors Furnishing Stores Ltd* [1956] 2 QB 78

118 *H.L. Bolton (Engineering) Co. Ltd v T. J. Graham & Sons Ltd* [1957] 1 QB 159

119 *Yoga for Health Foundation v Guest and Utilini* [2002] EWHC 2658

120 *Dolgellau Golf Club v Hett* [1988] 2 EGLR 75

121 *Yoga for Health Foundation v Guest and Utilini* [2002] EWHC 2658

122 *Espresso Coffee Machine Co Ltd v Guardian Assurance Co Ltd* [1959] 1 WLR 250

123 *Betty's Cafes Ltd v Phillips Furnishing Stores Ltd* [1959] AC 20

124 Romer LJ in *Joel v Swaddle* [1957] 1 WLR 1094

125 *Wessex Reserve Forces and Cadets Association v White* [2005] All ER (D) 310

126 *Yoga for Health Foundation v Guest and Utilini* [2003] EWHC 2658

127 *Gilmour Caterers Ltd v St. Bartholomew's Hospital Governors* [1956] 1 QB 387

128 *Atkinson v Bettison* [1995] 1 WLR 1127

129 *Barth v Pritchard* [1990] 20 EG 65

130 *Romulus Trading Co Ltd v Henry Smith's Charity Trustees* [1990] 2 EGLR 75

131 *Pumperninks of Piccadilly Ltd v Land Securities Ltd* [2002] EWCA Civ 621; and *Ivorygrove Ltd v Global Grange Ltd* [2003] EWHC 1409

132 Park J in *Marazzi v Global Grange Ltd* [2002] EWHC 3010

133 *Housleys Ltd v Bloomer-Holt Ltd* [1966] 1 WLR 1244

134 *Pumperninks of Piccadilly Ltd v Land Securities Ltd* [2002] EWCA Civ 621

135 *Lawrence Frederick Ltd v Freeman Hardy & Willis Ltd* [1959] Ch 731

136 *Bentley & Skinner (Bond Street Jewellers) Ltd v Searchmap Ltd* [2003] EWHC 1621

137 *Method Developments Ltd v Jones* [1971] 1 WLR 168

138 *Hillil Property & Investment Co. Ltd v Naraine Pharmacy Ltd* [1979] 2 EGLR 65

139 *Zafiris & another v Liu* [2005] All ER (D) 261 (Jan)

140 *London Hilton Jewellers Ltd v Hilton International Hotels Ltd* [1990] 1 EGLR 112

141 *Willis v Association of Universities of the British Commonwealth* [1965] 1 QB 140

Chapter 8

142 *Felber Jurker and Co Ltd v Sabreleague Ltd* (unreported, Chancery Division, Master Moncaster, 31/8/05)
143 HM Court Service website www.hmcourts-service.gov.uk

Chapter 9

144 HM Courts Service website *www.hmcourts-service.gov.uk/ infoabout/fees/county.htm*
145 Civil Justice Council website *www.civiljusticecouncil.gov.uk*
146 *Stevens v Gullis* [2000] 1 All ER 527
147 *Phillips v Symes* (No 2) [2004] EWHC 2330
148 *Hajigeorgiou v Vasiliou* [2005] EWCA Civ 236
149 Department for Constitutional Affairs *www.dca.gov.uk*
150 *Stanton v Callaghan* [2000] QB 75
151 *Arthur JS Hall & Co v Simons* [2002] 1 AC 615
152 *Phillips v Symes* [2004] EWHC 2330
153 *Chartered Surveyors Acting as Advocates:* RICS guidance note, RICS Books, Oct 1999 (ISBN 0 85406 952 6)
154 *Jackson v Marley Davenport Ltd* [2004] EWCA Civ 1225, CA
155 *Lucas v Barking, Havering & Redbridge Hospitals NHS Trust* [2003] EWCA Civ 1102
156 *Taylor v Bolton Heath Health Authority* (unreported, Queens Bench Division, Morland J, 14/1/00))
157 *Daniels v Walker* [2000] 1 WLR 1382

Chapter 10

158 Lewison QC., Ed., *Woodfall's Law of Landlord and Tenant* (28th edition), Sweet and Maxwell, January 1978 (ISBN 0 42122 820 2); and Furber, J., Ed., *Hill and Redman's Guide to Landlord and Tenant Law*, Lexis Nexis, June 1999 (ISBN 0 40692 675 1)
159 *Bacchiocchi v Academic Agency Ltd* [1998] 1WLR 1313 CA
160 *Sight and Sound Education Ltd v Books Etc. Ltd* [1999] 3 EGLR 45
161 Reynolds, K., and Clark, W., *Renewal of Business Tenancies* (2nd edition), Sweet and Maxwell, 2004 (ISBN 0 42182 960 5) paragraph 11.4.1.2

Chapter 11

162 RICS website *www.rics.org*
163 *Dunnett v Railtrack Plc.* [2002] EWCA Civ 302
164 The Law Society *www.lawsociety.org.uk*; RICS *www.rics.org*; and CEDR *www.cedr.co.uk*

Index